The Story c

The Cross of Cashel

All Ireland Under 21 Hurling Finals 1964 - 2014

ACKNOWLEDGEMENTS

A publication of this nature would not be feasible without the assistance of so many hurling followers. I am especially indebted to PJ Maxwell of Nenagh and formerly of Clonoulty. His advice and assistance were unwavering and his encouragement ensured the completion of this project. I am also eternally grateful to Ollie Byrnes (Ennis), Tom Greene (Galway), Tom Morrison and Tony Sheehan (Cork), Patrick O'Sullivan (Ballyhale), Patrick Donegan (Lusmagh), Donie McGettigan (Killenaule), Martin Bourke (Tipperary) Ian McCormack (Kilmeaden) and Bill Rooney (Clonroche). John Costigan has written an informed introduction as a former player at this grade and as a high ranking GAA official.

The match reports in both local and national newspapers contributed greatly to an understanding of the history of this great U-21 All-Ireland hurling championship. My gratitude also to photographers John Quirke, Tom O'Neill, Eoin Hennessy, John McIlwaine, Bridget Delaney, Tom Brett, John Kelly, Sportsfile, the Clare Express and the Irish Examiner studios. Photographers who could not be identified are also thanked.

As with my previous GAA book on the Dan Breen Cup, this publication would not be possible without the assistance of Gerry O'Neill, compiler annually of the Kilkenny GAA Yearbook. I am hugely indebted to Gerry for his I.T. skills but also for his time, effort and unfailing courtesy. Thanks also to his wife Anne for her genuine warmth and welcome, every time I visited their home.

Jim Fogarty.

FRONT COVER:
13 September 2014; The Wexford and Clare teams during the All Ireland U21 Final pre-match Parade. Plcture credit: Ray McManus / SPORTSFILE

BACK COVER:

Tipperary, First All Ireland U21 Hurling Champions 1964.
Clare, All Ireland U21 Hurling Champions 2014 (Photo Stephen McCarthy / SPORTSFILE)

First published 2015.
Copyright Jim Fogarty.
ISBN 978-0-9931823-0-3
Design & Layout: Gerry O'Neill.
Printed by Walsh's of Castleisland.

CONTENTS

INTRODUCTION

"A Half a Century of Under 21 Hurling"

On County Final day 2014 in Semple Stadium Jim Fogarty approached me and said how he was in the process of completing a book on fifty years of (u-21) hurling. He was aware of my involvement with Tipperary in the initial years of the competition and he asked me if I would write a small introductory piece for it. I was extremely honoured to be asked and as it was a competition I grew up with I was delighted to contribute. Incidentally over the past six or seven years the (u-21) grade in both hurling and football has come under scrutiny and there is a belief in certain quarters that the grade has outlived its usefulness. Many people are of the opinion that there is a proliferation of competitions in that age bracket between eighteen and twenty one. This is putting extra pressure on young players and is leading to burn out and the shortening of their careers.

About seven years ago a motion came to Congress looking to have the (U-21) age bracket changed or to have the competition suspended. The motion met with a resounding no at the annual gathering. I have certain reservations whether we can continue to have the competition as it was hereto fore but just the same I don't believe we will see any change in its format in the foreseeable future.

The (U-21) hurling competition was introduced in 1964 and at that time it filled a huge vacuum and evolved into a marvellous competition. It has provided many classic encounters over the years and it has been beneficial to counties in developing teams to compete for the McCarthy Cup subsequently. As the competition evolved it caught the public imagination and crowds between twenty and thirty thousand became commonplace for the provincial and All Ireland contests.

In the early sixties as players emerged from the minor scene it was felt that a majority of them were unfit to compete at senior hurling level as the game was more physical and not as regulated as it is today. At that time the number of boys attending third level education was quite small and for Fitzgibbon Cup purposes only four Colleges competed, U.C.D. U.C.C. University College Galway and Queens University Belfast. The powers to be at administrative level in the GAA decided that the introduction of the (U-21) grade as a transition from minor to senior was the road to travel. It gave hurlers in that age bracket space to compete against their own age group and get the experience needed to step up to senior level. In my opinion it was an inspired decision at that point in time.

Having competed at minor level myself with Tipperary in 1963 I was personally involved as a player in the first three years of the (U-21) competition and I can recall great excitement amongst players on its introduction.

When Tipperary won the inaugural All Ireland in 1964 I happened to be peripherally involved. I played in the All-Ireland Semi-Final v Roscommon as the full back was injured and did not figure in the final versus Wexford.

In 1965 I was a permanent fixture on the team that having won the Munster Final beating Galway in Ballinsloe came up against Wexford in Nowlan Park on a very wet September Sunday in the All-Ireland Final. Wexford were comprehensive victors and thus won the counties only (U-21) title to date. I was also involved with Tipperary at (U-21) level in 1966 when an Eamonn Cregan inspired Limerick ended Tipp's interest in that years Munster Semi Final.

Because of my early involvement, the (U-21) competition is of special interest to me. As I reflect on it I can see how success in the grade has led to further success at Senior Level.

The great Cork four in a row successes from(1968-1971) introduced players that became household names in the Rebel County and contributed in no small way to the three in a row victories (1976-78) at Senior level. The names that spring to mind are legends like Ray Cummins, Pat Hegarty, Willie Walsh, John Horgan, Seanie O Leary, Martin Doherty and one of Cork's greatest ever dual stars Jimmy Barry Murphy.

I believe the (U-21) grade helped Galway hurling. For years due to their geographical position Galway had only one or two senior championship games each year and it was extremely difficult to build up momentum towards an All-Ireland senior victory in that scenario. Competing at (U-21) level showed them that their hurling and their hurlers were on par with the best and their All Ireland (U-21) victories in 1972 and 1978 gave them the belief that they could win an All-Ireland Senior Title which they achieved in 1980. The victories achieved at (U-21) level helped in no small way players like Conor Hayes, Steve Mahon, Iggy Clarke, Bernie Forde, Frank Bourke, PJ Molloy and Joe McDonagh to capture the McCarthy Cup.

Further success at (U-21) level in 1983 and 1986 blooded further players that helped the tribesmen to McCarthy Cup victories in 1987 and 1988.

The (U-21) grade has been very helpful in Tipperary hurling. In the late seventies and early eighties Tipperary were unable to win a first round game in the Munster Senior hurling championship and as a result morale was quite low in the Premier County. The (U-21) grade came to the rescue and victories in the 1979, 80, 81 and 85 All Ireland Finals raised the confidence and self-belief in the developing players and enabled them to bounce back and win All Irelands at senior level in 1989 and 1991. A number of Munster Final victories at senior level during that period raised the profile of hurling once more in Tipperary. This era in Tipp hurling gave us great players like Nicky English, Pat Fox, the Bonner brothers, Aidan and Bobby Ryan, Declan Ryan and Ken Hogan just to mention but a few.

Kilkenny has used the (U-21) grade to their advantage over the years and many of their great players over the decades like the Fennellys, Brian Cody, Ger. Henderson, Joe Hennessy, DJ Carey, J.J. Delaney, Richie Hogan, Henry Shefflin and many others too numerous to mention collected (U-21) All Ireland Medals as a prelude to multiple senior awards.

Even though Offaly failed to win an All Ireland (U-21) title following their three minor successes in the late eighties they used the (U-21) grade to develop their excellent talent and were unlucky in 1989 and 1992 not to capture the Cross of Cashel trophy.

The grade further enhanced the education of great players like the Whelahans, the Troys, the Dooleys, Michael Duignan and others and they reaped their harvest with All Ireland Senior Hurling victories in 1994 and 1998.

When Limerick captured three (U-21) All Ireland titles between (2000 –2002) it gave rise to great expectations on Shannonside. Many believed that the elusive McCarthy Cup was destined for Limerick for the first time since 1973. They had a marvellous group of players and for whatever reason they failed to maximise their potential. This failure is still regretted by the passionate hurling people in the county.

Wexford's All Ireland (U-21) victory in 1965 was hugely significant. It gave the county players like the Quigleys, the Jacobs, Tony Doran, the late Jack Berry, Willie Murphy and Mick Kinsella who went on to capture the All Ireland senior title in 1968, and backbone a Wexford team that were very competitive for the best part of a decade.

The Waterford (U-21) victory in 1992 was a great boost for hurling in the county. The team was captained by the evergreen Tony Browne and included Fergal Hartley and Paul Flynn who helped Waterford to provincial senior hurling honours and a National League title in the subsequent decade and a half.

In the past six years we have witnessed the emergence of Clare as a powerful force in (U-21) grade. The winning of four All Ireland Titles in that period is significant. Already many players from those successful teams have played a huge role in Clare's all Ireland senior victory in 2013.

The stars of those successful (U-21) teams, players like Kelly, Galvin, Conlon, Honan, McInerney, McGrath and Paudge Collins could bring unprecedented success to the Banner at senior level.

In conclusion we can say that hurling has been enriched by the presence of the (U-21) grade over the last half century. Personally I believe that its presence is not as necessary as it was when introduced over fifty years ago. There is no doubt but the grade has been hugely significant in the history of hurling to date and it looks like continuing that way in the immediate future.

"Go n-éirí go geal leat, Jim le do fhoilseachán"

John Costigan
Chairman of Tipperary County Board GAA (2006 to 2008)
Delegate to Munster Council of GAA.

Preface.

The All-Ireland u-21 hurling championship has been competed for from 1964 to 2014. It is perhaps timely to produce a history of the grade for all hurling enthusiasts. Sporting history is all about great games and names. We love to recall the heroes and epics of the past. It is my fervent wish that this history will do justice to those who have embellished the u-21 grade over the past 51 years. The book is entitled "The Cross of Cashel" and it should be noted that this cup was first presented in 1967.

My own background is that of a Tipperary native who was County and City Librarian in Kilkenny from 1980 to 2008. On taking early retirement in 2008, I published my first GAA book in 2012 on "The Dan Breen Cup – Tipperary County SH Finals, 1931 to 2011". Greatly encouraged by the positive reaction to that book, I have enjoyed working on my current effort, "The Cross of Cashel Cup". I hope that it will be of interest to hurling followers everywhere.

Jim Fogarty.

Dedication

To my deceased parents Jim and Betsy, to my sister Betty and to my wife, Marie. Also to all the players at Under 21 grade, who have given such pleasure down through the years.

CHAPTER 1
ALL IRELAND U21
HURLING FINALS
1964-1969

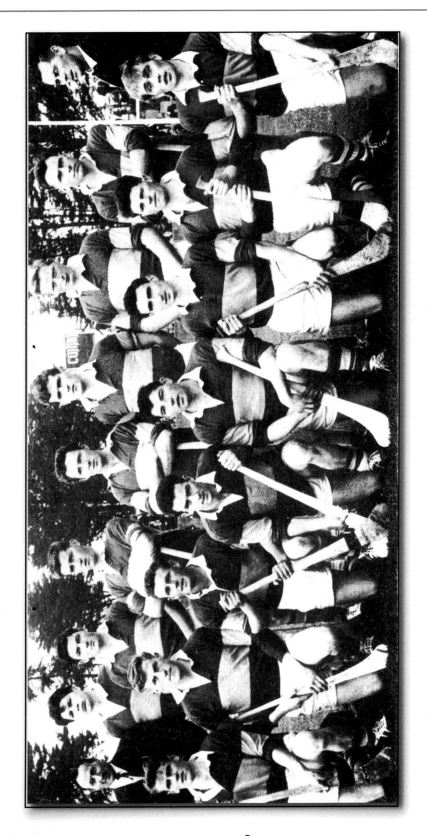

Tipperary - U21 All Ireland Champions 1964
Back: Ossie Bennett, W. Smyth, N. O'Gorman, J. Dillon, O. Killoran, M. Roche, T. Butler, N. Lane, J. Doyle.
Front: T. Brennan, C. O'Dwyer, P. O'Sulivan, F. Loughnane, M. Keating, L. Gaynor, J. Fogarty, M. O'Meara.

1964 FINAL
PREMIER COUNTY WIN FIRST ALL-IRELAND U-21 HURLING FINAL.
4/10/1964 AT NOWLAN PARK, KILKENNY.
Tipperary 8-9. Wexford 3-1

This game was infinitely more entertaining than the final score would suggest. Tipperary would have won by a even greater margin but for the heroic efforts of Wexford full-back Dan Quigley. Tipp's superiority stemmed from their superb midfield pairing of Mick Roche and Joe Fogarty and the sheer brilliance of centre-forward Michael Keating, who bamboozled the opposition at will. Tipp's midfield duo scored three goals, Fogarty two and Roche one. Others who starred for the Premier county were goalkeeper Peter O'Sullivan, Willie Smith, Noel O'Gorman, Owen Killoran, Noel Lane, Francis Loughnane and TJ Butler. Wexford battled with great heart, but it was all in vain against a much superior team.

Tipperary led by 4-2 to 0-1 after 16 minutes, due largely to a spell of Keating hurling magic. Wexford, however, appeared to find strength in adversity and limited the winners to a further point in the remainder of the half, while scoring a goal themselves. Thus Tipp led at the interval by 4-3 to 1-1. Wexford scored another goal within four minutes of the restart. However, in the space of six minutes, Tipp scored a further 2-3 and the game was as good as over.

Others to play well for Wexford, apart from Dan Quigley, were Vincent Staples, Willie Murphy, Con Dowdall and Christy Jacob. Keating was undoubtedly the star for Tipperary. His stickwork and economy of movement were impeccable. The Tipp defence was an extremely solid unit. Full-back Noel O'Gorman and left half-back Len Gaynor were particularly impressive.

The referee was Aubrey Higgins of Galway.

Tipperary scorers; Michael Keating 2-3 (0-1f), Joe Fogarty 2-0, Noel Lane 2-0, TJ Butler 1-1, Mick Roche 1-0, Francis Loughnane 0-3, Tommy Brennan 0-2.

Wexford scorers; Con Dowdall 2-1 (1-1fs), Christy Jacob 1-0.

Tipperary team. Peter O'Sullivan (CashelKing Cormacs), Willie Smith (Clonakenny), Noel O'Gorman (Newport), Michael O'Meara (Lorrha), Owen Killoran (Roscrea), Conor Dwyer (Borrisokane), Len Gaynor (Kilruane McDonaghs), Mick Roche (Carrick Davins), Joe Fogarty (Golden), Noel Lane (Lorrha), Michael Keating (Ballybacon-Grange), Francis Loughnane (Roscrea) Capt, John Dillon (Roscrea), TJ Butler (Clonoulty-Rossmore), Tommy Brennan (Ballingarry).
Subs; PJ Ryan (Carrick Davins) for O'Meara. Jimmy Ryan (Carrick Davins), Richard Buckley (Moycarkey-Borris), Barney Hogan (Roscrea), Seamus Shinnors (Newport).

Wexford team. Michael Jacob (Oulart-the-Ballagh), Jim Dunne (Davidstown), Dan Quigley (Rathnure), Bernard Doyle (Faythe Harriers), Vincent Staples (St. Martin's), Jim Berry (Kilmore),

Capt, **Willie Murphy (Faythe Harriers), Martin Byrne (Rathnure), Joe Doran (Buffer's Alley), Con Dowdall (Faythe Harriers), Christy Jacob (Oulart-the-Ballagh), Oliver Cullen (Liam Mellows), Seamus Barron (Rathnure), Tony Maher (St. Aidan's), Pat Quigley (Rathnure).**
Subs; Michael Kinsella (Wolfe Tones), for Dunne. Basil Murray (St. Martin's) for Byrne. Pat O'Connor (Oulart-the-Ballagh) for Maher.

1964
LEINSTER FINAL: *Wexford 4-7, Laois 2-2*
MUNSTER FINAL: *Tipperary 8-9, Waterford 3-1*
ULSTER FINAL: *Antrim only team entered*
CONNACHT FINAL: *Galway are the only team to win the Connacht championship and it has only been played on 8 occasions due to a lack of a competitive side to compete with in Connacht. Otherwise, Galway have been nominated to represent the province, apart from Roscommon who played in the early years. From 1959 to 1969, Galway competed in Munster.*
ALL IRELAND SEMI FINALS: *Tipperary 11-6, Roscommon 2-6; Wexford 5-8, Antrim 2-3.*

◆ *The scores in the Munster & All Ireland Finals were identical.*

1965 FINAL
WEXFORD GAIN REVENGE FOR PREVIOUS YEAR.
12/9/1965 AT NOWLAN PARK, KILKENNY.
Wexford 3-7. Tipperary 1-4.

Wexford gained revenge for their loss in the senior final of 1965 and the previous year's loss in the U-21 final by trouncing Tipperary in the All-Ireland final at Kilkenny, before an attendance of 5,000. With rain falling for most of the hour, the standard of hurling suffered. The supporters also had to endure floundering in the mud surrounding the stadium, due to reconstruction work. The Wexford supporters enjoyed the occasion, despite the conditions, as their team completely dominated.

The Wexford goalkeeper Mick Jacob gave an outstanding exhibition, although standing in a goalmouth of mud in the second half.

Right through the field Wexford played with supreme confidence. Despite the appalling conditions within five minutes of the start they led by 1-2 to 0-0. By the interval they had an advantage of 3-4 to 1-1. Wexford full-forward Tony Doran played his heart out. Con Dowdall was another to do well, while Tony Maher gave the impression that had the conditions been better, he would have improved on his total of 0-2.

Tipperary never got going in the rain. Michael Keating did get one good goal and looked about the best of their forwards. Noel O'Gorman played well in their defence, but their backs as a unit were

Wexford- U21 All Ireland Champions 1965

Back: Pat QuigLey, Eddie Furlong, Bernard Doyle, Tony Maher, Paddy Roche, Seamus Barron , Willie O'Neill, Jack Berry, Willie Bernie,
Dan Quigley, Mick Kinsella, Con Dowdall.
Front: Liam Griffin, Tony Doran, Aidan Somers, Joe Doran, Eugene Ryan,   Vinny Staples, Willie Murphy, Mick Jacob , Christy Jacob.

well beaten by a more eager set of Wexford forwards. Tipp made poor use of their midfield dominance and much good work by PJ Ryan went for nought. There were some stirring duels between Tipp full-back John Costigan and Tony Doran.

The Wexford full-forward line were very active and by exploiting gaps in the Tipperary defence early on laid the foundations for victory. Wexford had more senior inter-county players in action and this helped to sway the game in their favour. The experience of Dan Quigley coupled with the splendid work of Willie O'Neill added strength to the full-back line. In the half-back line Vincent Staples and Willie Murphy had a little too much class for their opponents. With so much material at their disposal the future of the game in the Model county looked assured.

The referee was Jimmy Duggan of Galwaay.

Wexford scorers; Tony Doran 1-2, Con Dowdall 1-2 (fs), Jack Berry 1-1, Tony Maher 0-2.

Tipperary scorers; Michael "Babs" Keating 1-0 (f), PJ Ryan 0-1, Philip Ryan 0-1, Gerry Quinlan 0-1, Tommy Brennan 0-1.

Wexford team. Mick Jacob, (Oulart-the-Ballagh), Willie O'Neill (Kilmore), Capt, Dan Quigley (Rathnure), Aidan Somers (Rathnure), Vincent Staples (St. Martin's), Michael Kinsella (Wolfe Tones), Willie Murphy (Faythe Harriers), Eugene Ryan (St. Patrick's), Joe Doran (Buffer's Alley), Con Dowdall (Faythe Harriers), Pat Quigley (Rathnure), Seamus Barron (Rathnure), Tony Maher (St. Aidan's), Tony Doran (Buffer's Alley), Jack Berry (Kilmore).
Subs; Christy Jacob (Oulart-the-Ballagh) for Barron. Colm Doran (Buffer's Alley).

Tipperary team. Seamus Shinnors (Newport), Michael Flanagan (Moycarkey-Borris), John Costigan (Clonakenny), Denis Burke (Fethard), Owen Killoran (Roscrea) Capt, Noel O'Gorman (Newport), Len Gaynor (Kilruane McDonaghs), PJ Ryan (Carrick Davins), Gerry Quinlan (Ne nagh Eire Og), Francis Loughnane (Roscrea), Michael Keating (Ballybacon-Grange), Philip Ryan (Moneygall), Jack Ryan (Moneygall), TJ Butler (Clonoulty-Rossmore), Tommy Brennan (Ballingarry).
Subs; Michael O'Meara (Lorrha) for Flanagan.

1965
LEINSTER FINAL: *Wexford 7-9, Dublin 1-5*
MUNSTER FINAL: *Tipperary 4-9, Galway 3-3*
ULSTER FINAL: *Antrim 5-8, Down 4-7*
ALL IRELAND SEMI FINALS: *Tipperary 8-16, Roscommon 0-4; Wexford 8-13, Antrim 0-4.*

1966 FINAL

BARRY RESCUES CORK AS GREAT FINAL ENDS IN DRAW.
2/10/1966 AT NOWLAN PARK, KILKENNY.
Cork 3-12. Wexford 5-6

A scintillating hour of classy fare, before an attendance of 20,000, climaxed with Cork hitting the equalising point in the last second. There could have been no better result to a great final at sun-drenched Nowlan Park. Neither team deserved to lose. The hurling was of superlative quality. Right from the start, both sides showed exceptionally clever touches. The large attendance thrilled to a tempestuous second half. In that period, Wexford played as men inspired to turn an interval deficit of 1-7 to 2-8, to a lead of four points with five minutes to play.

Just when Wexford seemed poised for a successful defence of their title, back came Cork with a goal and a point in less than two minutes to level the scores. Wexford's full-forward Seamus Barron with two minutes to play, gave his side the lead with a point from a 50 yard free. A second after the 30th minute, Cork's Seanie Barry split the posts with a point. The full time whistle came with the puck out.

It was fitting that Barry should have the final say, for he was the outstanding figure on the field, accounting for 2-8 of Cork's total. Little behind him, however, was midfielder Justin McCarthy, who laid on some of Barry's long-range points with precision passes. Others to show up well for Cork were Willie Murphy, Barry Wylie and Pat O'Sullivan in defence and Charlie McCarthy and Eddie O'Brien in attack. Tadhg Falvey and senior captain Gerald McCarthy came on as late subs in the last quarter and contributed to Cork's comeback.

Best for Wexford in a first half when Cork were on top, were defenders Willie O'Neill, Michael Kinsella and John Murphy. In Wexford's storming display in the second half, Michael Gardiner, Pat Quigley, Tony Doran and John Quigley starred for the Model County. Reckless bravado led to Donal Clifford of Cork and John Murphy of Wexford being sent off. However, it was anything but a dirty game. The pulling was fierce, the tackling severe, but there was no real rancour. The attack on the referee Donie Nealon at the end was utterly uncalled for. Players from both sides went to his aid and no damage was done.

During the course of the game, there was a goal of unusual origin. The Cork corner-back Willie Murphy, whilst trying to stave off a fierce Wexford onslaught, tried to deflect a ball out for a seventy, but from about fifteen yards out drove it into his own net.

The referee was Donie Nealon of Tipperary.

Cork scorers; Seanie Barry 2-8 (1-1fs), Eddie O'Brien 1-0, Jack Russell 0-1, Pat O'Riordan 0-1, Justin McCarthy 0-1, Charlie McCarthy 0-1.

Cork - U21 All Ireland Champions 1966 (First Game)

Back: Con Roche, Jack Barrett (Sel.), Dona! Clifford, John Mitchell, Seanie Barry, Justin McCarthy, Brian McKeown, Barry Wylie, Eddie O'Brien, Jim Barry (trainer).

Front: Willie Murphy, Pat O'Riordan, Tadhg Falvey, Peter Curley, Charlie McCarthy , Paddy O'Sullivan, Jack Russell.

Wexford scorers; Tony Doran 2-0, Michael Gardiner 1-1 (0-1f), Eddie Cousins 1-0, Con Dowdall 0-2, Barry Ronan 0-1, John Quigley 0-1, Seamus Barron 0-1 (f), Willie Murphy (Cork) 1-0 (og).

Cork team. John Mitchell (Blarney), Willie Murphy (Ballincollig), Brian McKeown (St. Finnbarr's), Kevin O' Farrell (Castletownroche), Con Roche (St. Finnbarr's), Barry Wylie (Carrigaline), Pat O'Sullivan (Midleton), Justin McCarthy (Passage), Donal Clifford (Cloyne), Seanie Barry (Rathcormac), Jack Russell (Ballyhea), Pat O'Riordan (White's Cross), Charlie McCarthy (St. Finnbarr's), Eddie O'Brien (Passage), Peter Curley (Brian Dillon's).
Subs; Gerald McCarthy (St. Finnbarr's), Captain, for Russell. Tadhg Falvey (Blackrock) for McKeown.

Wexford team. Mick Jacob (Oulart-the-Ballagh), Willie O'Neill (Kilmore), Mick Nolan (Oylegate), Aidan Somers (Rathnure), Vincent Staples (St. Martin's), Michael Kinsella (Wolfe Tones), John Murphy (Geraldine O'Hanrahan's), Pat Quigley (Rathnure), Ternie Murphy (Buffer's Alley), Con Dowdall (Faythe Harriers), Tony Doran (Buffer's Alley), Capt, Michael Gardiner (Geraldine O'Hanrahan's), John Quigley (Rathnure), Seamus Barron (Rathnure), Eddie Cousins (St. Martin's).
Subs; Barry Ronan (Geraldine O'Hanrahan's) for T. Murphy.

1966 FINAL REPLAY
TITANIC STRUGGLE ENDS IN ANOTHER DRAW.
23/10/1966 AT GAELIC GROUNDS, LIMERICK.
Cork 4-9. Wexford 4-9.

It is almost a maxim of sport that replays fail to live up to expectation. This was most certainly not the case in this replay in Limerick, as 18,000 spectators were enthralled by the speed and elegance of both teams. When Cork led by 1-7 to 1-1 after 19 minutes, due mainly to the splendour of their midfielders, Justin and Gerald McCarthy, it appeared that they would go on to victory. However, Wexford had wise mentors and three crucial switches involving the Quigley brothers, Pat and John and Barry Ronan, transformed their side.

Wexford put much more grit and vigour into their play in the last forty minutes. John Quigley, who had broken the hearts of the Cork minors at Croke Park on the previous Sunday, illuminated the game for Wexford. Within eight minutes of taking up duty on the "forty", he made two goals to give Wexford an interval lead of 3-2 to 1-7. Cork forged a 2 point lead within two minutes of the restart, but after eight minutes scores were again level. There followed a period of Cork dominance which brought 1-1, but between the 13th and 23rd minutes Wexford scored 1-4 and seemed secure.

In quicker time than it takes to relate, Cork levelled with a goal. With time running out Wexford once more went in front by a point. Thirty seconds later Cork got on terms with a point from a free by Seanie Barry. Every neutral in the attendance must have been charmed that neither side lost in

Cork Team 1966 - First Replay
Back: Pat O'Riordan, Barry Wiley, Andrew Flynn, Justin McCarthy, Jim Casey, Tony Maher,
Brian McKeoghn, Tadhg Falvey.
Front: Seanie Barry, Gerald McCarthy, Charlie McCarthy, Peter Curley, Jack Russell,
Paddy O'Sullivan, Denis Coughlin.

a memorable contest. On four occasions in all in that thrilling second half, scores were level. The Quigleys, especially teenager John, Vinnie Staples who policed Seanie Barry out of the game, Michael Kinsella, Tony Doran, Con Dowdall, Michael Nolan, Seamus Barron and Aidan Somers stood out in the Wexford side.

Along with Justin and Gerald McCarthy, Cork were magnificently served by goalie John Mitchell, Jack Russell, Charlie McCarthy, Andrew Flynn and Eddie O'Brien.

The referee was Gerry Fitzgerald of Limerick.

Andrew Flynn, scorer of 3-0, had scored 2-0 for Cork in their All-Ireland minor victory over Laois in 1964.

Cork scorers; Andrew Flynn 3-0, Seanie Barry 0-5 (4fs), Charlie McCarthy 1-2, Justin McCarthy, 0-1, Peter Curley 0-1.

Wexford scorers; Tony Doran 1-2, Con Dowdall 1-1, Seamus Barron 0-4 (2fs), Pat Quigley 1-0, Eddie Cousins 1-0, Michael Gardiner 0-1, Noel Rochford 0-1.

Cork team. John Mitchell (Blarney), Willie Murphy (Ballincollig), Tadhg Falvey (Blackrock), Pat Sullivan (Midleton), Con Roche (St. Finnbarr's), Barry Wylie (Carrigaline), Denis Coughlan (Glen Rovers), Justin McCarthy (Passage), Gerald McCarthy (St. Finnbarr's), Capt, Seanie Barry (Rathcormac), Jack Russell (Ballyhea), Peter Curley (Brian Dillons), Charlie McCarthy

(St. Finnbarr's), Andrew Flynn (Glen Rovers), Eddie O'Brien (Passage).
Subs. Tom Browne (Carrigtwohill) for O'Brien.

Wexford team. Mick Jacob (Oulart-the-Ballagh), Paddy O'Brien (Rosslare), Michael Nolan (Oylegate), Aidan Somers (Rathnure), Willie O'Neill (Kilmore), Michael Kinsella (Wolfe Tones), Vincent Staples (St. Martin's), Barry Ronan (Geraldine O'Hanrahan's), Seamus Barron (Rathnure), Con Dowdall (Faythe Harriers), Pat Quigley (Rathnure), John Quigley (Rathnure), Michael Gardiner (Geraldine O'Hanrahan's), Tony Doran (Buffer's Alley), Capt, Eddie Cousins (St.Martin's).
Subs. Noel Rochford (Kilmore) for Ronan. Ronan for Rochford.

1966 FINAL 2ND REPLAY.
CORK FINALLY CLINCH FIRST TITLE.
13/11/1966 AT CROKE PARK.
Cork 9-9. Wexford 5-9.

This second replay, before an attendance of 27,268, fell a long way short of the high standard of the previous two games. The signs were false, however, as the first half was a thriller. After 15 minutes in bad weather conditions, Cork led by 2-2 to 0-3. A Wexford surge followed and by the 18th minute the sides were level. Cork led by a point at half-time, 2-4 to 1-6. Both sides got a standing ovation as they left the field.

At the end of the third quarter, Cork led by 4-8 to 2-8. By the 18th minute of the second half Wexford had cut the gap to 2 points.

The Cork forwards now began to cut through the Wexford defence, which was in disarray. In the last eleven minutes Cork scored five goals and a point. The Wexford defenders were under severe pressure and suddenly cracked like a dry twig, as Justin McCarthy and Gerald McCarthy totally dominated the midfield area for the winners. The Cork men took their scores neatly from long and short range, while Wexford had to work extremely hard for their scores. Cork played power hurling for the full hour and always seemed to have that sixth sense, which told them when to pull first-time or when to lift and strike.

The midfield McCarthys were not the only Cork stars. John Mitchell was a top-class and courageous goalkeeper. Jack Russell, on this occasion starting at centre-back, added much stability to a defence in which Denis Coughlan and Con Roche also gave outstanding displays. All of the Cork forwards were outstanding with perhaps, Peter Curley the best of the sextet.

An injury to Wexford's John Quigley, in the first minute of the game, rendered him ineffective for the whole match. This was a big blow to the men from the Model County, as he had been the star player in the first replay. Michael Kinsella, Vincent Staples, Tony Doran, Willie O'Neill and Seamus Barron all battled bravely for the losers.

The referee was Gerry Fitzgerald of Limerick.

Gerald McCarthy had the unique distinction of captaining both Cork seniors and U-21's to All-Ireland victories in 1966.

Cork scorers; Charlie McCarthy 2-2 (0-2fs), Peter Curley 2-1, Eddie O'Brien 2-1, Andrew Flynn 2-0, Seanie Barry 1-2, Justin McCarthy 0-3 (fs).

Wexford scorers; Seamus Barron 2-4 (1-4fs), Mick Jacob 1-1, Pat Quigley 1-0, Tony Doran 1-0, Con Dowdall 0-2, Eddie Cousins 0-1, Michael Gardiner 0-1.

Cork team. John Mitchell (Blarney), Willie Murphy (Ballincollig), Tadhg Falvey (Blackrock), Pat O'Sullivan (Midleton), Con Roche (St. Finnbarr's), Jack Russell (Ballyhea), Denis Coughlan (Glen Rovers), Justin McCarthy (Passage), Gerald McCarthy (St. Finnbarr's), Capt, Seanie Barry (Rathcormac), Tom Browne (Carrigtwohill), Peter Curley (Brian Dillons), Charlie McCarthy (St. Finnbarr's), Andrew Flynn (Glen Rovers), Eddie O'Brien (Passage).
Subs. Brian McKeown (St. Finnbarr's) for Falvey. Anthony Maher (St. Finnbarr's) for O'Sullivan.

Wexford team. Henry Butler (Buffer's Alley), Willie O'Neill (Kilmore), Michael Nolan (Oylegate), Aidan Somers (Rathnure), Billy Bowe (Horeswood), Michael Kinsella (Wolfe Tones), Vincent Staples (St. Martin's), Mick Jacob (Oulart-the-Ballagh), Con Dowdall (Faythe Harriers), Seamus Barron (Rathnure), Pat Quigley (Rathnure), John Quigley (Rathnure), Pierce Butler (Buffer's Alley), Tony Doran (Buffer's Alley), Capt, Eddie Cousins (St. Martin's).
Subs. Enda Murphy (Ferns) for Bowe. Michael Gardiner (Geraldine O'Hanrahan's) for P. Butler. Noel Rochford (Kilmore) for Jacob.

1966
LEINSTER FINAL: Wexford 7-10, Laois 2-8
MUNSTER FINAL: Cork 5-12, Limerick 2-6
ULSTER FINAL: Antrim 4-5, Down 0-8
ALL IRELAND SEMI FINALS: Cork 11-18, Roscommon 5-1; Wexford 4-13, Antrim 1-5.

◆ *Each side had a tally of 21 points in the draw and replay*
◆ *At the end of first replay, both sides made a decision not to play extra time.*

1967 FINAL
DUBLIN WASTE CHANCES AS TIPP TAKE SECOND U-21 TITLE.
10/9/1967 AT CROKE PARK.
Tipperary 1-8. Dublin 1-7.

Although scores were level six times in the hour---three times in each half--- and the finish was conducted in a welter of excitement, this final never reached the expected heights. At no stage was there more than two points between the teams but the fare was dour rather than brilliant. Tipp led by 1-3 to 0-5 at the interval, thanks to a goal from Pat O'Connor in the 27th minute.

Dublin jumped into the lead in the 38th minute, when Tom Grealish goaled after the Tipp goalkeeper Henry Condron, had pushed Len Hennebury's long-range shot against the crossbar and the ball rebounded into play. Jack Ryan equalised with a pointed free in the 40th minute. Scores were level twice subsequently before John Flanagan shot the winning point for the Munster champions in the 59th minute. With time almost up and Tipp clinging on to that single point lead, Eugene Davey, the Dublin centre-forward, had his shot for goal saved by Condron. The most exciting part of the game was in that final five minutes.

Best for Tipperary were Seamus Ryan, John Kelly, Tadhg O'Connor, Seamus Hogan, PJ Ryan and Pat O'Connor. Dublin tackled as if their lives depended on it and their striking throughout the field matched that of their rivals. Had they a more penetrative full-forward line they might have won. Their best performers were Mick Hannick, Pat Martin, Fergus Cooney, Gay O'Driscoll, Noel Kinsella, Tom Grealish and Eugene Davey.

The referee was Aubrey Higgins of Galway.

Tipperary scorers; Pat O'Connor 1-3, John Flanagan 0-2 (1f), Jack Ryan 0-2 (1f), Timmy Delaney 0-1.

Dublin scorers; Tom Grealish 1-1, Harry Dalton 0-2 (1f), Eamon McGrath 0-1, Eugene Davey 0-1, Len Hennebury 0-1 (f), Noel Kinsella 0-1 (f).

Tipperary team. Henry Condron (Moneygall), Seamus Ryan (Moycarkey-Borris), John Kelly (Cappawhite), Dan O'Grady (Moyne-Templetouhy), Martin Esmonde (Moyne-Templetouhy), Tadhg O'Connor (Roscrea), Seamus Hogan (Kiladangan), PJ Ryan (Carrick Davins), Capt, Conor Davitt (Cashel King Cormacs), Noel O'Dwyer (Borris-Ileigh), John Flanagan (Moycarkey-Borris), Jacky Walsh (Carrick Davins), Pat O'Connor (Cashel King Cormacs), Phil Lowry (Upperchurch-Drombane), Jack Ryan (Moneygall).
Subs. Timmy Delaney (Borris-Ileigh) for O'Dwyer. Michael Nolan (Moneygall) for Esmonde. Michael Delaney (Toomevara).
Dublin team. Michael Behan (Na Fianna), Mick Hannick (St. Vincent's), Pat Martin (St. Columba's), Colm Brennan (New Ireland), Willie Markey (Rialto Gaels), Fergus Cooney (Good Counsel), Gay O'Driscoll (St. Vincent's), Harry Dalton (Good Counsel), Fergus McDonnell (St.

Columba's), Eamon McGrath (Commercials), Eugene Davey (Clanna Gael), Len Hennebury (St. Columba's), Tom Grealish (St. Columba's), Christy Moran (Ballyfermot), Noel Kinsella (Colmcille's).

Subs. M. Kennedy (Na Fianna) for Moran. Patsy Cunningham (Ballyfermot), Mick Cunningham (O'Toole's), S. Blake (Fr. Murphy's), P.Cassells (St. Columba's), M. Donovan (Ballyfermot).

First Presentation of the Cross of Cashel Trophy 1967
Tipperary captain, PJ Ryan receives the Cross of Cashel trophy from Most Rev Dr Morris who donated the trophy to the the the GAA.

1967
LEINSTER FINAL: *Dublin 2-10, Offaly 2-9*
MUNSTER FINAL: *Tipperary 3-9, Galway 3-5*
ULSTER FINAL: *Antrim 3-8, Down 2-7*
ALL IRELAND SEMI FINALS: *Dublin 3-13, Antrim 0-7. (Only one semi-final in 1967)*

◆ *Match winner John Flanagan was laid low with the flu in the week prior to the final.*
◆ *Tipperary's Jack Ryan was son of GAA President Seamus O'Riain.*

Tipperary - U21 All Ireland Champions 1967

Back: Jackie Walshe, Pat O'Connor, Seamus Hogan, Henry Condron, John Kelly, Conor Davitt, Dan O'Grady, Seamus Ryan.

Front: Noel O'Dwyer, Tadgh O'Connor, Phil Lowry, P. J. Ryan, John Flanagan, Jack Ryan, Martin Esmonde.

1968 FINAL
MEADE THE HERO, AS CORK CLINCH SECOND TITLE.
8/9/1968 AT WALSH PARK, WATERFORD.
Cork 2-18. Kilkenny 3-9.

This decider started rather tamely but finished with displays of top class hurling. The Noresiders were rather lethargic in a sloppy first half, marked by a succession of misses by both sets of forwards. After a bright opening by Cork, a torpor descended on their play until they began to hid their stride again entering the second quarter. With Pat Moylan dominating at midfield, Cork built up a lead of 0-10 to 1-1 at the interval.

Kilkenny chopped and changed at the break. These switches appeared to be working as Willie Harte notched three points in the first three minutes of the second half. Kilkenny now played their best hurling, reducing the arrears to four points with twelve minutes remaining. If Cork had their lanky right-half forward Bernard Meade as their sharpshooter, so too did Kilkenny in Willie Harte, also operating on the right wing. However, every time Kilkenny looked like drawing level, Cork retaliated with some fine scores. Meade's goal four minutes from time, when the Kilkenny goalkeeper advanced at the wrong moment, sealed the issue.

The 1968 final will always be associated with the stylish Passage wing forward Bernard Meade. Not alone did he score 1-12, but his clever stickwork, his well placed passes to colleagues and his lightning fast solo runs marked him out as the outstanding player on the field. Pat Hegarty, who starred in attack, midfield and defence, also contributed handsomely to Cork's win. However, it was their defence which really stood out in the closing stages when the stripey men piled everything into attack. Brian Tobin shone as brightly as the white boots he wore, while behind him Brendan Hurley had a cat-like save to stop what looked like a certain goal.

The Kilkenny full-forward line was very weak and only full-forward Pat Keyes scored, when he lashed a 21 yard free to the net. Kilkenny looked a most disjointed side in the first half. Their half-back line rarely looked happy. Willie Harte was the only forward upon whom Kilkenny could rely. John Kinsella played well when switched to midfield. Liam Byrne and Niall Morrissey tried hard in their defence. Senior inter-county man Frank Cummins did not reach his usual high standard at midfield.

The referee was Seamus Power of Waterford.

Cork scorers; Bernard Meade 1-12 0-9fs), Peter Curley 1-2, Pat Hegarty 0-2, Pat Moylan 0-1, Richard Lehane 0-1.
Kilkenny scorers; Willie Harte 1-8, Pat Lalor 1-0, Paddy Keyes 1-0 (f), John Kinsella 0-1.

Cork team. Bernard Hurley (Blackrock), Willie Murphy (Ballincollig), Brian Tobin (Blackrock), Frank Norberg (Blackrock), Noel Dunne (Cloughduv), Willie Walsh (Youghal), Ray Cummins (UCC), Donal Clifford (Cloyne), Pat Moylan (Blackrock), Bernard Meade (Passage), Simon Murphy (Blackrock), Pat Hegarty (Youghal), Capt, Henry O'Sullivan (Inniscarra), Peter Curley

Cork- U21 All Ireland Champions 1968
Back: Brian Tobin, Richard Lehane, Henry O'Sullivan, Paddy Ring, Simon Murphy, Joe Murphy, Bernie Meade, Noel Dunne,
Frank Norberg, Bernard Hurley, Jimmy Barrett.
Front: Willie Walsh, Ray Cummins,Peter Curley, Pat Hegarty capt, Donal Clifford. Pat Moylan. Mick McCarthy
Mick Malone, Willie Murphy.

(Brian Dillons), Paddy Ring (Cloyne).
Subs. Mick McCarthy (Na Piarsaigh) for Dunne. Richard Lehane (Blackrock) for Ring. Joe Murphy (Passage) for Clifford). Henry O'Brien (Inniscarra), Jimmy Barrett (Nemo Rangers), Gerard Cronin (Tracton), Mick Malone (Eire Og).

Kilkenny team. John Nolan (*Coon*), Liam Byrne (*Graigue*), Conor O'Brien (*Bennettsbridge*), Mick Leahy (James Stephens), John O'Shea (Clara), Niall Morrissey (James Stephens), Paddy Kealy (Bennetsbridge), Frank Cummins (Blackrock), Pat Lalor (Bennettsbridge), Willie Harte (Galmoy), Fergus Farrell (Johnstown), John Kinsella (Bennettsbridge), Patsy Dowling (James Stephens), Paddy Keyes (Paulstown), Brendan O'Sullivan (Thomastown).
Subs. Sean Brennan (James Stephens) for Farrell. Sean Kearney (Thomastown) for Dowling. Tommy Grant for O'Shea. Maurice Mason (Ballyhale Shamrocks), E. Murphy, W. Dillon (Muckalee), Murty Coonan (Coon).

1968
LEINSTER FINAL: *Kilkenny 4-10, Dublin 5-4*
MUNSTER FINAL: *Cork 4-10, Tipperary 1-13*
ULSTER FINAL: *Down 7-6, Armagh 2-9*
(This was Roinn 'B' final. Antrim represented province in All-Ireland series.)
ALL IRELAND SEMI FINALS: *Cork 4-17, Antrim 2-4. (Only one semi-final in 1968)*

◆ *Willie Murphy collected his second All-Ireland U-21 medal.*
◆ *Peter Curley and Donal Clifford were other survivors of the 1966 team.*

1969 FINAL
CORK'S LATE SURGE DEFLATES GALLANT WEXFORD.
14/9/1969 AT WALSH PARK, WATERFORD.
Cork 5-13. Wexford 4-7.

With no fewer than fourteen of the selection who won the previous year's All-Ireland U-21 hurling championship, Cork were strong favourites for the 1969 final. In an entertaining game, before an attendance of 5,000, the Leesiders opened up with a goal after 30 seconds. The losers kept in touch when Tom Royce goaled from a 21 yard free at the end of the first quarter. Then, Wexford's Mick Butler had two snap goals within ten minutes. Moments before half-time, Mick Dalton goaled to leave Wexford leading by two points at the break, 4-6 to 3-7.

There was nothing between the sides until the final quarter, when Cork made an astute switch. Centre forward Willie Walsh and full forward Ray Cummins swapped positions. While Cummins continued to be the most dangerous Cork forward, Walsh found his true form and with that the rest of the attack began to work really well. It was still very close seven minutes from the end, when Bernie Meade put Cork ahead with a point from a 21 yard free. From then until the final whistle, Cork completely dominated eventually winning by nine points. The surge to victory was sparked

Cork- U21 All Ireland Champions 1969

Back: Frank Keane, Mick McCarthy, Seamus Looney, Pat Moylan, Bernie Meade, Simon Murphy, Noel Dunne, Willie Walsh.
Front: Ray Cummins, Frank Norberg, Teddy O'Brien, Donal Clifford, Brian Tobin, Brendan Cummins, Bernard Hurley, Paddy Cooney.

off by a wonderful goal off the ground by Willie Walsh, almost immediately after Meade's point. Another goal followed from Simon Murphy seconds from full time.

For Cork, Ray Cummins and his brother Brendan showed uncanny ability in their fielding with Ray finishing with 2-4 to his credit. Bernie Meade was very accurate from frees. Cork's midfield pairing of Pat Moylan and Simon Murphy, although challenged by Ned Buggy, were dominant for most of the game. Donal Clifford and Michael McCarthy were best of the winners' defence.

Mick Butler, Tom Royce and John Quigley did well in the Wexford attack. In the losers' defence, Jack Russell had a very fine first half, while Eddie McDonald also impressed.

The referee was Paddy Johnson of Kilkenny.

Cork scorers; Ray Cummins 2-4, Bernie Meade 0-5, Simon Murphy 1-1, Willie Walsh 1-1, Brendan Cummins 1-0, Pat Moylan 0-1, Frankie Keane 0-1.

Wexford scorers; Mick Butler 2-0, Tom Royce 1-3 (1-0f), Mick Dalton 1-0, Ned Buggy 0-3, Martin Quigley 0-1.

Cork team. Bernard Hurley (Blackrock), Michael McCarthy (Na Piarsaigh), Capt, Brian Tobin (Blackrock), Frank Norberg (Blackrock), Seamus Looney (St. Finnbarr's), Donal Clifford (Cloyne), Teddy O'Brien (Glen Rovers), Simon Murphy (Blackrock), Pat Moylan (Blackrock), Bernie Meade (Passage), Willie Walsh (Passage), Noel Dunne (Cloughduv), Frankie Keane (Youghal), Ray Cummins (UCC), Brendan Cummins (Blackrock).
Subs. Pat McDonnell (Inniscarra), for Looney. Tom BuckleyGlen Rovers), Paddy Geary (Blackrock), Jimmy Barrett (Nemo Rangers), Mick Malone (Eire Og).

Wexford team. Pat Cox (St. Aidan's), Eddie McDonald (St. Martin's), Enda Murphy (Ferns St. Aidan's), Billy Butler (Geraldine O'Hanrahan's), Eddie Walsh (Faythe Harriers), Jack Russell (Geraldine O'Hanrahan's), Liam Bennett (Faythe Harriers), Capt, Mick Dalton (Geraldine O'Hanrahan's), Ned Buggy (Faythe Harriers), Tom Royce (Oulart-the-Ballagh), Martin Quigley (Rathnure), Matt Browne (Shamrocks), John Quigley (Rathnure), Mick Butler (Buffer's Alley), Colm Doran (Buffer's Alley).
Subs. Tom Byrne (Oulart-the-Ballagh) for Doran. Martin Casey (Buffer's Alley).

1969
LEINSTER FINAL: *Wexford 3-16, Kilkenny 4-3*
MUNSTER FINAL: *Cork 3-11, Tipperary 1-5*
ULSTER FINAL: *Down 5-17, Antrim 2-11*
ALL IRELAND SEMI FINALS: *Wexford 12-10, Down 2-1. (Only one semi-final in 1969)*

CHAPTER 2
ALL IRELAND U21
HURLING FINALS
1970-1979

1970 Final
Draw was a fitting result to a great game.
11/10/1970 at Croke Park.
Cork 3-8. Wexford 2-11.

In what was the best All-Ireland hurling final of 1970, Cork and Wexford were on level terms at the final whistle. Few in the attendance would quibble with the result for it gave them another opportunity of seeing two well-matched teams do battle in the replay. Cork, holders of the title for the previous two years and pre-match favourites got a rare fright. From the start it was apparent that the challengers would not be easily beaten. The evenly contested first half ended with Wexford leading by 0-6 to 0-5.

Cork equalised on the resumption and it was 0-7 each by the 34th minute. Three minutes later, Martin Quigley left his only imprint on the game, when bursting through the centre for a Wexford goal. It looked like Wexford had got the winning advantage in the 43rd minute, when Mick Butler's shot from the right-hand touchline deceived Cork goalkeeper Martin Coleman and dropped under the bar to the net. The champions' reply was swift and devastating. On 45 minutes, Paddy Ring goaled from a twenty one yard free. Almost immediately the best move of the hour saw Brendan Cummins and Jimmy Barrett combine to place substitute Seanie O'Leary for the equalising goal. Mick Butler(free) and Connie Kelly traded points to leave the score at 2-8 each. Two points from Butler, one from play, inched Wexford ahead once more before Ring's second goal from a twenty one yard free gave Cork the lead for the first time in the 55th minute. Within a minute, Butler had the teams on level terms for the seventh time. Two minutes from time, Butler missed his only free of the hour and there was no further scoring.

Defences on both sides dominated. Best of a very solid Cork defensive unit were Mick McCarthy, Pat McDonnell, John Horgan and Teddy O'Brien, who did a very good policing job on Martin Quigley. Senior county man Seamus Looney had a very quiet game at midfield, where the Rebels were dependent on the efforts of Pat Moylan. Up front, Cork were well served by Jimmy Barrett and the two substitutes, dynamic minor Seanie O'Leary and Connie Kelly.

All of the Wexford backs played well, with Jack Russell, Eddie McDonald, Larry Byrne and Liam Bennett particularly impressive. Tom Byrne and Colm Doran played well at midfield. In attack, Wexford were too dependent on Mick Butler.

Cork scorers; Paddy Ring 2-2 (fs), Seanie O'Leary 1-0, Connie Kelly 0-2, Kevin McSweeney 0-2, Simon Murphy 0-1, Seamus Looney 0-1.

Wexford scorers; Mick Butler 1-10 (0-9fs), Martin Quigley 1-0, Liam Bennett 0-1 (f).

Cork team. Martin Coleman (Ballinhassig), Mick McCarthy (UCC), Pat McDonnell (Inniscarra), Brian Tobin (Blackrock), Simon Murphy (Blackrock), John Horgan (Blackrock), Teddy O'Brien (Glen Rovers), Capt, Seamus Looney (UCC), Pat Moylan (Blackrock), Jimmy Barrett (UCC),

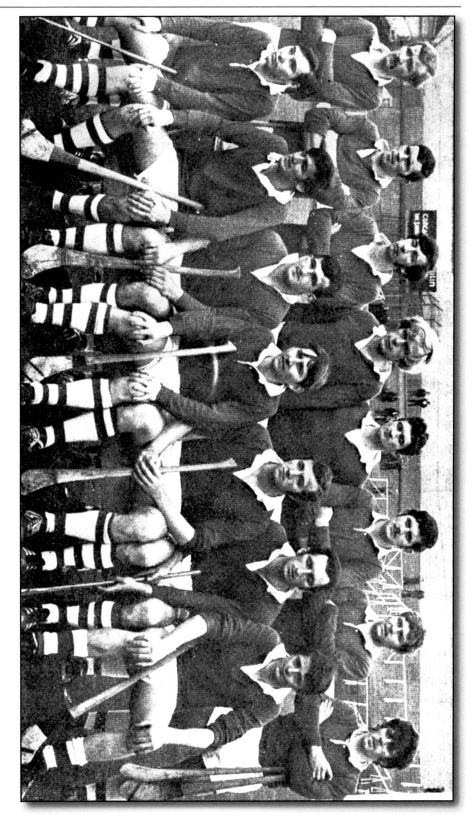

Cork- *U21 All Ireland Champions 1970*
Back: B. Tobin, Pat McDonnell, S. Looney, J. Horgan, P. Moylan, M. McCarthy, P. Ring, M. Coleman.
Front: S. O'Leary, B. Cummins, C. Kelly, T. O'Brien (Captain), J. Barrett, S. Murphy, K. McSweeney.

Jim Nodwell (Mayfield), Kevin McSweeney (Castletownroche), Mick Malone (Eire Og), Brendan Cummins (Blackrock), Paddy Ring (Cloyne).
Subs. Connie Kelly (Cloughduv) for Nodwell. Seanie O'Leary (Youghal) for Malone.

Wexford team. Pat Cox (St. Aidan's), Jim Prendergast (Oulart-the-Ballagh), Jack Russell (Geraldine O'Hanrahan's), Eddie McDonald (St. Martin's), Ger Collins (Shamrocks), Larry Byrne (St. Anne's, Rathangan), Liam Bennett (Faythe Harriers), Capt., Tom Byrne (Oulart-the-Ballagh), Colm Doran (Buffer's Alley), Martin Quigley (Rathnure), Martin Casey (Buffer's Alley), Enda Murphy (Ferns St. Aidan's), Pat Byrne (Shamrocks), Mick Butler (Buffer's Alley), Brendan Murphy (Faythe Harriers).
Subs. Aidan Kerrigan (St. Patrick's) for P. Byrne. Pat Byrne for Brendan Murphy.

1970 FINAL REPLAY
CORK ROMP TO VICTORY IN VERY DISAPPOINTING REPLAY.
1/11/1970 AT CROKE PARK.
Cork 5-17. Wexford 0-8.

In this very disappointing replay, the last ten minutes of the first half completely decided the result. Wexford had drawn level by the 20th minute, but Cork crashed home 4-4 between there and the interval to lead by fifteen points at the break, 4-9 to 0-6. That was the end of the contest. The Cork dominance started with a Jimmy Barrett point, followed by another from Paddy Ring. Then Connie Kelly scored their first goal. Within a minute, Brendan Cummins had another goal. A point from Ring, a goal by Barrett from a melee, another goal by Kelly from a free left Wexford reeling.

Through the second half Cork could do nothing wrong and Wexford nothing right. When Seanie O'Leary added Cork's fifth goal shortly after the resumption, the attendance had nothing else to wonder at except the splendour of Cork's subsequent hurling and the amazing goalkeeping of Martin Coleman who defied the Wexford attack right to the end.

Coleman had great protection from Pat McDonnell, Mick McCarthy, Simon Murphy, Teddy O'Brien and John Horgan. Cork took control at midfield after the end of the first quarter, when Kevin McSweeney moved out to join Pat Moylan. In attack, Paddy Ring's accuracy was an added asset to Connie Kelly's brilliance.

For Wexford, who fell apart as a team, only Eddie McDonald, Liam Bennett, Colm Doran, Mick Butler and Martin Quigley met the standard they had set themselves in the drawn game.
The referee was Jim Dunphy of Waterford.

Cork scorers; Connie Kelly 2-7 (1-2fs), Paddy Ring 0-7 (0-3fs), Jimmy Barrett 1-1, Brendan Cummins 1-0, Seanie O'Leary 1-0, John Horgan 0-1, Pat Moylan 0-1.

Wexford scorers; Mick Butler 0-4 (fs), Martin Casey 0-2, Martin Quigley 0-1, Liam Bennett 0-1 (70).

The referee for both games Jim Dunphy of Waterford.

Cork team. Martin Coleman (Ballinhassig), Mick McCarthy (U.C.C.), Pat McDonnell (Inniscara), Brian Tobin (Blackrock), Simon Murphy (Blackrock), John Horgan (Blackrock), Teddy O'Brien (Glen Rovers), Capt., Seamus Looney (U.C.C.), Pat Moylan (Blackrock), Connie Kelly (Cloghduv), Brendan Cummins (Blackrock), Kevin McSweeney (Castletownroche), Seanie O'Leary (Youghal), Jimmy Barrett (U.C.C.), Paddy Ring (Cloyne).
Subs. P. Lawton (Killeagh), T. O'Shea (Passage), Jim Nodwell (Mayfield), Mick Malone (Eire Og), P. Kavanagh (Blackrock).

Wexford team. Pat Cox (St. Aidan's), Jim Prendergast (Oulart-the-Ballagh, Jack Russell (Geraldine O'Hanrahan's), Eddie McDonald (St. Martin's), Ger Collins (Shamrocks), Larry Byrne (St. Anne's, Rathangan), Liam Bennett (Faythe Harriers), Capt., Tom Byrne (Oulart-the-Ballagh), Colm Doran (Buffer's Alley), Martin Quigley (Rathnure), Martin Casey (Buffer's Alley), Enda Murphy (Ferns St. Aidan's), Pat Byrne (Shamrocks), Mick Butler (Buffer's Alley), Brendan Murphy (Faythe Harriers).
Subs. Aidan Kerrigan (St. Patrick's) for B. Murphy. Phil Kennedy (Horeswood) for P. Byrne. Eddie Walsh (Faythe Harriers) for E. Murphy.

1970

LEINSTER FINAL: Wexford 2-15, Kilkenny 5-4
MUNSTER FINAL: Cork 3-11, Tipperary 2-7
ULSTER FINAL: Antrim 6-12, Down 2-10
ALL IRELAND SEMI FINALS: Cork 3-10, Antrim 1-4; Wexford 8-22, Galway 2-9.

♦ Cork won their 4th All-Ireland title of the season, Senior and Minor Hurling and the two U-21 titles.
♦ Simon Murphy, Seamus Looney, Teddy O'Brien and Jimmy Barrett all completed the U-21 double of football and hurling.
♦ Simon Murphy and Seamus Looney each won their 3rd All-Ireland medal of the year.
♦ John Horgan, Pat McDonnell and Martin Coleman also won Senior All-Ireland hurling medals.
♦ Seanie O'Leary also won a Minor All-Ireland hurling medal in 1970.

1971 FINAL
FOUR GOAL ROTHWELL DESTROYS WEXFORD IN LAST QUARTER.
12/9/1971 AT CROKE PARK.
Cork 7-8 Wexford 1-11.

Before a very small attendance, Cork trailed by a point as the game moved into the last quarter, yet won by 15 points, thanks to an amazing scoring feat of 5 goals in just over 7 minutes. The man who destroyed Wexford and gave Cork their 4th successive title was full-forward, John Rothwell from Blackrock.

The winners settled down quickly and went into an early lead. Wexford improved in the second quarter. They were 5 points in front at one stage, before Cork hauled them back to level pegging at the interval, Wexford 1-7, Cork 2-4. On the resumption Cork took an early lead, but Wexford then took control. Faulty shooting deprived them of what could have been a sizeable lead. The outlook was bleak for Cork, when with Wexford leading by 2 points, they lost senior star Seamus Looney, who was replaced at midfield by Pat Kavanagh from Blackrock.

Kavanagh immediately scored a fine point, which halved the Wexford lead. A minute later, John Horgan, who had just discarded boots and stockings, sent a long-range free into the Wexford goalmouth. Though closely marked, Rothwell backhanded the ball to the Wexford net. Thirty seconds later, the full forward set up Brendan Cummins for another goal. Liam Bennett interrupted the Cork scoring riot, with a point from out the field – Wexford's last score. Inside a minute, Rothwell scored 2 more goals. When a drive from Cummins came off the crossbar, he smashed the rebound to the Wexford net. Next he connected with Noel Crowley's high lob for his own 4th and Cork's 6th goal.

When the ball was running for them in the last quarter, Cork looked a team of all the talents. Goalkeeper Martin Coleman, his brother Brendan at left half-back and full back Pat McDonnell were best of a very sound defence. Cork were dominant at midfield, where Noel Crowley was outstanding. In attack, Rothwell was the scoring hero but accurate free-taker Seanie O'Leary also shone.

For Wexford, who fell away in the last quarter, goalkeeper Pat Cox, Larry Kinsella, Liam Bennett, Martin Quigley, Tom Byrne, Mick Butler and Martin Casey all had their moments. All except Bennett were swamped, when Cork cut loose.

The referee was Paddy Buggy of Kilkenny.

Cork scorers; John Rothwell 4-0, Seanie O'Leary 2-4 (1-4fs), Brendan Cummins 1-0, Pat Kavanagh 0-2, Mick Malone 0-1, Kevin McSweeney 0-1.

Wexford scorers; Mick Butler 1-2 (0-2fs), Martin Casey 0-3, Tom Byrne 0-2, Liam Bennett 0-2 (0-1f), Brendan Dunne 0-1, Jack Russell 0-1.

Cork team. Martin Coleman (Ballinhassig), Martin Doherty (Glen Rovers), Pat McDonnell (U.C.C.) Capt, Brian Murphy (Nemo Rangers), S. O'Farrell (Midleton), John Horgan (Blackrock), Brendan Coleman (Ballinhassig), Noel Crowley (Bandon), Seamus Looney (U.C.C.), E. Fitzpatrick (U.C.C.), Mick Malone (Eire Og), Kevin McSweeney (Castletownroche), Brendan Cummins (Blackrock), John Rothwell (Blackrock), Seanie O'Leary (Youghal).
Subs. Pat Casey (Blackrock) for O'Farrell, Donal Collins (Blackrock) for Fitzpatrick. Pat Kavanagh (Blackrock) for Looney, Pat Lawton (Killeagh), Mick Bohane (St. Finbarr's).

Wexford team. Pat Cox (St.Aidan's-Shamrocks), Jim Higgins (Rathnure), George O'Connor (Faythe Harriers), Peter O'Brien (Ferns St. Aidan's), Aidan Kerrigan (St. Patrick's), Larry Kinsella (Bunclody St. Vincent's), Liam Bennett (Faythe Harriers), Martin Quigley (Rathnure), Capt, Andy Dwyer (Ferns St. Aidan's), Brendan Dunne (Rathgarogue-Cushenstown), Tom Byrne

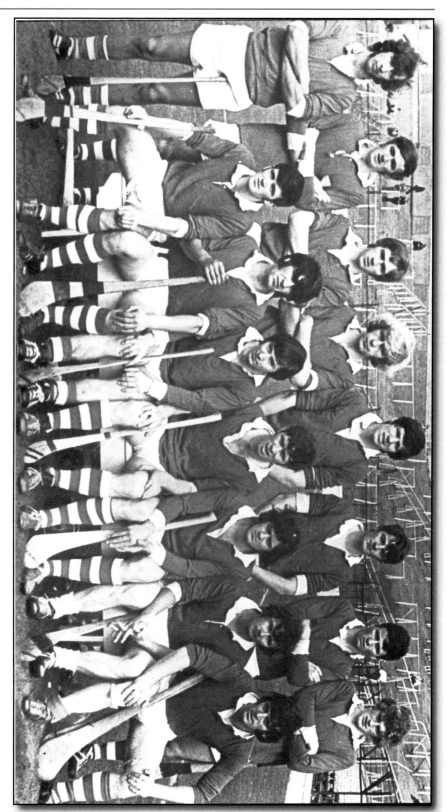

Cork - U21 All Ireland Champions 1971
Back: Seamus Looney, Brendan Cummins, Noel Crowley, John Horgan, Martin O'Doherty, Kevin McSweeney, Brian Murphy, Seamus O'Farrell.
Front: Brendan Coleman, Mick Malone, Sean O'Leary, Pat McDonnell capt., John Rothwell, Eamon Fitzpatrick, Martin Coleman.

(Oulart-the-Ballagh), Seanie Kinsella (St. Enda's Gorey), Pat Flynn (Rathnure), Martin Casey (Buffer's Alley), Mick Butler (Buffer's Alley).

Subs. Jack Russell (Geraldine O'Hanrahan's) for Dwyer. Brendan Murphy (Faythe Harriers) for Higgins. T. McCormack (Oulart-the-Ballagh), P. O'Connor (Oulart-the-Ballagh), T. Walsh (Faythe Harriers).

1971
LEINSTER FINAL: *Wexford 2-16, Kilkenny 2-9*
MUNSTER FINAL: *Cork 5-11, Tipperary 4-9*
ULSTER FINAL: *Down 5-11, Antrim 2-9*
ALL IRELAND SEMI FINALS: *Cork 11-10, Down 2-11; Wexford 4-8, Galway 0-9.*

♦ *Looney and Doherty did the double at u-21 in 1971.*
♦ *Mick Malone won 4 successive medals at u-21 hurling.*
♦ *Looney, McDonnell, Horgan and Cummins won 3 successive u-21 hurling medals.*
♦ *Doherty and Looney each added an 8th All-Ireland medal to their collection.*
♦ *Wexford's Martin Casey was Kerry born.*

1972 FINAL
EXCELLENT LAST QUARTER DISPLAY WINS FIRST U-21 HURLING TITLE FOR GALWAY.
10/9/1972 AT GAELIC GROUNDS, LIMERICK.
Galway 2-9. Dublin 1-10.

To the delight of their large contingent of supporters, Galway won their first u-21 title at a windy Gaelic Grounds in Limerick. Despite a promising start which gave them a lead of 4 points in as many minutes, the Tribesmen were unimpressive in an opening half in which the hurling though lively, was often mediocre. Despite the backing of a very stiff wind in the first half, they only led by 6 points, 2-3 to 1-0 at the interval, having registered 13 wides.

When Dublin had reduced the lead to a goal with only 6 minutes of the second period gone, Galway's prospects looked anything but bright. From there on the Galwegians began to find their best form. Dublin too raised their game and the standard improved dramatically. At the end of the third quarter, Dublin had cut the margin to one point. Galway now hurling with great determination into wind and sun, stretched their margin to safer proportions. They then survived a great late onslaught headed by Mick Holden, who had come out of goal to try and save the day, as he did in the Leinster final. Seconds from time , a Dublin forward missed a splendid opportunity of scoring the winning goal. Galway, on their second half showing, well deserved the honours. Galway's substitute, P.J. Molloy inspired his colleagues in the second half. Over the hour, the winners' best forward was Gerry Holland. Other stars for the winners were goalkeeper Eamonn Campbell, Lukie Glynn, Liam Shields, Frank Donoghue and Tony Brehony in defence. Long-striking Gerry Glynn was impressive at midfield.

Vinny Lambe, Jim Brennan, Gerry Ryan, Pascal Lee, the captain Jim Kealy and P.J. Holden were best for Dublin. They had a stroke of bad luck ten minutes from time, when P.J. Holden's cracking shot came back off an upright.

The referee was Sean O'Grady of Limerick.

Galway scorers; Gerry Holland 1-4 (0-1f), P.J. Molloy 0-3, Andy Fenton 1-0, Gerry Glynn 0-1, Marty Barrett 0-1.

Dublin scorers; Brian Sweeney 1-0, Jim Kealy 0-3 (fs), Pascal Lee 0-2, Gerry Whelan 0-2, P.J. Holden 0-2 (0-1f), G. O'Connor 0-1.

Galway team. Eamonn Campbell (Kiltormer), Lukie Glynn (Athenry), Gerry Kelly (Athenry), Liam Shields (Ballinderreen), Iggy Clarke (Mullagh), Capt, Frank Donoghue (Tommy Larkin's), Tony Brehony (Tommy Larkin's), Gerry Glynn (Castlegar), Frank Burke (Turloughmore), Mick Coen (Ballinderreen), Andy Fenton (Kiltormer), Mick Donoghue (Craughwell), Marty Barrett (Ballymacward), Tom Donoghue (Killimordaly), Gerry Holland (Turloughmore).
Subs. P.J.Molloy (Athenry) for Coen. Joe McDonagh (Ballinderreen) for Barrett.

Dublin team. Mick Holden (Cuala), Mick Leonard (St. Vincent's), Noel Quinn (Crumlin), Vincent Lambe (St. Vincent's), Gerry Ryan (Kevin's), Jim Brennan (St. Brendan's), Eamon Rheinisch (Craobh Chiarain), P.J. Holden (Cuala), Martin Greally (Crumlin), Pascal Lee (St. Vincent's), Vinnie Holden (Cuala), Jim Kealy (Crumlin), Capt, Canice Hennebry (Crumlin), Brian Sweeney (Craobh Chiarain), Gerry Whelan (O'Toole's).
Subs. G.O'Connor (Eoghan Ruadh) for Greally. D. O'Donovan (Crumlin) for Lee. Denis Kealy (Craobh Chiarain), D. Moody (Sts. Michael & James), C. McGrath (Colmcilles), J. Norton (Fianna), C. Kealy (Cuala).

1972
LEINSTER FINAL: *Dublin 2-11, Offaly 0-15*
MUNSTER FINAL: *Tipperary 4-10, Clare 3-10*
ULSTER FINAL: *Antrim 4-9, Down 1-11*
ALL IRELAND SEMI FINALS: *Dublin 4-12, Antrim 2-8; Galway 2-11, Tipperary 1-11.*

♦ *Galway sub Joe McDonagh was later GAA President.*
♦ *He is the only President to win senior All-Ireland, NHL, Railway Cup and U21 hurling medals.*

Galway - All-Ireland U21 Champions 1972
Back: GerryKelly, Gerry Glynn, Gerry Holland, Frank Donoghue, Andy Fenton, Michael Donoghue, Frank Burke.
Front: Luke Glynn, Liam Shiel (RIP), Ned Campbell, Michael Coen, IggyClarke (Captain), Tom Donoghoe, Tony Brehony, Marty Barrett.

Cork - All Ireland U21 Champions 1973.
Back: Jim Coughlan sel., Jack Barrett, Tony Murphy, Denis Burns, Brian Murphy, Liam Kelly, Tim Crowley, Mick Corbett, Brian Cotter.
Front: John Buckley, Sean O'Leary, Pat Kavanagh, Frank O'Sullivan, Martin O'Doherty, Dan Relihan, Seamus O'Farrell, Tom Fogarty.

1973 FINAL
DECIDED ADVANTAGE IN PHYSIQUE A KEY FACTOR IN YET ANOTHER
U-21 TITLE FOR CORK.
11/11/1973 AT CARRICK-ON-SUIR.
Cork 2-10. Wexford 4-2.

This final was played on a quite cold day in perfect conditions on a Carrick-on-Suir pitch which was in excellent trim. An exciting hour's hurling was served up before Cork emerged victorious by a two point margin. Cork were red hot favourites but the game could easily have ended in a draw. Sheer determination and first time pulling compensated for the moderate standard of hurling.

In the first half, it looked as if Cork's inadequate defence would lead to a Wexford victory. Three times in the first 19 minutes, Wexford found the Cork net. However, Cork's centre-back John Buckley and corner-back Brian Murphy suddenly found their rhythm and steadied the Rebels' backline. Wexford found it difficult to score points from easy range and thus led by only a point at half time, 3-0 to 1-5.

In the second half, Cork gradually got on top and by the 43rd minute had opened up a 5 point advantage. Two pointed frees by P.J. Harris brought Wexford back into the game. During the next 8 minutes Wexford attacked incessantly but were repelled by the brilliance of Buckley and Murphy. In the 56th minute, Cork sub Jimmy Barry-Murphy hit a point which was quickly followed by another from Seanie O'Leary. A gap of 5 points had opened again. In the last 3 minutes Nicky Walsh goaled for Wexford and a couple of other efforts almost found the Cork net.
In addition to Cork seniors Brian Murphy and John Buckley, others to play well for them were Pat Kavanagh, Tom Fogarty and Seanie O'Leary. The outstanding player of the final was Wexford goalkeeper John Nolan. He made a number of brilliant saves and earned many a round of applause. In the Slaneysiders' half back line John Moloney and Eddie Breen were magnificent. P.J. Harris was the best midfielder on view. The Wexford attack's inability to score points from play was fatal, but the overhead goals from Wexford forwards John Allen and Sean Storey were beautifully taken.

The referee was John Moloney of Tipperary.

Cork scorers; Seanie O'Leary 0-5 (0-4fs), Tom Fogarty 1-1, Pat Kavanagh 0-3, Tommy Sheehan 1-0, Jimmy Barry-Murphy 0-1.

Wexford scorers; John Allen 2-0, Nicky Walsh 1-0, Sean Storey 1-0, P.J. Harris 0-2 (fs).

Cork team. Frank O'Sullivan (Glen Rovers), Mick Corbett (Glen Rovers), Liam Kelly (Bandon), Brian Murphy (Nemo Rangers), Martin Doherty (Glen Rovers), Capt, John Buckley (Newtownshandrum), Denis Burns (St. Finnbarr's), Tim Crowley (Newcestown), Brian Cotter (Sarsfields), Pat Kavanagh (Blackrock), Seamus O'Farrell (Midleton), Tony Murphy (Blackrock), Dan Relihan (Castletownroche), Tom Fogarty (Kinsale), Seanie O'Leary (Youghal).

*Subs. Tommy Sheehan (Mallow) for T. Murphy. Jimmy Barry-Murphy (St. Finnbarr's) for Cotter.
Tim Murphy (Blackrock), Dan Joe Foley (Sarsfields), Andy Creagh (Blackrock), Vincent Twomey
(Na Piarsaigh), Pat Buckley (Mallow).*

Wexford team. John Nolan (Geraldine O'Hanrahan's), Michael Hickey (Adamstown), Sean
Byrne (Faythe Harriers), Pat Dempsey (Oulart-the-Ballagh), John Moloney (Adamstown), Eddie
Breen (Horeswood), Robert Lambert (St. Martin's), Rory Kinsella (St.Enda's, Gorey), P.J.Harris
(Oulart-the-Ballagh), John Murphy (Crossabeg/Ballymurn), Andy Dwyer (Ferns St. Aidan's),
Paddy Keogh (Cloughbawn), Nicky Walsh (Faythe Harriers), John Allen (Geraldine
O'Hanrahan's), Sean Storey (Oulart-the-Ballagh).

Subs. Michael Carty (Liam Mellows) for Dempsey. Sean Murphy (Rathnure) for Dwyer.

1973
LEINSTER FINAL: *Wexford 2-13, Offaly 2-10*
MUNSTER FINAL: *Cork 4-11, Limerick 2-7*
ULSTER FINAL: *Antrim 1-6, Down 1-6; Antrim 3-19, Down 3-3 (Replay)*
ALL IRELAND SEMI FINALS: *Cork 2-16, Galway 1 -8; Wexford 2-9, Antrim 0-7. (Abandoned after
50 minutes. Wexford awarded match.)*

♦ *Seanie O'Leary scored 2-14(1-11fs) in the semi-final versus Galway.*
♦ *Brian Murphy of Cork who won his second medal in 1973, has the unique distinction of winning
All-Ireland medals at Minor, Under-21 and Senior in both codes.*

1974 FINAL
FITZPATRICK'S LATE POINT WINS FIRST TITLE FOR KILKENNY.
8/9/1974 AT SEMPLE STADIUM, THURLES.
Kilkenny 3-8. Waterford 3-7.

In a thrilling final, Kilkenny just prevailed against their neighbours from across the Suir before an attendance of 9,000. Waterford made the running for almost 50 minutes before Kilkenny rallied in the closing stages. The Suirsiders had the backing of the wind in the first half. They appeared to have squandered that advantage when held to level scores, 0-5 to 1-2, at the interval. Waterford put in a storming third quarter and led by 6 points as the game entered the last ten minutes. Conditions at this stage were difficult following a hail shower after the interval on an already heavy pitch. Both teams were not deterred by this and there was some grand striking as the decisive minutes were battled out. Billy Fitzpatrick reduced Kilkenny's arrears to a goal in the 50th minute. The cats soon drew level and then ten seconds from the end of normal time, Fitzpatrick put over the winning point.

Kilkenny - All Ireland U21 Champions 1974

Back: Tom McCormack, Malachy Hogan, John Dowling, Mick Tierney, Ger Henderson, Brian Cody, Kevin Fennelly, Shem Brophy.
Front: Ger Woodcock, Tony Teehan, Pat Kearney, Ger Fennelly, Nicky Brennan, Billy Fitzpatrick, Jimmy Dunne.

Kilkenny had a fine goalkeeper in Kevin Fennelly and a solid full back line in which Jimmy Dunne was outstanding. Their half backs finished on a high note. Midfield was never more than adequate. Billy Fitzpatrick, Ger Woodcock, Ger Fennelly and substitutes Bobby Sweeney and Pat Mulcahy were best in an attack, that lost Tony Teehan with a broken jaw before the interval.

The chief reason for Waterford's defeat was a very inept full forward line. This trio collectively failed to raise a flag. Waterford's most impressive performers were Tom Casey, who displayed all the talents which made him such a wonderful minor, Eamon Ryan, Pat Egan, Brendan Mansfield, Kieran Ryan, John Galvin, Pat McGrath, Willie Ryan and Liam O'Brien. Lack of balance in attack undoubtedly cost Waterford.

The referee was Sean O'Grady of Limerick.

Kilkenny scorers; Billy Fitzpatrick 1-2, Bobby Sweeney 1-1, Ger Woodcock 1-0, Ger Fennelly 0-3 (0-2fs), Pat Mulcahy 0-1, Nicky Brennan 0-1.

Waterford scorers; Tom Casey 1-2 (0-1f), Liam Power 1-1, Brendan Mansfield 1-1, John Galvin 0-1, Pat McGrath 0-1, Eamon Ryan 0-1.

Kilkenny team. Kevin Fennelly (Ballyhale Shamrocks), Tom McCormack (James Stephens), Malachy Hogan (Dunamaggin), Jimmy Dunne (Dunamaggin), Ger Henderson (Fenians), Brian Cody (James Stephens), Mick Tierney (Rower-Inistioge), John Dowling (Bennettsbridge), Shem Brophy (St.Patrick's), Nicky Brennan (Conahy Shamrocks), Ger Woodcock (Danesfort), Ger Fennelly (Ballyhale Shamrocks), Capt, Pat Kearney (Thomastown), Tony Teehan (Coon), Billy Fitzpatrick (Fenians).
Subs. Bobby Sweeney (Tullaroan) for Teehan. Pat Mulcahy (Dicksboro) for Brennan. Nicky Brennan for Brophy. Pat Dunphy (Rower-Inistioge), Tom Barry, Liam Galavan, Sean Reid, Paddy Grace, Tom Kinsella.

Waterford team. Willie Ryan (Fourmilewater), Frank McCarthy (Cappoquin), Michael Flynn (Abbeyside), Kieran Ryan (Tallow), Liam O'Brien (Tallow), John Galvin (Portlaw), Eamon Ryan (Mount Sion), Capt, Pat Egan (Cappoquin), Pat McGrath (Mount Sion), Tom Casey (Dunhill), Liam Power (Ballyduff), Brendan Mansfield (Ballydurn), Patsy O'Keefe (Ballinameela), Michael McNamara (Ballyduff), Paul Moore (Ferrybank).
Subs. L.Aherne for Moore. E. Kehoe for McNamara.

1974
LEINSTER FINAL: *Kilkenny 3-8, Wexford 1-5*
MUNSTER FINAL: *Waterford 2-5, Clare 1-3*
ULSTER FINAL: *Antrim 3-8, Down 0-3*
ALL IRELAND SEMI FINALS: *Kilkenny 4-12, Galway 3-6; Waterford 3-18, Antrim 1-2.*

1975 FINAL
KILKENNY COMPLETE GRAND SLAM OF HURLING TITLES.
12/10/1975 AT FRAHER PARK, DUNGARVAN.
Kilkenny 5-13. Cork 2-19.

In a classic final, Kilkenny completed their grand slam of hurling successes, adding to the titles already won in the senior and minor grades. This was no easy victory as Cork rose magnificently to the occasion and at times threatened to overrun the opposition. However, Kilkenny showed their fighting spirit in battling back from adversity.

The attendance of over 12,000 thrilled to every stroke in the game. The frequency of the scores and the lead changing hands on seven occasions ensured that this final was a thriller all the way through. Kilkenny were five points clear by the 18th minute of the first half. Up to then Brian Cody at centre half back had been the dominant figure for the Noresiders. In a shrewd move, the Cork mentors moved Jimmy Barry-Murphy to centre forward and there was an immediate transformation. Cork reduced the deficit to a single point in the 21st minute. The Rebels then drew level when John Fenton hit a long range point.Two points by Bertie Og Murphy for Cork were answered by a hat-trick of points from John Lyng for Kilkenny. Thus, Kilkenny led at the break, 2-7 to 0-12.

Cork went four points clear in the first quarter of the second half. Then Ger Fennelly pointed a free for Kilkenny. In the 17th minute Bobby Sweeney threw himself at a cross from Billy Fitzpatrick and diverted the ball into the net. After Fenton pointed for Cork, Terry Brennan netted from close range for the lead and Lyng's long range point gave Kilkenny further breathing space. They preserved their hard earned lead despite some determined efforts from the Cork attack.

The outstanding player on the field was Kilkenny's Ger Henderson, who, when moved to midfield, gave one of the most whole-hearted displays ever seen in this grade. He was ably assisted by Joe Hennessy who was seen at his best when moved to defence. Others to shine were Ger and Kevin Fennelly, Dick O'Hara, Brian Cody, John Lyng, Terry Brennan and Billy Fitzpatrick.

Defensive lapses cost Cork dearly. Best for them were the outstanding John Crowley, Jimmy Barry-Murphy, who continually created openings for his fellow forwards, the clean-striking John Fenton, Kieran Murphy, Bertie Og Murphy and Tadhg Murphy.

The referee was Sean O'Meara of Tipperary.

Kilkenny scorers; Terry Brennan 2-0, John Lyng 0-5, Bobby Sweeney 1-1, Mick Tierney 1-1 (1-0f), Brian Cody 1-1 (1-0 "70", 0-1f), Ger Fennelly 0-3 (fs), Billy Fitzpatrick 0-2 (0-1f).

Cork scorers; John Fenton 0-9 (0-8fs), Bertie Og Murphy 0-7 (0-4fs), Sean O'Farrell 1-2, Tadhg O'Sullivan 1-0, Finbarr Delaney 0-1.

Kilkenny - All Ireland U21 Champions 1975

Back: John Marnell, Dick O'Hara, Ger Henderson, Jim Moran, Mick Tierney, Billy Fitzpatrick, Ger Fennelly, Brian Cody.

Front: Joe Hennessy, John Lyng, James Grace, John Dowling, Terry Brennan, Kevin Fennelly (Capt.), Bobby Sweeney.

Kilkenny team. Kevin Fennelly (Ballyhale Shamrocks) Capt, John Marnell (Dicksboro), Jim Moran (St. Martin's), Dick O'Hara (Thomastown), Ger Henderson (Fenians), Brian Cody (James Stephens), Jim Grace (Rower-Inistioge), John Dowling (Bennettsbridge), Ger Fennelly (Bally hale Shamrocks), Joe Hennessy (James Stephens), Mick Tierney (Rower-Inistioge), John Lyng (Rower-Inistioge), Terry Brennan (Erin's Own), Bobby Sweeney (Tullaroan), Billy Fitzpatrick (Fenians).

Subs. Kevin Robinson (O'Loughlin's) for Grace. Joe O'Sullivan (Piltown) for Dowling. Ger Woodcock (Danesfort), Pat Dunphy (Rower-Inistioge), John Dunne (Lisdowney), Richie Reid (Ballyhale Shamrocks), Paddy O'Brien (James Stephens), Maurice Healy Ballyhale Shamrocks), Peter Prendergast (Graignamanagh), Sylvie Lester (Rower Inistioge).

Cork team. Frank O'Sullivan (Glen Rovers), Capt, John Kennefick (Glen Rovers), Des Hurley (Midleton), Joe O'Herlihy Newtownshandrum), Con Brassil (Ballyhea), Kieran Murphy (Nemo Rangers), John Crowley (Bishopstown), Finbarr Delaney (Blackrock), John Fenton (Midleton), Bertie Og Murphy (Sarsfields), Sean O'Farrell (Watergrasshill), Tadhg Murphy (Sarsfields), Eamonn O'Sullivan (Blackrock), Jimmy Barry-Murphy (St. Finbarr's), Tom Collins (Glen Rovers).

Subs. Tadhg O'Sullivan (Bantry) for Collins. Richie Fitzgerald (Sarsfields), John Dennehy (Rathluirc), Bill Geaney (Glen Rovers), Pat Horgan (Glen Rovers), Daithi Cooney (Youghal).

1975
LEINSTER FINAL: *Kilkenny 3-14, Wexford 0-8*
MUNSTER FINAL: *Cork 3-12, Limerick 2-6*
ULSTER FINAL: *Down 3-10, Antrim 1-3*
ALL IRELAND SEMI FINALS: *Cork 4-14, Down 1-4; Kilkenny 3-13, Galway 2-9.*

♦ *Tadhg and Bertie Óg Murphy were brothers.*
♦ *For Cork, Tadhg Murphy was a late replacement for Richie Fitzgerald. They were also missing Tom Cashman.*
♦ *For Kilkenny, Joe Hennessy started in place of the injured Ger Woodcock.*

1976 FINAL
CORK REVERSE PREVIOUS YEAR'S RESULT AND WIN SEVENTH TITLE.
19/9/1976 AT WALSH PARK, WATERFORD.
Cork 2-17. Kilkenny 1-8.

The attendance of 8,000, thoroughly drenched in the second-half downpour, waited in vain for this game to ignite. It was difficult to play good hurling because although the grass was wet, the ground underneath was rock hard. The standard suffered and it was not nearly as good a final as the previous year's, when the same counties met. Cork's first-half dominance should have yielded better rewards than a four point interval lead, 0-7 to 0-3. The Rebels had eight wides

Cork - All Ireland U21 Champions 1976.

Back: Kieran Murphy, Finbarr Delaney, John Allen, Bill Geaney, John Crowley, Pat Horgan, Con Brassil, Jerry Cronin.

Front: Danny Buckley, Ritchie McDonnell, John Fenton, Tadhg Murphy capt., Dermot McCurtain, Sylvie O'Mahony, Tom Cashman.

in that first half. Despite the wides Cork fans must have been reasonably confident at the half-way stage. The Leesiders were fitter and faster than their opponents.

Kieran Murphy shook the Kilkenny net to put Cork 1-8 to 0-4 ahead after six minutes of the second half. Pat Horgan increased their lead with a point in the 37th minute. The Leinster champions now proceeded to make their most determined bid to retain their All-Ireland crown. In the following five minutes they scored 1-3 without reply and reduced the deficit to two points. A goal then from Pat Horgan, following good work by their captain Tadhg Murphy, set Cork on the victory road. In the last quarter, hurling with great confidence, they fired over eight points. A demoralised Kilkenny could only reply with a Kieran Brennan point in the 53rd minute. Cork were fully deserving of their eventual twelve point victory margin.

For the winners, the contributions of Tadhg Murphy, John Fenton and John Crowley were most significant. Murphy played a captain's part in attack. Fenton showed repeated flashes of his immense class. Crowley was soundness personified in Cork's full-back line. Of the rest, Tom Cashman, Finbarr Delaney, Con Brassil, Pat Horgan and Richie McDonnell caught attention most frequently in what was a real team performance.

Kilkenny goalkeeper Kevin Fennelly could be faulted for Pat Horgan's goal. In front of him, John Marnell, Dick O'Hara and Harry Ryan tried hard. Their midfield was never really happy where neither Joe Hennessy nor Kevin Robinson could match Cork's Con Brassil and Sylvie O'Mahony. Were it not for some fine free-taking by John Lyng in the Kilkenny attack, Cork would have won by even more.

The referee was Gerry Kirwan of Offaly.

Cork scorers; Pat Horgan 1-5 (0-4fs), Tadhg Murphy 0-6 (0-5fs), Kieran Murphy 1-1, Danny Buckley 0-2, Richie McDonnell 0-1, Con Brassil 0-1, John Fenton 0-1 (lb).

Kilkenny scorers; John Lyng 0-6 (0-5fs), Brendan Fennelly 1-0, Joe Hennessy 0-1, Kieran Brennan 0-1.

Cork team. **Jerry Cronin (Newmarket), Johnny Crowley (Bishopstown), Bill Geaney (Glen Rovers), Dermot McCurtain (Blackrock), John Fenton (Midleton), Tom Cashman (Blackrock), Finbarr Delaney (Blackrock), Sylie O'Mahony (Castlemartyr), Con Brassil (Ballyhea), John Allen (Aghabullogue), Richie McDonnell (Na Piarsaigh), Pat Horgan (Glen Rovers), Tadhg Murphy (Sarsfields), Capt, Kieran Murphy (Nemo Rangers), Danny Buckley (Blackrock).**
Subs. Billy Reidy (St. Finnbarr's) for Geaney. Joe Herlihy (Newtownshandrum), Donald O'Herlihy (Newtownshandrum), Richard O'Mahony (Glen Rovers), John Higgins (Watergrasshill), Finbarr Crowley (Bandon), Jerry McCarthy (St. Finnbarr's), Tom O'Neill (Glen Rovers).

Kilkenny team. **Kevin Fennelly (Ballyhale Shamrocks), John Marnell (Dicksboro), Dermot Tyrrell (O'Loughlin Gaels), Dick O'Hara (Thomastown), Harry Ryan (Clara), Jim Moran (St. Martin's), Richie Reid (Ballyhale Shamrocks), Kevin Robinson (O'Loughlin's), Joe Hennessy**

(James Stephens), John Lyng (Rower-Inistioge) Captain, Michael Lyng (Rower-Inistioge), Kieran Brennan (Conahy Shamrocks), Brendan Fennelly (Ballyhale Shamrocks), Ger Tyrrell (James Stephens), Ollie Bergin (O'Loughlin Gaels).
Subs. Brian Waldron (St.Lachtain's) for Robinson. Murty Kennedy (St. Lachtain's) for Reid. Pat Dunphy (Rower-Inistioge) for Waldron.

1976
LEINSTER FINAL: *Kilkenny 3-21, Wexford 0-5*
MUNSTER FINAL: *Cork 2-11, Clare 3-6*
ULSTER FINAL: *Antrim 1-9, Down 0-4*
ALL IRELAND SEMI FINALS: *Cork 1-16, Galway 2-6; Kilkenny 4-15, Antrim 1-8.*

♦ *Kilkenny and Cork each had 6 players who started in the previous year's final.*

1977 FINAL
KILKENNY'S SECOND HALF DISPLAY AGAINST THE WIND EARNS THEM THEIR THIRD TITLE.
9/10/1977 AT SEMPLE STADIUM, THURLES.
Kilkenny 2-9. Cork 1-9.

After an uncertain opening quarter, in which they drove six wides and scored just one point, Kilkenny eventually prevailed against Cork, before an attendance of 15,000 at a windy and rain-swept Semple Stadium. At the start of the second quarter, a point from a free by Brian Waldron was quickly followed by a goal from Richie Power. A long puck out was then goaled by Brendan Fennelly to put eight points between the sides. A long drive by Tom Cashman ended with an opportunist Cork goal from Tom Lyons. Points were then exchanged which left Kilkenny leading at the break by 2-4 to 1-2.

With the aid of the wind, the losers cut the arrears to a goal, seven minutes into the second half. Kilkenny now produced their most effective hurling with the half back line of Joe Hennessy, Dick O'Hara and Richie Reid driving them on. Waldron pointed free after free with unerring accuracy into the wind. Kilkenny were five points clear in the closing minutes. Cork brought Cashman and Johnny Crowley to midfield. They had a goal from Davy Keane controversially disallowed in the 26th minute of that second half. That was the margin by which they lost, when the final whistle was blown.

For Kilkenny, John Henderson and Paddy Prendergast were very sound behind a great half back line. Murty Kennedy was outstanding at midfield. Brian Waldron and Brendan Fennelly were best of the attack.

Killkenny - All Ireland U21 Champions 1977
Back: Joe Hennessy, Murty Kennedy, Ger Tyrrell, Dick O'Hara, Richie Reid, Richie Power, Paddy Prendergast, John Henderson.
Front: Eddie Mahon, Jimmy Lennon, Brendan Fennelly, Brian Waldron, Michael Lyng (Capt), Paudie Lennon, Joe Wall.

The Cork goalkeeper Jerry Cronin made some outstanding saves. Johnny Crowley defended well and Tom Cashman scored two wonderful points. Donal O'Herlihy hurled very well at midfield. Tom Lyons, Tadhg Murphy and Richie McDonnell were best of a disappointing attack.

The referee was Jimmy Rankins of Laois.

Kilkenny scorers; Brendan Fennelly 1-2, Brian Waldron 0-5 (fs), Richie Power 1-0, Kieran Brennan 0-1, Paudie Lannon 0-1.

Cork scorers; Tom Lyons 1-1, Tadhg Murphy 0-3 (0-1f), Tom Cashman 0-2 (0-1f), Johnny Crowley 0-1, Pat Horgan 0-1, Richie McDonnell 0-1.

Kilkenny team. Eddie Mahon (Erin's Own), Jim Lennon (Bennetsbridge), John Henderson (Fenians), Paddy Prendergast (Clara), Joe Hennessy (James Stephens), Dick O'Hara (Thomastown), Richie Reid (Ballyhale Shamrocks), Paudie Lannon (Thomastown), Murty Kennedy (St. Lachtain's), Richie Power (Carrickshock), Michael Lyng (Rower-Inistioge), Capt, Brian Waldron (St. Lachtain's), Brendan Fennelly (Ballyhale Shamrocks), Ger Tyrrell (James Stephens), Joe Wall (Mooncoin).
Subs. Kieran Brennan (Conahy Shamrocks) for Power. Gerry Stapleton, Harry Ryan (Clara), Anthony Bergin (O'Loughlin's), Josie O'Brien, Michael Dempsey (Ballyhale Shamrocks), Frank Holohan (Ballyhale Shamrocks), Anthony O'Driscoll (O'Loughlins), Jim Coady (Graignamanagh), John Power (Fenians), Christy Heffernan (Glenmore).

Cork team. Jerry Cronin (Newmarket), Jerry Murphy (St. Finnbarr's), Johnny Crowley (Ballincollig), Finbarr Delaney (Blackrock), Con Brassil (Ballyhea), Tom Cashman (Blackrock), Dermot McCurtain (St. Finnbarr's), Capt, Donal O'Herlihy (Newtownshandrum), Joe O'Brien (Harbour Rovers), Pat Horgan (Glen Rovers), Tom Lyons (Blackrock), Paul Crowley (Blackrock), Tadhg Murphy (Sarsfields), Richie McDonnell (Na Piarsaigh), Danny Buckley (Blackrock).
Subs. Davy Keane (Passage) for O'Brien. David Ryan (Ballyhea) for T. Murphy. Ger McEvoy (Sarsfields) for P. Crowley. Brian Dineen (Brian Dillons), Denis Mulcahy (Midleton), Joe Hegarty (Blackrock).

1977
LEINSTER FINAL: *Kilkenny 3-11, Wexford 1-10*
MUNSTER FINAL: *Cork 5-9, Limerick 1-8*
ULSTER FINAL: *Down 3-7, Antrim 0-9*
ALL IRELAND SEMI FINALS: *Cork 1-8, Galway 0-5; Kilkenny 4-19, Down 1-2*

♦ *Cork had 10 of the previous year's winning side and 6 panellists from the All-Ireland winning Senior team.*

1978 FINAL
STERLING PERFORMANCE FROM BOURKE SAVES TIPPERARY.
8/10/1978 AT GAELIC GROUNDS, LIMERICK.
Galway 3-5. Tipperary 2-8.

Though this final ended in a welter of excitement, it could not disguise the fact that there was a lot of poor play for the attendance of 15,000 at Limerick. The first half was particularly poor, the highlight of which was Seamus Bourke's goal for Tipperary in the 24th minute. At that stage Galway were leading by 1-3 to 0-2. Bourke received a pass from Michael Doyle. Striking the ball with ferocious power from thirty yards out, he gave the Galway goalkeeper Gerry Smith no chance. The same player concluded the first half with a lovely long range point to leave Galway ahead by 1-4 to 1-3 at the interval.

Tipperary resumed with the backing of the blustery breeze and within a minute they were level as Bourke pointed from close in. A long range effort from John Grace put Tipperary ahead for the only time in the 36th minute. Within thirty seconds Galway had regained the lead as Mattie Conneely goaled. Tipp had a disallowed goal from Eamonn O'Shea in the 41st minute as he was adjudged to have been in the small square. John Ryan first-timed a goal for Galway in the 48th minute, which put the Tribesmen ahead by 3-5 to 1-6. The Premier County were back in contention after 53 minutes when Bourke goaled from a free. A memorable point from sub Kevin Fox and another from Eamonn O'Shea ensured that the sides would finish level.

Galway's goalkeeper Gerry Smith made some excellent saves. Michael Headd, Conor Hayes and Joe Greaney marshalled the Galway defence splendidly. Their forwards apart from Mattie Conneely and John Ryan were disappointing.

John Doyle and Gerry Stapleton were excellent in the Tipperarydefence. Seamus Bourke was their outstanding forward, ably assisted by Michael Doyle and Eamonn O'Shea. Substitutes Kevin Fox and Michael Murphy made important contributions in the closing stages.

The referee was Noel O'Donoghue of Dublin.

Galway scorers; Mattie Conneely 2-2, John Ryan 1-2, Michael Kilkenny 0-1 (f).

Tipperary scorers; Seamus Bourke 2-2 (1-0f), Pat Ryan 0-1, John Grace 0-1, Eamonn O'Shea 0-1, Tommy Grogan 0-1, Kevin Fox 0-1, Tommy Walsh 0-1 (f).

Galway team. Gerry Smith (Ahascragh), Conor Hayes (Kiltormer), Michael Headd (Killimor), P.J.Burke (Tynagh), Joe Greaney (Turloughmore), Michael Earls (Killimordaly), Seamus Coen (Mullagh), Steve Mahon (Kilbecanty), Gerry Linnane (Ardrahan), Michael Kilkenny (Kiltormer), John Goode (Kiltormer), Pascal Ryan (Killimordaly), Bernie Forde (Ardrahan), Capt, Mattie Conneely (Sarsfields), John Ryan (Killimordaly).

Galway - All Ireland U21 Champions 1978
Back : Conor Hayes, Michael Headd, Steve Mahon, Gerry Kennedy, Gerry Smith, Mattie Conneely, John Goode, Seamus Coen.
Front:: John Ryan, Fr. Michael Kilkenny, Michael Earls, Pascal Ryan, Bernard Forde, Joe Greaney, P.J. Burke.

Subs. John Coen (Mullagh) for Mahon. Sean Forde (Kinvara) for Kilkenny.

Tipperary team. Vincent Mullins (St. Mary's Clonmel), Purdy Loughnane (Roscrea), Joe Minogue (Cashel), Johnny Doyle (Holycross), Pat Fitzelle (Cashel) Captain, Gerry Stapleton (Borris-Ileigh), Joe O'Dwyer (Killenaule), Pat Ryan (Borris-Ileigh), John Grace (Silvermines), Tommy Walsh (St. Mary's Clonmel), Michael Doyle (Holycross), Eamonn O'Shea (Kilruane McDonaghs), Tommy Ryan (Sean Treacy's), Seamus Bourke (Clonmore), Tommy Grogan (Cashel).

Subs. Kevin Fox (Annacarthy) for T. Ryan. Michael Murphy (Templederry) for T.Walsh. Enda Hogan (Kilruane McDonaghs) for Minogue. Paudie O'Neill (Clonmel), Joe Hannigan (Shannon Rovers), Michael Stapleton (Templederry), Jimmy Cunningham (Roscrea), Tony Slattery (Cashel), John Stone (Roscrea), Jim Bourke (Upperchurch).

1978 Final Replay
Impressive Greaney the star of Galway victory.
29/10/1978 at Gaelic Grounds, Limerick.
Galway 3-15. Tipperary 2-8.

Galway's victory before an attendance of 13,986 at Limerick was even more impressive than the scoreline indicates, as Tipperary scored a last-minute goal from Seamus Bourke. Many of Galway's points were struck from fifty and sixty yards. Their tackling was terrier-like and they had a brilliant half back line, led by Joe Greaney. The unhappy Tipp defence was caught badly for Galway's first goal from Mattie Conneely. The same player palmed a second goal just before the interval. Galway had registered five wides by half time, at which stage they led by 2-7 to 1-6. For thirty minutes it had been a superb replay---rich in free-flowing hurling, great scores, solid stickwork and raw courage.

It is a reflection on Tipp's attack and a tribute to the Galway defence that the men from the Premier County only scored 1-2 in the second half. Galway were 2-11 to 1-8 in front ten minutes from time, when team captain Bernie Forde was beaten in a tackle by one of the opposing defenders. Forde dispossessed his opponent and then ran twenty yards before goaling. This incident typified Galway's spirit.

In the Galway defence, the half back line of Greaney, Earls and Coen were outstanding, as was left full back P.J. Burke. Steve Mahon was superb at midfield. In their attack, the Ryan twins, Gerry Kennedy, Mattie Conneely and Bernie Forde were very effective.

John Doyle and Gerry Stapleton had fine games in the Tipp defence, until the latter was sent off eight minutes from the end. His dismissal was a little harsh and possibly the result of frustration. Pat Ryan played very well at midfield but only Eamonn O'Shea and Seamus Bourke impressed in the losers' attack.

The referee was Noel O'Donoghue of Dublin.

Galway scorers; Gerry Kennedy 0-8, Mattie Conneely 2-0, Pascal Ryan 0-3, Bernie Forde 1-0, John Ryan 0-3, Michael Kilkenny 0-1.

Tipperary scorers; Seamus Bourke 1-4, Eamonn O'Shea 0-3, Tommy Ryan 1-0, Tommy Grogan 0-1 (f).

Galway team. Gerry Smith (Ahascragh), Conor Hayes (Kiltormer), Michael Headd (Killimor), P.J.Burke (Tynagh), Joe Greaney (Turloughmore), Michael Earls (Killimordaly), Seamus Coen (Mullagh), Steve Mahon (Kilbecanty), Michael Kilkenny (Kiltormer), Gerry Kennedy (Tommy Larkins), John Goode (Kiltormer), Pascal Ryan (Killimordaly), Bernie Forde (Ardrahan), Capt, Michael Conneely (Sarsfields), John Ryan (Killimordaly).
Sub. Tommy Breheny (Tynagh) for Forde.

Tipperary team. Vincent Mullins (St. Mary's Clonmel), John Doyle (Holycross), Joe O'Dwyer (Killenaule), Purdy Loughnane (Roscrea), Michael Stapleton (Templederry), Pat Fitzelle (Cashel) Captain, Gerry Stapleton (Borris-Ileigh), John Grace (Silvermines), Pat Ryan (Borris-Ileigh), Tommy Walsh (St. Mary's Clonmel), Michael Doyle (Holycross), Eamonn O'Shea (Kilruane McDonaghs), Tommy Ryan (Sean Treacys), Seamus Bourke (Clonmore), Tommy Grogan (Cashel).
Subs. Enda Hogan (Kilruane McDonaghs) for M.Stapleton. Kevin Fox (Annacarthy) for T. Walsh. Tony Slattery (Cashel) for Loughnane). John Stone (Roscrea), Jimmy Cunningham (Roscrea), Michael Murphy (Templederry), Joe Hannigan (Shannon Rovers), Joe Minogue (Cashel), Paudie O'Neill (Clonmel), Jim Bourke (Upperchurch), PJ Maxwell (Clonoulty-Rossmore).

1978
LEINSTER FINAL: Offaly 2-14, Laois 2-7
MUNSTER FINAL: Tipperary 3-13, Cork 4-10
Tipperary 3-8, Cork 2-9
ULSTER FINAL: Antrim 5-18, Down 3-9
ALL IRELAND SEMI FINALS: Galway 2-13, Offaly 2-9; Tipperary 3-9, Antrim 1-8.

♦ *Mattie Conneely was brother of Galway's senior goalkeeper, Michael.*
♦ *John Ryan and Pascal Ryan were twins.*

Tipperary - All Ireland U21 Champions 1979

Back: J Sheedy, J Ryan, B Heffernan, P Power, E Hogan, V Mullins, E O'Shea, J O'Dwyer, T Slattery, J Ryan, P Loughnane.
Middle: D. O'Connell, P. Ryan, M. Murphy, B. Mannion, G. Stapleton, M. Doyle (Capt.), T. Grogan, Pat Fox, G. O'Connor.
Front: P. Looby, M. McGrath, M. Stapleton, C. Bonner, R. Coffey, T. Floyd, J. Stone.

1979 FINAL
TIPP'S TITLE AFTER TWELVE BARREN YEARS.
23/9/1979 AT O'MOORE PARK, PORTLAOISE.
Tipperary 2-12. Galway 1-9.

Tipperary gained revenge for the previous year's defeat before a large attendance at sunny O'Moore Park. The first half was a powerful advertisement for hurling as evenly matched sides gave a delightful display of uncompromising, often skilful fare. Tipp took control early on but Galway eased ahead for the first time some seven minutes from the interval. The Premier County got back on level terms on 0-7 each at the interval.

Within 90 seconds of the restart, Tipperary led by four points. Tommy Grogan pointed and then Pat Looby goaled following a fine passing movement involving Ger O'Connor and Michael Murphy. Galway retaliated with a fine point from John Coen.

The Tipp mentors then made a master move by introducing Pat Ryan. Ryan's raking deliveries from midfield tested the resolve of the western defenders. After Tipp's Tony Slattery had sent an eighty yard free over the bar, their captain Michael Doyle ran on to a superb pass from supersub Ryan and slipped the ball past the Galway goalkeeper Tony Carr.

With seven minutes remaining, John Ryan soloed through the defence and palmed the ball into the Tipperary net. Conor Hayes added a great point from a long range free. Tipperary had sufficient leeway on the scoreboard to withstand the late Galway rally.

On this display, Tipperary looked a side without weakness. Slightly ahead of the rest of the side were Purdy Loughnane, Enda Hogan, Gerry Stapleton, Pat Fox, Michael Doyle, Eamonn O'Shea, Pat Looby and substitute Pat Ryan, who showed class and fire in abundance.

Galway, who should have moved team captain Conor Hayes outfield earlier, had other outstanding players in Headd, Seamus Coen, Earls, John Coen, Syl Dolan and the Ryan twins.

The referee was Noel Dalton of Waterford.

Tipperary scorers; Michael Doyle 1-2, Pat Looby 1-1, Tommy Grogan 0-3 (0-1f), Michael Murphy 0-2, Eamonn O'Shea 0-2, Brian Mannion 0-1, Tony Slattery 0-1 (f).

Galway scorers; John Ryan 1-2, John Coen 0-4 (0-1f), Sean Davoren 0-1, Pascal Ryan 0-1, Conor Hayes 0-1 (f).

Tipperary team. Vincent Mullins (St. Mary's Clonmel), Purdy Loughnane (Roscrea), John Ryan (Holycross), Enda Hogan (Kilruane McDonaghs), Tony Slattery (Cashel), Joe O'Dwyer (Killenaule), Gerry Stapleton (Borris-Ileigh), Ger O'Connor (Roscrea), Pat Fox (Annacarty), Michael Murphy (Templederry), Eamonn O'Shea (Kilruane McDonaghs), Tommy Grogan

(Cashel), Brian Mannion (Lorrha), Michael Doyle (Holycross), Capt, Pat Looby (Drom-Inch). *Subs. Pat Ryan (Borris-Ileigh) for Grogan. Joe Kennedy (Lorrha), John Stone (Roscrea), Brian Heffernan (Nenagh), Pat Power (Boherlahan).*

Galway team. Tony Carr (Kiltormer), Tom Brehony (Tynagh), Michael Headd (Killimor), Conor Hayes (Kiltormer), Capt, Seamus Coen (Mullagh), Michael Earls (Killimordaly), Eddie Reilly (Tynagh), Sean Davoren (Rahoon), Michael Donoghue (St. Thomas), John Coen (Mullagh), Gerry Linnane (Gort), Pascal Ryan (Killimordaly), Syl Dolan (Ardrahan), David Burke (Portumna), John Ryan (Killimordaly).
Subs. Gerry Dempsey for Donoghue. Jarlath Hanlon (Turloughmore) for Linnane. Vincent Kelly for Headd.

1979

LEINSTER FINAL: *Wexford 0-14, Kilkenny 2-8; Wexford 1-8, Kilkenny 0-10 (Replay)*
MUNSTER FINAL: *Tipperary 1-13, Cork 2-7*
ULSTER FINAL: *Antrim 9-13, Armagh 2-2*
ALL IRELAND SEMI FINALS: *Galway 1 -12, Wexford 2-8; Tipperary 7-13, Antrim 4-6.*

♦ *Pat Ryan had only returned the previous week from a working holiday in the U.S.A.*
♦ *Brother O'Grady was the Tipperary coach. .*

CHAPTER 3
ALL IRELAND U21
HURLING FINALS
1980-1989

Tipperary – All Ireland U21 Champions 1980

Back: P. Power, M. Kennedy, D. O'Connell, J. Kennedy, V. Mullins, B. Heffernan, B. Ryan, C. Bonnar.
Front: M. Murphy, P. McGrath, P. Fox, J. O'Dwyer, P. Kennedy, M. Ryan, A. Buckley. (Mascot: Stephen Fallon).

1980 Final
END-TO-END GAME SEES TIPPERARY WIN FOURTH TITLE.
14/9/1980 AT WALSH PARK, WATERFORD.
Tipperary 2-9. Kilkenny 0-14.

This superb final featured every thing that is best in hurling before an appreciative attendance of 15,000.Tipperary had first use of the strong wind as they played into the city end. They took time to avail of this advantage as Kilkenny whipped first time into every tackle. This was a contributory factor to plenty of fast end-to-end play. When fifteen minutes had elapsed and the sides were level at 0-2 each, Tipp looked in trouble. Two minutes later Michael Murphy put them ahead with a goal from a powerfully struck free. Pat McGrath added a point from a seventy to leave the Munster men ahead by 1-4 to 0-4 at the interval.

Kilkenny had the advantage of the wind for the second half and the sides shared two points each in the early minutes. The came five Kilkenny points in succession. The Leinster champions were now three points ahead at the three quarters stage, The Premier men refused to yield. They scored the next three points. Billy McEvoy then put Kilkenny back in front. Next came the decisive score. From a centre by Michael Murphy, which was misjudged by the Kilkenny goalkeeper, Austin Buckley found the net. Murphy and Eamonn Wallace exchanged points. Tom Lennon reduced the margin to one point, but that was the second last stroke of the hour, as the final whistle blew after the puckout.

Pat McGrath and Pat Fox were outstanding in the winners' defence that featured a rock solid half back line. Others to shine for Tipperary were Michael Murphy, Joe Kennedy, Donie O'Connell, when at midfield, Pat Power and Austin Buckley.

Kilkenny could not be faulted for lack of effort and in midfielder Eamonn Wallace they had the most effective performer on view. Bill Doherty and Bill O;Hara were best of the losers' defence. The most eye-catching of the Kilkenny forwards were the left wing pair, Michael Nash and Willie Purcell, who got eight of their points. Billy McEvoy on the other flank of attack also had a very good game, scoring three points.

The referee was John Denton of Wexford.

Tipperary scorers; Michael Murphy 1-1 (1-0f), Pat Power 0-3, Joe Kennedy 0-3, Austin Buckley 1-0, Pat McGrath 0-2 (0-1,70).

Kilkenny scorers; Willie Purcell 0-4, Michael Nash 0-4 (0-1f), Billy McEvoy 0-3, Tom Lennon 0-1, Eamonn Wallace 0-1, Lester Ryan 0-1.

Tipperary team. Vincent Mullins (St. Mary's Clonmel), Michael Ryan (Borris-Ileigh), Cormac Bonnar (Cashel), Pat Fox (Annacarty), Brian Heffernan (Nenagh), Joe O'Dwyer (Killenaule), Pat McGrath (Loughmore), Michael Kennedy (Nenagh), Philip Kennedy (Nenagh), Capt, Michael Murphy (Templederry), Bobby Ryan (Borris-Ileigh), Austin Buckley (Cappawhite), Joe Kennedy (Lorrha), Donie O'Connell (Killenaule), Pat Power (Boherlahan).

Subs. Alan Kinsella (Silvermines) for M. Kennedy, Donal Flannery (Kildangan), Peter Brennan (Loughmore), Roger Coffey (Nenagh), Michael Gleeson (Portroe), PJ Maxwell (Nenagh), Mick Ryan (Clonmore), John Sheedy (Portroe), Mick Ryan (Ballinahinch), Connie Maher (Thurles Sars).

Kilkenny team. Michael Walsh (Dicksboro), Mick Morrissey (St Lachtain's), Michael Meagher (John Lockes), Bill O'Hara (Thomastown), Tom Lennon (St Lachtain's), Bill Doherty (Glenmore), Sean Fennelly (Ballyhale Shamrocks), Eamonn Wallace (Erin's Own), Gordon Ryan (Clara), John Mulcahy (O'Loughlins), Richard Murphy (Thomastown), Michael Nash (Erin's Own), Billy McEvoy (Lisdowney), Lester Ryan (Clara), Willie Purcell (Fenians).
Subs. Jimmy Heffernan (Tullogher Rosbercon) for Murphy, G.Ryan (Freshford), D. Connolly (Clara), Pat Gannon (St Patrick's), N.Wall (Lisdowney), J. Murphy (Glenmore), C. Mackey (Dunamaggin), Mick Cleere (O'Loughlins), P. Heffernan (Tullogher), Eugene Deegan (O'Loughlins), Aidan Brophy (St Patrick's).

1980
LEINSTER FINAL: *Kilkenny 2-14, Wexford 2-9*
MUNSTER FINAL: *Tipperary 4-11, Cork 2-9*
ULSTER FINAL: *Antrim 4-16, Down 0-9*
ALL IRELAND SEMI FINALS: *Kilkenny 2-13, Antrim 1-11; Tipperary 3-11, Galway 2-12.*

♦ *Michael and Philip Kennedy were brothers.*

1981 FINAL
SCINTILLATING TIPPERARY DISPLAY WINS THIRD TITLE IN SUCCESSION.
13/9/1981 AT WALSH PARK, WATERFORD.
Tipperary 2-16. Kilkenny. 1-10.

Tipperary won their third successive All-Ireland u-21 title in decisive fashion at Walsh Park, Waterford, before an attendance of 20,000. Although champions for the previous two years, they hurled throughout as if they were chasing their first title. They were quicker to the ball and lightning sharp in the tackle. Tipperary were leading by 0-6 to 0-2 in the 22nd minute, when Donie O'Connell gained possession just fifteen yards out and scored their first goal. Both sides added two points each before the interval, at which Tipp led by 1-8 to 0-4. Kilkenny's first score from play hadn't arrived until the 25th minute when M.J.Ryan pointed. The leaders had also driven seven wides in the first half to Kilkenny's one.

After just three minutes of the second half the Munster champions had added 1-1 to their tally. Ger O'Neill struck a splendid point within 45 seconds of the restart. Two minutes later, O'Connell goaled again following a goalmouth scramble. Kilkenny now had their best period of the final. Billy Walton put over three points in quick succession, two from frees. With just six minutes remaining, Willie Purcell was fouled in the square. Walton hammered the resultant penalty to the net. That left the score at 2-14 to 1-8 and the sides exchanged two points each before the final whistle.

Tipperary - All Ireland U21 Champions 1981

Back: D. Hayes, A. Buckley, P. McGrath, J. Maher, L. Conroy, P. Maher, J. McIntyre, C. Maher, D. O'Connell, J. Farrell,
B. Ryan, M. McGrath, B. Heffernan.
Front: J. Sullivan, N. Byrne, J. Butler, P. Brennan, P. Fox, P. Kennedy, M. Ryan, N. English, A. Kinsella, G. O'Neill, S. Moran.

All fifteen of the winning team, which remained unchanged throughout, played superbly. The full back line of Michael Ryan, Peter Brennan and Pat Fox held their opponents scoreless. Most of Tipp's scores came from the distribution of Pat McGrath and Philip Kennedy. Ger O'Neill and Donie O'Connell were the top scorers from play in an excellent attack. O'Neill was the star performer as he picked off six points from play and forced Kilkenny to make several unsuccessful positional changes. Kilkenny were well served in defence by goalkeeper Michael Walsh, Pat Ryan and Bill O'Hara. In their attack, M.J.Ryan and Billy Walton did their utmost for the Leinster champions.

The referee was Neilly Duggan of Limerick.

Tipperary scorers; Donie O'Connell 2-1, Ger O'Neill 0-6, Martin McGrath 0-5 (fs), Nicky English 0-2, Bobby Ryan 0-1, Pat McGrath 0-1, 65).

Kilkenny scorers; Billy Walton 1-7 (1-0 pen., 0-5fs), Matty Byrne 0-1, M.J. Ryan 0-1, Pat Gannon 0-1 (65).

Tipperary team. John Farrell (Knockavilla), Michael Ryan (Borris-Ileigh), Peter Brennan (Loughmore), Pat Fox (Annacarty), Ian Conroy (Borrisokane), John McIntyre (Lorrha), Pat McGrath (Loughmore), Alan Kinsella (Silvermines), Philip Kennedy (Nenagh), Capt, Nicky English (Lattin-Cullen), Bobby Ryan (Borris-Ileigh), Martin McGrath (Knockavilla), Ger O'Neill (Cappawhite), Donie O'Connell (Killenaule), Austin Buckley (Cappawhite).
Subs. Noel Byrne (Thurles Sarsfields), Paddy Maher (Thurles Sarsfields), Jim O'Sullivan (Nenagh), Dominic Hayes (Knockavilla), Joe Butler (Roscrea), Jack Moran (Borrisokane), Brian Heffernan (Nenagh), Jim Maher (Loughmore, Michael Ryan (JK Brackens), John Sheedy (Portroe), Donie Flannery (Kildangan), Peter Brennan (Loughmore), Roger Coffey (Nenagh), Connie Maher (Thurles Sars), Michael Ryan (Ballinahinch), Paddy O'Meara (Lorrha).

Kilkenny team. Michael Walsh (Dicksboro), Pat Ryan (Gowran), Eddie Aylward (Glenmore), Jimmy Holden (Mooncoin), Sean Norris (Piltown), Bill O'Hara (Thomastown), Mick Cleere (O'Loughlin's), Pat Gannon (Ballyragget), Matty Byrne (Gowran), Billy McEvoy (Lisdowney), M.J.Ryan (Galmoy), Billy Walton (James Stephens), Johnny Murphy (Glenmore), John O'Dwyer (Callan), Capt, Willie Purcell (Fenians).
Subs. Seanie Tyrrell (O'Loughlin's) for Holden. Eddie Crowley (Mooncoin) for Murphy. John Brennan (Thomastown), Ger Fitzpatrick (O'Loughlin's), John Mahon (Mooncoin), Richard Moloney (Coon), Michael O'Connor (Glenmore), John Holland (St Pat's Ballyragget).

1981
LEINSTER FINAL: *Kilkenny 6-11, Wexford 2-10*
MUNSTER FINAL: *Tipperary 1-15, Cork 0-10*
ULSTER FINAL: *Antrim 2-9, Down 1-5*
ALL IRELAND SEMI FINALS: *Kilkenny 3-23, Antrim 0-3; Tipperary 3-17, Galway 0-7.*
- ◆ *Philip Kennedy captained Tipperary to victory for the second successive year.*
- ◆ *Tipp's selectors were Coach, Mick Minogue(Roscrea), Paddy O'Meara(Lorrha), Danny Morrissey(Knockavilla), Willie Carroll(St. Mary's Clonmel), Phil Lowry(Holycross).*

1982 FINAL
CORK PREVAIL BY A POINT IN ABSORBING FINAL.
12/9/1982, AT BIRR.
Cork 0-12. Galway 0-11.

In an entertaining final, during which scores were level on nine occasions, before an attendance of 4,500, Cork's winning point came with less than 15 seconds left. Cork won the toss but chose to play against the strong breeze. They opened a two point lead but Galway fought back and edged in front. The Rebels levelled just before the interval. The score at half time was 0-6 each. Cork appeared to be in the better position as they would have the wind in the second half.

However, on the resumption the Tribesmen opened with tremendous spirit and skill. Only a minute had passed before Peter Murphy put them a point ahead. On four occasions, Cork goalkeeper Ger Cunningham made brilliant saves that prevented Galway from increasing their tally. Galway were undaunted and went 3 points ahead within eight minutes of the restart, with further points from John Murphy and Michael Haverty. Two points for Cork from Tony O'Sullivan and another from Tony Coyne had the sides level at 0-9 each with fifteen minutes left. Five minutes without a score followed before O'Sullivan and John Murphy exchanged points. In the 24th minute, to the great joy of the Galway supporters, Michael Haverty with a point regained the lead for the men from the west. Their hopes were dashed when Cork scored twice in the last two minutes. First Ned Brosnan whipped a ground ball over the bar from 25 yards and then Kevin Hennessy first timed the ball over the bar for the winning score.

Best for Cork were Ger Cunningham, Martin McCarthy, Michael Boylan, Colm O'Connor, Kevin Hennessy, Tony Coyne and Denis Walsh.

Most prominent for Galway were Tommy Coen, Peter Casserley, Tom Nolan, Ollie Kilkenny, Michael Haverty, Pierse Piggott, Peter Murphy and John Murphy.

The referee was Gerry Kirwan of Offaly.

Cork scorers; Tony O'Sullivan 0-4 (0-3fs), Kevin Hennessy 0-2, Tony Coyne 0-2, Denis Walsh 0-2, Ned Brosnan 0-1, Martin O'Sullivan 0-1.

Galway scorers; Michael Haverty 0-5 (0 3fs), Peter Murphy 0-3, John Murphy 0-2, Michael McGrath 0-1.

Cork team. Ger Cunningham (St. Finbarr's), Martin McCarthy (Na Piarsaigh), Capt, Mick Boylan (Midleton), John Hodgins (St. Finbarr's), Willie Cashman (St. Finbarr's), Kieran O'Driscoll (St. Finbarr's), Colm O'Connor (Cobh), Kevin Hennessy (Midleton), Donie Curtin (Shanballymore), Tony O'Sullivan (Na Piarsaigh), Tony Coyne (Youghal), Denis Walsh (Cloughduv), Ned Brosnan (Meelin), Martin O'Sullivan (Na Piarsaigh), Ger Motherway (St. Ita's). Subs. Pat Deasy (Blackrock), for O'Driscoll. Tomas Mulcahy (Glen Rovers) for Motherway. Gabriel McCarthy (Bishopstown) for M O'Sullivan. Pat Hartnett (Midleton), Diarmuid Scanlon (Banteer), Martin Hennessy (Aghada), Christy Coughlan (Na Piarsaigh), Michael Lyons

Cork - All Ireland U21 Champions 1982.

Back: T. Coyne, D. Curtain, K. O'Driscoll, W. Cashman, G. Cunningham, K. Hennessy, M. Boylan, G. Motherway.
Front: Colm O'Connor, J. Hodgins, Martin McCarthy (Captain), M. O'Sullivan, T. O'Sullivan, N. Brosnan, D. Walsh.

(Bishopstown), Tim Finn (St. Finbarr's).

Galway team. Tommy Coen (Mullagh), Michael Mooney (St. Thomas), Peter Casserley (Beagh), Denis Burke (Turloughmore), Paschal Healy (Athenry), Tom Nolan (Salthill), Ollie Kilkenny (Kiltormer), Aidan Staunton (Kiltormer), John Boland (Loughrea), Michael Haverty (Killimordaly), Pierse Piggott (Gort), Capt, Peter Murphy (Loughrea), John Murphy (Mullagh), Martin Grealish (Carnmore), Michael McGrath (Sarsfields).

Subs. Noel Morrissey (Sarsfields) for Boland. Tony Keady (Killimordaly) for Grealish. Thomas Fahy (Tommie Larkin's), Joe Callanan (Ardrahan), Michael Coleman (Abbeyknockmoy), Ger Fallon (Leitrim), Brendan Dervan (Kiltormer), Leo Kelly (Tommie Larkin's), Eanna Ryan (Killimordaly).

1982
LEINSTER FINAL: *Kilkenny 5-20, Offaly 2-6*
MUNSTER FINAL: *Cork 1-14, Limerick 1-4*
ULSTER FINAL: *Antrim 9-14, Down 4-5*
ALL IRELAND SEMI FINALS: *Cork 4-21, Antrim 1-10; Galway 1-13, Kilkenny 1-10.*

♦ *Three Cork players, Ger Cunningham, Tony O'Sullivan and Kevin Hennessy were on the vanquished Senior team at Croke Park, a week earlier.*

1983 FINAL
GALWAY U-21'S TOO STRONG FOR TIPPERARY.
11/9/1983 AT O'CONNOR PARK, TULLAMORE.
Galway 0-12. Tipperary 1-6.

A week after their minors won the All-Ireland title for the first time, the Galway u-21's made it a double by defeating Tipperary before an attendance of 6,050. Both Galway teams won their respective All-Irelands without scoring a goal. The blustery wind coming from the town end at Tullamore didn't make it easy for the teams. Ground hurling proved to be the best approach to the conditions. The Munster champions failed to score in the first half, when playing against the wind. They shot five wides in this period. The half time score was Galway 0-5, Tipperary 0-0.

Tipperary laid siege to the Galway goal in the second half. They scored a goal forty seconds after the restart, when a free from Martin McGrath was touched to the Galway net by Arthur Browne. Staunton replied with a point for the Tribesmen and their goalkeeper Tommy Coen deflected another effort from Browne over the bar after three minutes. When Martin McGrath reduced the deficit to one point in the tenth minute, the character of the Galway side then shone through. Pascal Healy took control at midfield and supplied his forwards with scoring opportunities. They quickly restored their three point advantage and though further scores were exchanged, that was the winning margin at the final whistle.

For Galway, the aforementioned Pascal Healy gave an exhibition of style, craft and commitment.

He was well supported by Ollie Kilkenny, Peter Finnerty and Peter Casserley in defence. There was some fine forward play from Aidan Staunton and Michael McGrath.

Were it not for the displays of Ian Conroy, Eddie Hogan, Colm Bonnar, Paddy Maher and goalie Ken Hogan, Tipperary would have suffered a heavier defeat. They lost because their key forwards failed to impress and their midfielders couldn't match the talent of their direct opponents.

The referee was Michael Kelleher of Kildare.

Galway scorers; Aidan Staunton 0-3, Albert Moylan 0-3 (0-2fs), Tony Keady 0-1, Michael Coleman 0-1, Michael Costello 0-1, Gerry Burke 0-1, Michael McGrath 0-1, John Murphy 0-1 (f).

Tipperary scorers; Arthur Browne 1-1, Martin McGrath 0-2 (fs), Philip Kenny 0-1, Conor O'Donovan 0-1, Ger O'Neill 0-1.

Galway team. Tommy Coen (Mullagh), Brendan Dervan (Kiltormer), Peter Casserley (Beagh), Capt, Martin Donoghue (Kilconieron), Peter Finnerty (Mullagh), Tony Keady (Killimordaly), Ollie Kilkenny (Kiltormer), Albert Moylan (Beagh), Pascal Healy (Athenry), Aidan Staunton (Kiltormer), Michael Coleman (Abbeyknockmoy), Michael Costello (Abbeyknockmoy), Gerry Burke (Turloughmore), John Murphy (Meelick), Michael McGrath (Sarsfields).
Subs. Eanna Ryan (Killimordaly) for Burke. Mattie Kenny (Abbey-Duniry) for Coleman. C.Hanberry (Tommie Larkin's), T. Kenny (Sarsfields), Tom Nolan (Salthill), J. Rodgers (Kiltormer), P.Neilan (Gort).

Tipperary team. Ken Hogan (Lorrha), Colm Bonnar (Cashel), Paddy Maher (Thurles Sarsfields), Eddie Hogan (Roscrea), Ian Conroy (Borrisokane), Nicholas English (Lattin-Cullen), Denis Finnerty (Nenagh), Capt, Joe Hayes (Clonoulty), Liam Bergin (Moycarkey), Philip Kenny (Borris-Ileigh), Conor O'Donovan (Nenagh), Martin McGrath (Knockavilla), Ger O'Neill (Cappawhite), Willie Peters (St. Mary's, Clonmel), Arthur Browne (Father Sheehy's).
Subs. John Kennedy (Clonoulty) for Peters. Jim Maher (Loughmore) for Hayes. Vivian Dooley (Borrisokane) for Kenny, Donal Flannery(Kildangan), Peter Brennan (Loughmore), Roger Coffey (Nenagh), Michael Gleeson (Portroe), Mick Ryan (Clonmore), John Sheedy (Portroe), Mick Ryan (Ballinahinch), Connie Maher (Thurles Sars)

1983
LEINSTER FINAL: *Laois 3-13, Wexford 4-8*
MUNSTER FINAL: *Tipperary 2-17, Clare 3-8*
ULSTER FINAL: *Down 2-7, Antrim 0-7*
ALL IRELAND SEMI FINALS: *Galway 2-10, Laois 1-7; Tipperary 1-16, Down 3-7.*

♦ *Three Dervan brothers had now collected a Senior medal (Jackie), an u-21 medal (Brendan) and a Minor medal (Pakie).*

Galway - All Ireland U21 Champions 1983
Back: Brendan Dervan, Pascal Healy, Aidan Staunton, Ollie Kilkenny, Martin Donoghue, Michael Costello, Tony Keady, Peter Finnerty.
Front: Michael Coleman, Gerry Burke, John Murphy, Tommy Coen, Michael McGrath, Peter Casserly, Albert Moylan.

Kilkenny - All Ireland U21 Champions 1984

Back: Liam Walsh, Denis Carroll, John McDonald, David Hoyne, Larry Cleere, Ray Heffernan, Pat Walsh, Brian Young.
Front: Liam McCarthy, Eddie O'Connor, Tommy Phelan, David Burke, Seamus Delehunty, Eddie Wall, Richard McCarthy

1984 Final
Burke's display sees Kilkenny through.
26/8/1984 at Walsh Park, Waterford.
Kilkenny 1-12. Tipperary 0-11.

An attendance of 9,000 watched a thrilling final in ideal conditions. When the final whistle blew, the talk amongst spectators was of the brilliant display of Kilkenny goalkeeper David "Stoney" Burke. He kept his side in the game during the opening quarter when Tipperary were most dangerous. Burke saved a penalty from Michael Scully and shortly afterwards foiled the same player after he had broken clean through. In the 19th minute of the first half, he made a double save from close range flicks. Kilkenny led by 1-5 to 0-6 at the interval despite having the worst of matters territorially. Their goal struck by Ray Heffernan from a penalty in the 5th minute was the crucial score.

In the second half, Kilkenny had established a definite superiority, but were unable to put distance between themselves and their tenacious opponents. In the 54th minute, they were leading by 1-9 to 0-10 when Willie Peters of the Munster champions was put clean through. The Tipp forward shot hard and accurately for what could have been the winning goal, but Burke dived full length to his right and his save averted the danger.

Apart from Burke's display, another key factor in the Noresiders' victory was the switch of Liam McCarthy to full forward after 20 minutes. He scored four points from that position. Brian Young and
David Hoyne were outstanding in the winners' defence. Tommy Phelan worked very hard at midfield and Pat Walsh at centre forward brought his forward colleagues into the game with intelligent play. Overall what contributed immensely to Kilkenny's victory was their first time hurling, the short flicked pass from the hurley and the palmed pass.

Ken Hogan was very sound in goal for the losers. Their defence as a whole was reasonably steady with Donal Kealy the most prominent player. John Kennedy and his clubmate, Joe Hayes, played well at midfield. Their attack faded after a promising start. They managed only one point from play during the second half.

The referee was Kevin Walsh of Limerick.

Kilkenny scorers; Ray Heffernan 1-4 (1-0open,0-3fs), Liam McCarthy 0-4, Denis Carroll 0-1, Pat Walsh 0-1, Pat Ryan 0-1, Michael Rafter 0-1.

Tipperary scorers; Michael Scully 0-5 (0-3fs), Joe Hayes 0-2, David Fogarty 0-2, Anthony Waters 0-1, Donal Kealy 0-1 (f).

Kilkenny team. David Burke (Emeralds), Eddie Wall (Lisdowney), Eddie O'Connor (Glenmore), Brian Young (Erin's Own), David Hoyne (Thomastown), Larry Cleere (Bennetsbridge), Liam

Walsh (O'Loughlin's), Tommy Phelan (Ballyhale Shamrocks), Ray Heffernan (Glenmore), Denis Carroll (Black & Whites), Pat Walsh (Windgap), John McDonald (Mullinavat), Liam McCarthy (Piltown), Richard McCarthy (Bennetsbridge), Seamus Delahunty (Mooncoin), Capt.
Subs. Pat Ryan (Emeralds) for R. McCarthy. Michael Rafter (Emeralds) for Carroll. John Dunphy (Mullinavat), Michael Morrissey (Graiguenamanagh), Des Dunne (Danesfort), Tom Leahy (James Stephens), Anthony Prendergast (Clara), Pat Nolan (Black & Whites), Pat Barron (Glenmore), Eddie O'Neill (James Stephens), Jimmy Doran (Bennetsbridge).

Tipperary team. Ken Hogan (Lorrha), John McKenna (Borrisokane), Eddie Hogan (Roscrea), Colm Bonnar (Cashel), Richard Stakelum (Borris-Ileigh), Donal Kealy (Roscrea), Capt, Jimmy Leahy (Moycarkey-Borris), John Kennedy (Clonoulty-Rossmore), Joe Hayes (Clonoulty-Rossmore), Aidan Ryan (Borris-Ileigh), Noel Sheehy (Silvermines), Philip Kenny (Borris-Ileigh), Michael Scully (Roscrea), Anthony Waters (Carrick Swans), David Fogarty (Moycarkey-Borris).
Subs. Willie Peters (St. Mary's,Clonmel) for Kenny, Michael Cunningham (Emly) for Scully, Rory Dwan (Holycross), John Flannery (Nenagh), Philip Hennessy (Nenagh), Seamus Hammersley (Clonoulty-Rossmore), John Harding (Lorrha), John Leamy (Golden-Kilfeacle).

1984
LEINSTER FINAL: *Kilkenny 0-18, Wexford 1-10*
MUNSTER FINAL: *Tipperary 0-12, Limerick 1-8*
ULSTER FINAL: *Down 1-14, Antrim 0-15*
ALL IRELAND SEMI FINALS: *Kilkenny 5-16, Down 1-9; Tipperary 3-10, Galway 2-8.*

1985 FINAL
INACCURACY ALMOST COST TIPPERARY DEARLY.
25/8/1985 AT WALSH PARK, WATERFORD.
Tipperary 1-10. Kilkenny 2-6.

This final, despite the scoreline, was not up to the standard of some previous finals in the grade. A crowd of 8,000 watched the game in sunny breezy conditions. Tipperary enjoyed first use of the wind. An early goal from John McGrath should have set them on their way. They dominated the opening half, but only led by 1-5 to 0-2 at the break. They shot thirteen wides before the interval to Kilkenny's five. They also had a goal by Michael Cunningham disallowed for a square infringement.

In the second half Tipperary resumed where they had left off and appeared to be cruising to a comfortable victory, when they led by 1-8 to 0-3 as the game approached the three quarter mark. However, in the 45th minute, Kilkenny's Joe Walsh with a one handed pull sent the sliotar flying to the net. Michael Scully then missed a simple free for the Munster champions, before Paul Cleere first timed Michael Dunne's cross for a Kilkenny goal. That left only two points between the teams.

Tipperary - All Ireland U21 Champions 1985
Back: John Kennedy, John McGrath, Noel Sheehy, John Cormack, Pat O'Donoghue, Michael Corcoran, Liam Stokes.
Front: Colm Bonnar, Donal Kealy, Michael Scully (capt.), John Leamy, Paul Delaney, Michael Cunningham, Noel McDonnell, Aidan Ryan.

Tipp's lead soon vanished as Tommy Bawle from long range and Eamon Morrissey(free) tied the scores. Tipp rallied and two points followed from Murty Bryan and Noel Sheehy. The losers' sole reply was a pointed 65 from Larry Cleere in the last minute.

Tipperary were worthy winners but suffered some nervous moments in the final quarter. They had a most dependable goalkeeper in John Leamy. Best in defence were Noel McDonnell, Michael Corcoran and Paul Delaney. Aidan Ryan had a tremendous game at midfield. In attack, Michael Scully landed some vital points from frees, but also missed some. Michael Cunningham and Noel Sheehy were the only others in an erratic forward line to impress.

Kilkenny's best player by far was Larry Cleere, who was dominant in the aerial duels and displayed some great fielding. Tommy Lannon, Kevin Ryan and substitute Tommy Bawle also made worthwhile contributions.

The referee was John Denton of Wexford.

Tipperary scorers; Michael Scully 0-5 (0-4fs), John McGrath 1-0, Donal Kealy 0-1, Aidan Ryan 0-1, Noel Sheehy 0-1, John Cormack 0-1, Murty Bryan 0-1.

Kilkenny scorers; Joe Walsh 1-0, Paul Cleere 1-0, Eamon Morrissey 0-3 (0-2fs), Richie Moran 0-1, Tommy Bawle 0-1, Larry Cleere 0-1 (65).

Tipperary team. John Leamy (Golden-Kilfeacle), Noel McDonnell (Toomevara), Pat O'Donoghue (Cashel), Colm Bonnar (Cashel), Michael Corcoran (Emly), Donal Kealy (Roscrea), Paul Delaney (Roscrea), John Kennedy (Clonoulty-Rossmore), Aidan Ryan (Borris-Ileigh), Michael Cunningham (Emly), John McGrath (Borris-Ileigh), Noel Sheehy (Silvermines), John Cormack (Loughmore-Castleiney), Liam Stokes (Kilsheelan), Michael Scully (Roscrea), Capt.

Action from the 1985 All Ireland U21 Final

Subs. Murty Bryan (Thurles Sarsfields) for Stokes. Seamus Collison (Moneygall), James Seymour (Portroe), Gerry Ryan (Upperchurch), Tom Leamy (Golden-Kilfeacle), Ger Bradley (Newport), Declan Carr (Holycross), John Flannery (Nenagh), John Bergin (Moyne-Templetouhy), John McKenna (Borrisokane).

Kilkenny team. Richard Dunne (Graiguenamanagh), Kevin Ryan (Clara), Capt, Eddie O'Connor (Glenmore), Peadar Healy (Erin's Own), Tommy Lannon (Bennettsbridge), Larry Cleere (Bennettsbridge), Larry O'Brien (Slieverue), Tommy Phelan (Ballyhale Shamrocks), John Scott (James Stephens), Richie Moran (Bennettsbridge), Seamus Delahunty (Mooncoin), Eamon Morrissey (St. Martin's), Michael Dunne (Graiguenamanagh), Michael Rafter (Emeralds), Joe Walsh (Mullinavat).

Subs. Paul Cleere (O'Loughlin's) for Rafter. Tommy Bawle (Dicksboro) for Phelan. Pat Barron (Glenmore) for Scott. John Dunphy (Mullinavat), PJ Greene (Tullogher-Rosbercon), Brian Barcoe (Clara), Brian Young (Erin's Own), Tom Leahy (James Stephens), John Power (John Lockes), Jim Whelan (Graiguenamanagh).

1985
LEINSTER FINAL: *Kilkenny 4-18, Wexford 1-4*
MUNSTER FINAL: *Tipperary 1-16, Clare 4-5*
ULSTER FINAL: *Down 1-12, Antrim 1-10*
ALL IRELAND SEMI FINALS: *Kilkenny 2-12, Down 0-4; Tipperary 1-15, Galway 2-7.*

◆ *Mick Minogue was Tipperary's trainer/coach for the seventh season. It was their fourth All-Ireland victory at the grade under his tutelage.*

1986 FINAL
GALWAY GAIN SOME CONSOLATION FOR SENIOR DEFEAT.
14/9/1986 AT SEMPLE STADIUM, THURLES.
Galway 1-14. Wexford 2-5.

This was never a final which had the 8,000 attendance enraptured, even though the movements were often swift, interspersed with some fine scores. Played in bright sunshine, Galway started well and some fine points from Michael Connolly helped them to a lead of 0-5 to 0-2 after the first quarter. In the 20th minute, Mark Morrissey managed to finish a centre from Pat Barden for a goal, which put Wexford on level terms. Joe Cooney then scored a Galway point from a free, but almost immediately Paul Carton's shot from twenty yards finished in the Galway net. Wexford then earned a penalty but Tom Dempsey's shot was deflected around the post for a 65. This was converted and left Wexford leading by 2-3 to 0-6 at the interval.

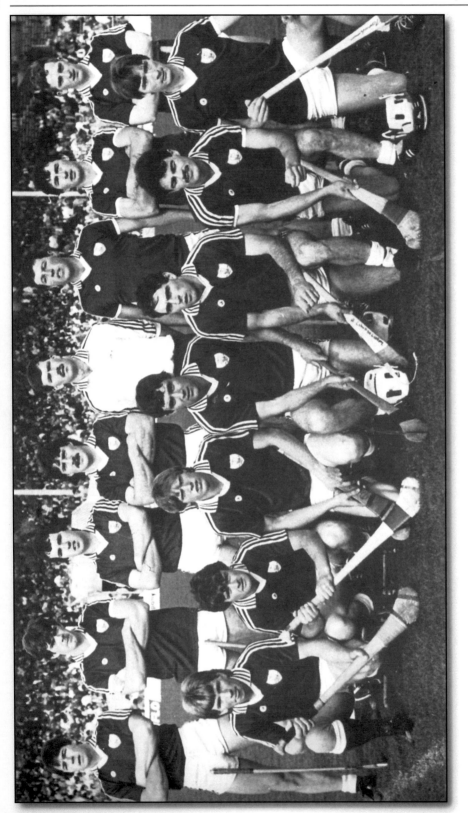

Galway - All-Ireland U21 Champions 1986.
Back: Pat Higgins, Michael Helebert, Pakie Dervan, Michael Connolly, John Commins, Martin Kelly, Declan Jennings and Pat Nolan.
Front: Aodh Davoren, Mick Flaherty, Joe Cooney, Pat Malone, Anthony Cunningham, Gerry McInerney and Tom Monaghan.

Within forty seconds of the restart Cooney landed a well taken point for Galway. Two minutes later came the crucial goal when Galway captain Anthony Cunningham was fouled. The Galway goalkeeper John Commins came the length of the field to lash the resultant penalty to the net. The Leinster champions only managed two points after the interval, one of these a free from Tom Dempsey. Galway in the second half showed their battling qualities. They took their points well to build up a commanding lead and withstood all the pressure, which Wexford threw at them in the final quarter.

Galway's half back line were immense all through. Michael Helebert, Pat Malone and Gerry McInerney formed a solid barrier to Wexford attacks. Joe Cooney enjoying far more freedom after moving to centre forward, was involved in most of Galway's attacking ventures. Michael Connolly, Pat Nolan and Aodh Davoren profited as good possession flowed their way.

Wexford, who were trying to win the title for the first time since 1965, were well served by Tom Dempsey, Paul Bridges and Joe Doyle in their defence. Pat Barden played well for them at midfield. Their weakness was in attack where only Paul Carton made any real impression.

The referee was Gerry Long of Tipperary.

Galway scorers; Joe Cooney 0-4 (0-2fs), Michael Connolly 0-3, John Commins 1-0 (pen), Pat Nolan 0-2, Declan Jennings 0-1, Aodh Davoren 0-1, Anthony Cunningham 0-1, Pakie Dervan 0-1 (65), Gerry McInerney 0-1 (f).

Wexford scorers; Paul Carton 1-1, Mark Morrissey 1-0, Tom Dempsey 0-2 (f,65), Pat Barden 0-1, Dermot Prendergast 0-1.

Galway team. John Commins (Gort), Pakie Dervan (Kiltormer), Martin Kelly (Killimor), Michael Flaherty (Gort), Michael Helebert (Gort), Pat Malone (Oranmore Maree), Gerry McInerney (Kinvara), Tom Monaghan (Killimor), Declan Jennings (Kiltormer), Michael Connolly (Craughwell), Anthony Cunningham (St. Thomas), Capt, Aodh Davoren (Moycullen), Pat Nolan (Castlegar), Joe Cooney (Sarsfields), Pat Higgins (Athenry).

Subs. Gary Elwood (Liam Mellows) for Higgins. Sean Keane (Beagh) for Monaghan). Billy Glynn (Gort), Nigel Harrington (Beagh), John Fox (Moycullen), John Blade (Abbeyknockmoy), Jimmy Burke (Turloughmore).

Wexford team. Paul Nolan (Rapparees), Joe Doyle (Rathnure), Michael Foley (Rapparees), Paul Bridges (Faythe Harriers), Larry O'Gorman (Faythe Harriers), Tom Dempsey (Buffer's Alley), Kevin Murphy (Faythe Harriers), Matt Foley (Buffer's Alley), Pat Barden (Adamstown), Eamon Sinnott (Buffer's Alley), Vincent Murphy (Ferns), Dermot Prendergast (Monageer/Boolavogue), Mark Morrissey (Rathnure), Paul Carton (Cloughbawn), Ray Murphy (Rath/Cushinstown).
Subs. Niall McDonald (Ballymurn/Crossabeg) for Foley. John Murray (Ferns St. Aidan's) for Prendergast. Colin Whelan (Buffer's Alley) for O'Gorman). John Kenny (Naomh Eanna). Michael Reck (Oylegate/Glenbrien).

1986
LEINSTER FINAL: *Wexford 2-9, Offaly 2-9*
Wexford 1-16, Offaly 0-10
MUNSTER FINAL: *Limerick 3-9, Clare 3-9*
Limerick 2-10, Clare 0-3
ULSTER FINAL: *Derry 2-9, Down 2-9*
Derry 3-9, Down 1-2
ALL IRELAND SEMI FINALS: *Galway 2-10, Limerick 2-6; Wexford 5-16, Derry 2-3.*

♦ *Anthony Cunningham also captained the victorious Galway minors in 1983..*

1987 FINAL
HISTORIC FIRST TITLE FOR LIMERICK.
21/6/1987 AT CUSACK PARK, ENNIS.
Limerick 2-15. Galway 3-6.

The 1987 final opened at a furious pace and treated the attendance of over 11,000 to extensive entertainment. Galway got off to an encouraging start with points from Michael Connolly and Dermot Coxe. However, with Ger Hegarty and Anthony Carmody quick to find their shooting form, Limerick responded to lead by 0-6 to 0-2 after fourteen minutes. They were threatening to pull away when Galway struck for a timely goal midway through the half. A Jimmy Burke free was doubled on to the net by Coxe. The Shannonsiders, despite a significant degree of wastage, were not rattled and went on to establish a five point lead at the interval, 0-11 to 1-3.

Within seconds of the restart, Connolly expertly pointed from a sideline cut to reduce the arrears. After a prolonged period of scoreless if exciting end to end hurling, Eamon Burke goaled for Galway in the 42nd minute from a 21 yard free. In the following four minutes points were exchanged by Michael Connolly(65) and Leo O'Connor(free) to leave Galway only one point adrift. The concluding stages, however, were more representative of Limerick's dominance throughout the field. Corner forward Leo O'Connor got a brace of goals between the 53rd and 55th minutes to put his team into a commanding lead. A goal for Galway by Ray Duane was answered by Limerick points from Hegarty and O'Connor. The Galway centre back Jimmy Burke was sent off just on full time as Limerick prepared to celebrate their first title in this grade.

The class of their senior players Ger Hegarty, Anthony Carmody and Gary Kirby was a major factor in Limerick's success. Yet at the end it was corner forward Leo O'Connor who emerged as the hero, with a contribution of 2-5. Others to shine for the Treaty side were John O'Neill, Don Flynn and Anthony Madden.

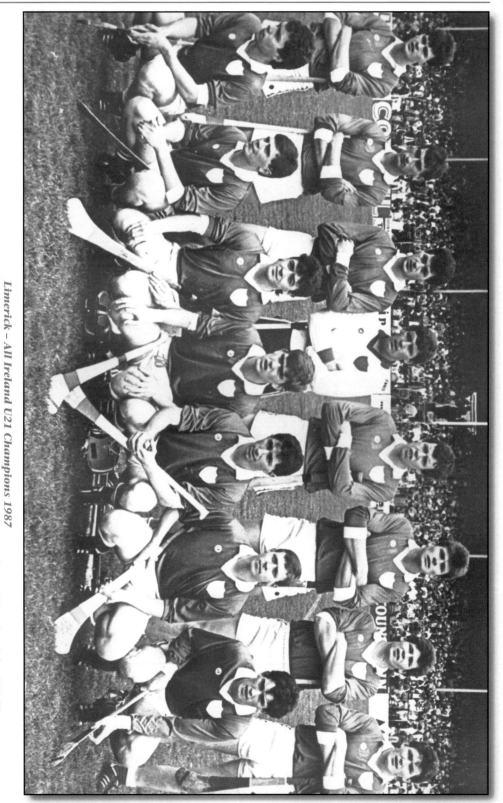

Limerick – All Ireland U21 Champions 1987
Back: Mike Reale, Anthony Carmody, Pa Carey, Val Murnane, Gary Kirby, Ger Hegarty, Anthony O'Riordan, John O'Neill.
Front : Joe O'Connor, Anthony Madden, Gussie Ryan, Leo O'Connor, Declan Nash, Pat Barrett, Don Flynn.

Best for the deposed champions Galway, were goalkeeper Michael Finnerty, Brendan Cooney, Tom Broderick, Sean Dolphin, Dermot Coxe and Michael Connolly.

The referee was Paschal Long of Kilkenny.

Limerick scorers; Leo O'Connor 2-5 (0-5fs), Ger Hegarty 0-5 (0-1f,0-1,65), Anthony Carmody 0-4, Joe O'Connor 0-1.

Galway scorers; Dermot Coxe 1-2, Michael Connolly 0-4 (0-1f,0-1,65,0-2lbs), Ray Duane 1-0, Eamon Burke 1-0 (f).

Limerick team. Val Murnane (Caherline), Anthony Madden (Bruff), Anthony O'Riordan (Bruff), Don Flynn (Killeedy), Declan Nash (South Liberties), Pa Carey (Patrickswell), Michael Reale (Bruff), Ger Hegarty (Old Christians), John O'Neill (Kilfinane), Anthony Carmody (Patrickswell), Gary Kirby (Patrickswell), Gus Ryan (Claughaun), Capt, Pat Barrett (Bruff), Joe O'Connor (Ballybrown), Leo O'Connor (Claughaun).

Subs. Declan Marren (Adare) for Barrett. Dan McKenna (Cappamore), Nicky O'Farrell (Na Piarsaigh), Brian Stapleton (Garryspillane), Brendan Heffernan (Adare), Andy Cunneen (Claughaun).

Galway team. Michael Finnerty (Craughwell), Brendan Cawley (Castlegar), Sean Dolphin (Mullagh), Brendan Cooney (Sarsfields), Tom Broderick (Killimordaly), Jimmy Burke (Turloughmore), Tom King (Castlegar), Dermot Coxe (Kiltormer), Gerry Coyne (Castlegar), Michael Connolly (Craughwell), Capt, Kevin Coen (Mullagh), Aodh Davoren (Moycullen), Michael Greaney (Annaghdown), Eamon Burke (Killimordaly), Ray Duane (Mullagh).
Subs. Enda Lyons (Ballinasloe) for Greaney. Padraig Killilea (Carnmore) for Broderick. Bosco Hurley (Turloughmore) for Coen. Noel Cooney (Killimordaly), Michael Kenny (Sarsfields), Owen Shaughnessy (Kilrickle).

1987
LEINSTER FINAL: *Wexford 4-11, Offaly 0-5*
MUNSTER FINAL: *Limerick 3-14, Cork 2-9*
ULSTER FINAL: *Down 3-12 Derry 2-9*
ALL IRELAND SEMI FINALS: *Galway 0-11, Wexford1 -7; Limerick 2-14, Down 1 -6.*

♦ *The majority of the Limerick u-21 team had won a minor All-Ireland three years previously in 1984.*
♦ *Galway had only two survivors from their victorious u-21 team of 1986, Aodh Davoren and Michael Connolly.*

1988 FINAL
CORK WIN NINTH TITLE IN ONE-SIDED FINAL.
11/9/1988 AT ST.BRENDAN'S PARK, BIRR.
Cork 4-11. Kilkenny 1-5.

This final lacked drama and excitement as Cork proved far too good on a cool but dry afternoon before 4,750 spectators, the great majority of whom were Kilkenny supporters. Cork were seeking their ninth title and Kilkenny their fifth. The Leesiders goaled after 16 seconds through John Fitzgibbon and steadily built on their bright start. By the 11th minute the Munster champions were 1-3 to 0-1 ahead. Kilkenny's Pat Hoban had pointed from play in the 4th minute, but that was their only score from play for the next 42 minutes. Cork scored further goals in the 21st and 25th minutes through Mark Foley and Dan O'Connell, respectively. The Rebels held an interval lead of 3-7 to 0-2.

A point from towering full forward Mark Foley was the first score of the second half. In the 42nd minute Cork scored their fourth goal. A free from 55 yards out was dropped by the Kilkenny goalkeeper only for Dan O'Connell to net and put the issue beyond all doubt. Kilkenny had a consolation goal in the 47th minute, when lively sub Tom Murphy and Tom O'Keefe combined to create an opening for John Feehan. This left the score at 4-9 to 1-4. Points were exchanged before the final whistle as Cork ran out easy winners.

Cork had a polished performer in Cathal Casey. He had able assistants in Liam Kelly, Ger Manley, Frank Horgan, Christy Connery, Pat Kenneally. Mark Foley and Dan O'Connell.

In a porous Kilkenny defence, Willie O'Connor tried hard. Bill Hennessy did his best and Tom Murphy made a useful contribution, when introduced.

The referee was John Moore of Waterford.

Cork scorers; Dan O'Connell 2-1, Mark Foley 1-1, Ger Manley 0-4 (0-1f), John Fitzgibbon 1-0, Frank Horgan 0-3, John Corcoran 0-1, Trevor Cooney 0-1 (f).

Kilkenny scorers; John Feehan 1-0, Tom O'Keefe 0-2 (fs), Liam Egan 0-1, Pat Hoban 0-1, Tom Murphy 0-1.

Cork team. Tom Kingston (Tracton), Christy Connery (Na Piarsaigh), Capt, Damien Irwin (Killeagh), Seamus O'Leary (St. Finbarrs), Cathal Casey (St. Catherines), Pat Kenneally (Newcestown), Tony O'Keefe (Erin's Own), Liam Kelly (Tracton), Trevor Cooney (Fermoy), John Corcoran (Erin's Own), Ger Manley (Inniscarra), Frank Horgan (Erin's Own), Dan O'Connell (Kilbritain), Mark Foley (Ardigeen Rangers), John Fitzgibbon (Glen Rovers).
Subs. Paddy Barry (Blackrock), Colman Quirke (Midleton), Kieran Keane (Glen Rovers), Ronan Sheehan (Mallow), Brian Cunningham (St. Finbarrs), John Tobin (St. Finbarrs), Barry Harte (Ardigeen Rangers).

Cork - All Ireland U21 Hurling Champions 1988

Back: *Pat Kennealy (Newcestown), Frank Horgan (Erins Own) , Damien Irwin (Killeagh), Tom Kingston (Tracton), Seamus O'Leary (St. Finbarrs), Cathal Casey (St. Catherines) , John Fitzgibbon (Glen Rovers), Mark Foley (Argideen Rangers).*
Front: *Dan O'Connell (Kilbrittain), Trevor Cooney (Fermoy), Liam Kelly (Tracton), John Corcoran (Erins Own), Christy Connery (Capt.) (Na Piarsaigh), Ger Manley (Inniscarra) , Tony O'Keeffe (EnnsOwn).*

Kilkenny Team. Tom Phelan (Fenians), Frankie Morgan (James Stephens), Capt, Willie O'Connor (Glenmore), Liam Drennan (Galmoy), Richie Minogue (James Stephens), Liam Keoghan (Tullaroan), Bill Hennessy (Tullaroan), Tommy Fogarty (James Stephens), Liam Egan (John Lockes), Tom O'Keefe (Thomastown), Michael Phelan (Glenmore), John Feehan (Conahy Shamrocks), Pat Hoban (Mullinavat), Seanie O'Mahoney (Conahy Shamrocks), John Larkin (James Stephens).

Subs. Pat Carroll (Dicksboro) for Drennan. Tom Murphy (Mooncoin) for Larkin. Liam Dowling (St. Martin's) for Fogarty. Pat Drea (Young Irelands), Declan Mullen (James Stephens), John Millea (James Stephens), John Teehan (Graigue/Ballycallan), Declan Killeen (St. Lachtains), Seamus McGuire (James Stephens), Jamesie Brennan (Erin's Own), Ned Kelly (Black&Whites), Jodi O'Dwyer (James Stephens), Donal Kennedy (O'Loughlins).

1988
LEINSTER FINAL: *Kilkenny 3-13, Offaly 2-5*
MUNSTER FINAL: *Cork 4-12, Limerick 1-7*
ULSTER FINAL: *Antrim 6-11, Down 1-4*
ALL IRELAND SEMI FINALS: *Cork 4-21, Antrim 1-3; Kilkenny 0-19, Galway 2-9.*

1989 FINAL
RECORD ATTENDANCE AS TIPPERARY WIN SECOND ALL-IRELAND TITLE IN A WEEK.
10/9/1989 AT O'MOORE PARK, PORTLAOISE.
Tipperary 4-10. Offaly 3-11.

An attendance of 35,000 witnessed a thrilling final at Portlaoise. Offaly won the toss and chose to face the strong wind. They were quicker to settle and Declan Pilkington goaled after two minutes. Offaly went on to lead by 2-3 to 0-2, when Billy Dooley goaled in the 16th minute. The Tipp full forward Dan Quirke then took centre stage. In the last eight minutes of the first half he scored 3-2. His first goal in the 22nd minute was struck low and hard inside the right hand post. The second goal after 28 minutes was hit from far out on the right wing. The third, 30 seconds from the interval, was an opportunist effort from Quirke after a free from Conor Stakelum rebounded from an upright. Tipperary led by 3-7 to 2-4 at half time.

In the early minutes of the second half, Offaly shot four points without reply. Then in the 42nd minute, Michael Nolan crashed home a Tipp goal from a penalty. Offaly refused to lie down. They

Tipperary - All-Ireland U21 Champions 1989:
Back: John Leahy, Padraic Hogan, Seamus Maher, Brendan Bane, Michael Ryan, John Madden, Dan Quirke, Liam Sheedy.
Front: Conor Stakelum, Tony Lanigan, Dinny Ryan, Don Lyons, Declan Ryan (capt), Conal Bonnar, George Frend.

continued to take their points and when Daithi Regan shot a goal in the 49th minute, they had reduced the leeway to the minimum. The Munster champions then created and took two excellent points. John Leahy placed Conor Stakelum for the first and following an incisive solo run from John Madden, Nolan scored the second. The Offaly full back Damien Geoghegan was sent off with six minutes remaining. The Leinster champions attacked for most of the last five minutes, but Tipperary prevailed by two points.

For Tipperary, Dan Quirke's performance in scoring 3-2 in the first half was vital. Of the other forwards, Conor Stakelum and Michael Nolan were most prominent. John Leahy and Declan Ryan did very well at midfield breaking Offaly's early dominance there. Of the backs, John Madden was in splendid form both on the wing and at centre back. Conal Bonnar showed glimpses of his brilliance. The full back line settled in after a shaky start and both Michael Ryan and George Frend finished very well.

Offaly lost nothing in defeat. They had contributed handsomely to one of the finest games not alone in the u-21 grade but in any grade. They had outstanding players in Gary Cahill, Johnny and Declan Pilkington, Michael Duignan, Daithi Regan and the Dooley brothers, Billy and Johnny. Tipperary had 12 wides to Offaly's 8.

The referee was Paschal Long of Kilkenny.

Tipperary scorers; Dan Quirke 3-2, Michael Nolan 1-1 (1-0pen), Conor Stakelum 0-3, Padraig Hogan 0-1, Dinny Ryan 0-1, Conal Bonnar 0-1 (f), John Leahy 0-1 (f).

Declan Ryan (capt.) is carried off the field after victory in the 1989 U21 All-Ireland Final

Offaly scorers; Daithi Regan 1-2, Johnny Dooley 0-5 (0-3fs), Billy Dooley 1-0, Declan Pilkington 1-0, Johnny Pilkington 0-2, Gary Cahill 0-1, Brian Whelehan 0-1 (65).

Tipperary team. Brendan Bane (JK Brackens), Liam Sheedy (Portroe), Michael Ryan (Upperchurch-Drombane), George Frend (Toomevara), John Madden (Lorrha), Conal Bonnar (Cashel), Seamus Maher (Thurles Sarsfields), John Leahy (Mullinahone), Declan Ryan (Clonoulty-Rossmore), Capt, Padraig Hogan (Borrisokane), Conor Stakelum (Borris-Ileigh), Dinny Ryan (Newport), Michael Nolan (Toomevara), Dan Quirke (Clonoulty-Rossmore), Tony Lanigan (Holycross/Ballycahill).
Subs. Jim Cahill (JK Brackens) for Maher. Don Lyons (Ballingarry) for Lanigan). Kevin Ryan (Clonoulty-Rossmore) for Cahill. Declan Ryan (St. Mary's), Noel Keane (Clonoulty-Rossmore), Seamus Bohan (Loughmore-Castleiney), Colm Egan (Kildangan), Jim Harvey (St. Mary's), Raymie Ryan (Cashel).

Offaly team. John Troy (Lusmagh), Brian Whelehan (Birr), Damian Geoghegan (Birr), Brian Hennessy (Birr), Roy Mannion (St.Rynagh's), Brendan Kelly (Lusmagh), Gary Cahill (Birr), Johnny Pilkington (Birr), Adrian Cahill (Birr), Billy Dooley (Seir Kieran), Daithi Regan (Faughs), Johnny Dooley (Seir Kieran), Ronnie Byrne (Lusmagh), Declan Pilkington (Birr), Michael Duignan (St.Rynagh's), Capt.
Subs. John Kilmartin (Kilcormac) for Byrne, Michael Hogan (Birr), Shane McGuckin (St. Rynagh's), Peter Nallen (St. Rynagh's), Padraig McGuinness (Kinnitty), Timmy Dooley (Killavilla), Alan Kelly (St. Rynagh's), Tommy Kilmartin (Kilcormac-Killoughey), John Troy (Kilcormac-Killoughey).

1989
LEINSTER FINAL: *Offaly 3-16, Kilkenny 3-9*
MUNSTER FINAL: *Tipperary 5-16, Limerick 1-6*
ULSTER FINAL: *Antrim 4-18, Derry 0-4*
ALL IRELAND SEMI FINALS: *Offaly 5-18, Antrim 0-9; Tipperary 1-14, Galway 1-7.*

♦ *Mick Minogue was again Tipperary's trainer/coach. It was their fifth All-Ireland title at the grade, under his tutelage.*

CHAPTER 4
ALL IRELAND U21
HURLING FINALS
1990-1999

Kilkenny - All Ireland U21 Champions 19901990

Back: John Conlon, Tom Murphy, Brian McGovern, Jimmy Lawlor, Paul Treacy, Patsy Brophy, Donal Carroll, Adrian Ronan.
Front: Johnny Holohan, Jamesie Brennan (Capt), Charlie Carter, Jimmy Conroy, Tommy Shefflin, DJ Carey, Pat O'Neill.

1990 FINAL
RONAN AND CAREY INSPIRE KILKENNY TO VICTORY.
9/9/1990 AT O'MOORE PARK, PORTLAOISE.
Kilkenny 2-11. Tipperary 1-11.

In bright sunshine and under a blue sky, 23,000 spectators enjoyed a memorable final between two fit and skilful teams. Apart from the first three minutes, Kilkenny were always in front. Their first big break came in the seventh minute when Paul Treacy goaled. DJ Carey hit their second goal in the 26th minute as Tipperary were down to fourteen men with Brendan Corcoran receiving attention for a head injury. Carey added a point three minutes later to put Kilkenny seven points ahead. In injury time of the first half Ger Deely scored a Tipperary goal. The Noresiders led by 2-5 to 1-4 at the break.

Encouraged by that goal, Tipperary took the game to Kilkenny in the early stages of the second half. By the 12th minute they had cut the deficit to the minimum. John Leahy was ruling midfield for the Munster champions and they looked like taking hold of the game. Kilkenny responded and scored three successive points. Tipperary never managed to get closer than that. Points were exchanged but at the final whistle, a goal separated the sides with Kilkenny victorious.

Kilkenny's senior players Adrian Ronan and DJ Carey were the stand out men for the Black and Amber side. Midfielder and captain, Jamesie Brennan was also hugely influential as were Patsy Brophy, Jimmy Conroy, Johnny Holohan and Paul Treacy.

Defensively Tipperary were secure enough. Liam Fallon held the highly rated Charlie Carter scoreless. Eoin Maher, Noel Keane and Brendan Corcoran formed a solid half back line.Tipperary's inter-county senior players John Leahy and Conal Bonnar played well at midfield. The losers could have done with Leahy in an attack, which relied far too heavily on Liam Sheedy's accuracy from frees.
Tipperary drove 14 wides to Kilkenny's 11.

The referee was Pat Delaney of Laois.

Kilkenny scorers; Adrian Ronan 0-6, DJ Carey 1-1, Paul Treacy 1-0, Jamesie Brennan 0-2 (0-1f), Jimmy Lawlor 0-1, Pat O'Grady 0-1.

Tipperary scorers; Liam Sheedy 0-7 (0-5fs), Ger Deely 1-1, Don Lyons 0-1, Paudie O'Brien 0-1, Cathal Egan 0-1.

Kilkenny team. Jimmy Conroy (James Stephens), Johnny Holohan (O'Loughlins), Pat O'Neill (Young Irelands), Donal Carroll (Dicksboro), Patsy Brophy (Erin's Own), Tom Murphy (Mooncoin), John Conlon (Bennettsbridge), Jamesie Brennan (Erin's Own), Capt, Brian McGovern (Slieverue), Adrian Ronan (Graigue/Ballycallan), Jimmy Lawlor (Ballyhale Shamrocks), Tommy Shefflin (Ballyhale Shamrocks), DJ Carey (Young Irelands), Paul Treacy

(Thomastown), Charlie Carter (Young Irelands).
Subs. Pat O'Grady (Black & Whites) for Shefflin. Jimmy Walton (Tullaroan) for McGovern. Donal Carroll (Dicksboro), Ger Henderson (Dicksboro), Brian Ryan (Fenians), John Buggy (Erin's Own), John Teehan (Graigue Ballycallan), Declan Forristal (James Stephens), Brendan Mason (Ballyhale Shamrocks), Declan Roche (John Lockes).

Tipperary team. Brendan Bane (JK Brackens), Liam Fallon (Roscrea), Michael Ryan (Upperchurch-Drombane), George Frend (Toomevara), Eoin Maher (Roscrea), Noel Keane (Clonoulty/Rossmore), Brendan Corcoran (Emly), John Leahy (Mullinahone), Capt, Conal Bonnar (Cashel), Colm Egan (Kildangan), Liam Sheedy (Portroe), Ger Deely (St. Mary's, Clonmel), Don Lyons (Ballingarry), Paudie O'Brien (Portroe), Anthony Wall (St. Mary's, Clonmel).
Subs. Michael O'Meara (Toomevara) for Egan. Cathal Egan (Kildangan) for Lyons. Kevin McCormack (Toomevara), Kevin Ryan (Clonoulty/Rossmore), Brendan Carroll (Thurles Sarsfields), Michael Hogan (Roscrea), Raymie Ryan (Cashel), Seamus Bohan (Loughmore-Castleiney), Owen Cummins (Fethard), Tom Duggan (Ballingarry), TJ Connolly (Cashel), Eamon Maher (Skeheennarinka).

1990
LEINSTER FINAL: *Kilkenny 2-9, Laois 1-10*
MUNSTER FINAL: *Tipperary 2-21, Limerick 1-11*
ULSTER FINAL: *Down 2-9, Antrim 2-6*
ALL IRELAND SEMI FINALS: *Kilkenny 2-16, Galway 1-13; Tipperary 6-13, Down 0-8.*

1991 FINAL
GALWAY'S SECOND HALF DOMINANCE OVERPOWERS OFFALY.
8/9/1991 AT GAELIC GROUNDS, LIMERICK.
Galway 2-17. Offaly 1-9.

Galway's dominance in the second half, was all too evident for the attendance of 16,000, who basked in the warm sunshine. The early tone for this final was set in the 3rd minute, when Liam Burke hammered a shot into the Offaly net. Offaly, showing typical resilience, rallied strongly to score a well struck penalty goal from Johnny Dooley. As the game entered its second quarter, a clever pass from Joe Rabbitte to Justin Campbell saw the latter goal. Offaly were within two points of the winners at the interval, as Galway led by 2-5 to 1-6.

Three minutes after half time, Offaly had levelled with two pointed frees from Johnny Dooley. In the remaining 27 minutes the losers could only muster one more point. That came from another free from Johnny Dooley. In contrast Galway scored twelve points, ten of them from play. The Connacht side went from strength to strength in the second half. Points flowed from the sticks of Francis O'Brien, Cathal Moran, Joe Rabbitte and Basil Larkin with all six forwards getting on the scoresheet. Offaly seemed to have no answer.

Galway – All Ireland U21 Champions 1991

Back: *Justin Campbell, Liam Burke, Christy Helebert, Richard Burke, Joe Rabbitte, Paul Hardiman, Francis O'Brien.*
Front: *Noel Power, Basil Larkin, Murty Killilea, Noel Larkin, Brendan Keogh, Brian Feeney, Gerry McGrath, Cathal Moran.*

The Galway defence was very strong. Christy Helebert was very impressive at right corner back. He got great assistance from Brian Feeney, Noel Power and Gerry McGrath. In their attack Francis O'Brien was a delight to watch. His four points from play made him a real thorn in the Offaly defence. Joe Rabbitte, apart from scoring three points, had a hand in many other scores.

Wing back Brian Whelehan led the Offaly resistance with a fiery display. Johnny Dooley, Adrian Cahill (until injured in the first half) and Johnny Pilkington, when switched to full forward, posed occasional threats to the Galway defence.

The referee was Terence Murray of Limerick.

Galway scorers; Liam Burke 1-2, Francis O'Brien 0-4, Cathal Moran 0-4 (0-3fs), Joe Rabbitte 0-3, Justin Campbell 1-0, Basil Larkin 0-1, Michael Curtin 0-1, Christy Helebert 0-1 (f), Brendan Keogh 0-1 (f).

Offaly scorers; Johnny Dooley 1-5 (0-4fs,1-0pen,), Johnny Pilkington 0-1, Pat Temple 0-1, Adrian Cahill 0-1, John Troy 0-1.

Galway team. Richard Burke (Oranmore-Maree), Christy Helebert (Ballindereen), Brian Feeney (Athenry), Capt, Murty Killilea (Carnmore), Gerry McGrath (Sarsfields), Paul Hardiman (Athenry), Noel Power (Tommy Larkins), Brendan Keogh (Athenry), Noel Larkin (Meelick-Eyrecourt), Liam Burke (Kilconieran), Justin Campbell (Kiltormer), Francis O'Brien (Padraig Pearses), Basil Larkin (Meelick-Eyrecourt), Joe Rabbitte (Athenry), Cathal Moran (Athenry).
Subs. Pat Egan (Castlegar) for Hardiman), Michael Curtin (Kinvara) for Larkin, Kevin Devine (Abbey-Duniry), Kevin Griffin(Loughrea), Michael Donnellan (Sylane), Liam Turley(Castlegar), Pat Coyne (Castlegar), John Dillon (Cappataggle), Martin Holland (Oranmore-Maree).

Offaly team. Damien Franks (Shinrone), Michael Hogan (Coolderry), Kevin Kinahan (Seir Kieran), Donal Franks (Ballyskenagh), David Dooley (Coolderry), Hubert Rigney (St. Rynagh's), Brian Whelehan (Birr), Johnny Pilkington (Birr), Pat Temple (Lusmagh), Johnny Dooley (Seir Kieran), Sean Grennan (Belmont Rangers), Adrian Cahill (Birr), John Troy (Lusmagh), John Brady (Raheen-Killeigh), Enda Mulhare (St. Rynagh's).
Subs. Oisin O'Neill (Birr) for Cahill. Damien Barron (Kilcormac-Killoughey) for Brady, Henry Kilmartin (Kilcormac-Killoughey), Joey Carroll (Kinnitty), Ray Dooley (Coolderry), Mark Gallagher (Tullamore), Eunan Martin (St. Rynagh's), Cathal Maher (Ferbane), Noel Hogan (Birr).

1991
LEINSTER FINAL: *Offaly 2-10, Kilkenny 0-12*
MUNSTER FINAL: *Cork 0-17, Limerick 1-7*
ULSTER FINAL: *Antrim 2-19, Down 2-6*
ALL IRELAND SEMI FINALS: *Galway 2-19, Cork 4-10;   Offaly 2-19, Antrim 1-8.*

1992 FINAL
PULSATING FINAL ENDS AS A DRAW.
13/9/1992 AT NOWLAN PARK, KILKENNY.
Waterford 4-4. Offaly 0-16.

A crowd of 25,000 witnessed an enthralling final at Nowlan Park. The first half bristled with the degree of urgency that makes a championship decider something special. After winning the toss, Waterford opted to play against the breeze. They more than contained Offaly during the opening twenty minutes and were only five points adrift at the interval. The Leinster champions led by 0-9 to 0-4. Both goals during the first half had charmed lives. Waterford shot six wides to Offaly's three.

After six minutes of the second half, Waterford got the first goal of the game. Anthony Fitzgerald placed Sean Daly, who made no mistake. The cheers of the Decies supporters had hardly died, when the lethal forward from Lismore struck again, after Kevin McGrath had delivered a perfect pass. Waterford thus took the lead for the first time. Slowly but surely Offaly regained the lead. Mark Gallagher and Johnny Dooley with points enabled them to go into the final quarter, 0-12 to 2-4 in front. Then Sean Daly got his third goal of the game. A brace of well-taken points from Offaly's midfielder Sean Og Farrell seemed to seal the Decies fate. Less than a minute from the end of normal time, minor star Paul Flynn goaled for Waterford. In this seesaw final Waterford had again taken the lead. In added on time, Brian Whelehan got the all-important two points(one from a sixty five) which secured a draw for Offaly.

Waterford had many stars. Ray Barry in goal was magnificent. His colleagues in defence, Mark O'Sullivan, Tony Browne and Fergal Hartley were outstanding. Johnny Brenner and Tom Fives did well at midfield. Their star in attack was three goal hero Sean Daly. He was the only starting Waterford forward to score.

In the Offaly team none stood out more prominently than team captain, Brian Whelehan. Damian Franks, Hubert Rigney, Sean Og Farrell, Johnny Dooley, Niall Hand and John Troy also contributed hugely to a gripping final.

The referee was Willie Barrett of Tipperary.

Waterford scorers; Sean Daly 3-0, Johnny Brenner 0-4 (0-3fs), Paul Flynn 1-0.

Offaly scorers; Johnny Dooley 0-6 (0-3fs), Sean Og Farrell 0-3, John Troy 0-2, Brian Whelehan 0-2 (0-1,65), Sean Grennan 0-1, Mark Gallagher 0-1, Niall Hand 0-1.

Waterford team. Ray Barry (Passage), Kevin O'Gorman (Lismore), Owen Dunphy (De La Salle), Mark O'Sullivan (Lismore), Tony Browne (Mount Sion), Capt, Pat Fanning (De La Salle), Fergal Hartley (Ballygunner), Tom Fives (Tourin), Johnny Brenner (De La Salle), Paul Power (Ballygunner), Michael Hubbard (Ballydurn), Anthony Fitzgerald (Passage), Noel Dalton (De

Waterford - All-Ireland U21 Champions 1992

Back: Pat Fanning, Owen Dunphy, Kevin McGrath, Johnny Brenner, Tom Fives, Anthony Fitzgerald, Sean Daly, Seamus Keating.
Front: Noel Dalton, Michael Hubbard, Fergal Hartley, Ray Barry, Mark O'Sullivan, Tony Brown (captain), Kieran O'Gorman.

Offaly - All-Ireland U21 Finalists 1992
Back: Michael Hogan, Sean Grennan, Kevin Kinahan,Kevin Martin, Brian Whelehan, Hubert Rigney, Raymond Dooley, Sean Óg Farrell.
Front: Henry Kilmartin, Niall Hand, John Troy, Oisfn O'Neill, Donal Franks, Damien Franks, Johnny Dooley.

La Salle), Sean Daly (Lismore), Kevin McGrath (Colligan).
Subs. Mark Geary (Tallow) for Power. Paul Flynn (Ballygunner) for Geary. Pat Haran (Ballygunner), Johnny Walsh (De La Salle), Seamus Keating (Passage), Colm Cunningham (Tallow), Michael O'Sullivan (Lismore), Paul Meany (Mount Sion), Fergal Cunningham (Dungarvan).

Offaly team. Damian Franks (Shinrone), Henry Kilmartin (Kilcormac/Killoughey), Kevin Kinahan (Seir Kieran), Donal Franks (Ballyskenagh), Kevin Martin (Tullamore), Hubert Rigney (St. Rynagh's), Brian Whelehan (Birr), Sean Og Farrell (Edenderry), Michael Hogan (Coolderry), Johnny Dooley (Seir Kieran), Sean Grennan (Belmont Rangers), John Troy (Lusmagh), Mark Gallagher (Tullamore), Niall Hand (Kilcormac/Killoughey), Oisin O'Neill (Birr).
Subs. Brian Gath (Drumcullen) for Hogan. Peadar Bergin (Kinnitty), Damien Barron (Kilcormac/Killoughey), Eunan Martin (Sarsfields, Cork), Shane Buggy (Ballinamere-Durrow), Raymond Dooley (Coolderry), Mark Moloney (Coolderry), Johnny Carroll (Birr), Liam Clear (Shinrone).

1992 FINAL REPLAY
WATERFORD WIN THEIR FIRST U-21 TITLE.
27/9/1992 AT NOWLAN PARK, KILKENNY.
Waterford 0-12. Offaly 2-3.

Some 28,000 spectators were in attendance in overcast conditions, when the ball was thrown in for this eagerly awaited replay. A quarter of the game had elapsed before Offaly got their first score. By that time Waterford had accumulated a tally of four points. At the start of the second quarter, Mark Gallagher goaled for Offaly, after receiving a diagonal pass from Johnny Dooley. Noel Dalton and Paul Flynn for Waterford, and Johnny Dooley and John Troy for Offaly, exchanged points. In the last minute of the first half, John Troy flashed a ball to the Decies net, to leave the interval score at Offaly 2-3, Waterford 0-6.

As the teams came out for the second half, little did the capacity attendance realise that the Leinster champions would not score again. From the start of the second half, Waterford took complete control but shot some very bad wides. As the half progressed Offaly found themselves repeatedly on the defensive. Fergal Hartley pointed a long range free in the 40th minute. Paul Flynn reduced the deficit to the minimum in the 42nd minute. Five minutes from time, Sean Daly got the equalising score. Ninety seconds later, young Paul Flynn pointed to give Waterford the lead. Johnny Brenner added another in the 57th minute. Just a minute later Flynn landed another minor to give the Munster champions a three point victory. Waterford emerged victorious despite shooting 16 wides to Offaly's 8.

The Waterford defence, particularly the half back line were magnificent. The manner in which this sector held the much vaunted Offaly attack scoreless in the second half ensured Waterford's success. Team captain Tony Browne led by deed and example. Pat Fanning was a tower of strength at centre back. Fergal Hartley had the game of his life, completely blotting out the Offaly dangerman Johnny Dooley. Brenner and Tom Fives were dominant at midfield. In contrast to the drawn game, all the Waterford forwards scored with Paul Flynn emerging as top scorer.

For Offaly, Brian Whelehan was again impeccable. Hubert Rigney, Damien Barron and Donal Franks also played well in the Offaly defence. John Troy was best of an outplayed forward sextet.

The referee was Willie Barrett of Tipperary.

Waterford scorers; Paul Flynn 0-5, Johnny Brenner 0-1, Anthony Fitzgerald 0-1, Michael Hubbard 0-1, Kevin McGrath 0-1, Sean Daly 0-1, Fergal Hartley 0-1 (f), Noel Dalton 0-1 (f).

Offaly scorers; John Troy 1-1, Mark Gallagher 1-0, Johnny Dooley 0-2 (0-1f).

Waterford team. Ray Barry (Passage), Kevin O'Gorman (Lismore), Owen Dunphy (De La Salle), Mark O'Sullivan (Lismore), Tony Browne (Mount Sion), Capt., Pat Fanning (De La Salle), Fergal Hartley (Ballygunner), Tom Fives (Tourin), Johnny Brenner (De La Salle), Anthony Fitzgerald (Passage), Michael Hubbard (Ballydurn), Kevin McGrath (Colligan), Noel Dalton (De La Salle), Sean Daly (Lismore), Paul Flynn (Ballygunner).
Subs. Paul Power (Ballygunner) for Dalton. Pat Haran (Ballygunner), Johnny Walsh (De La Salle), Colm Cunningham (Tallow), Mark Geary (Tallow), Michael Dunford (Colligan), Michael O'Sullivan (Lismore), Jerome O'Shea (St. Molleran's). Pat O'Connor (Passage), Mark Geary (Tallow) for Power. Paul Flynn (Ballygunner) for Geary. Pat Haran (Ballygunner).

Offaly team. Damian Franks (Shinrone), Henry Kilmartin (Kilcormac/Killoughey), Kevin Kinahan (Seir Kieran), Donal Franks (Ballyskenagh), Damien Barron (Kilcormac/Killoughey), Hubert Rigney (St. Rynagh's), Brian Whelehan (Birr), Capt., Sean Óg Farrell (Edenderry), Michael Hogan (Coolderry), Johnny Dooley (Seir Kieran), Sean Grennan (Belmont Rangers), John Troy (Lusmagh), Mark Gallagher (Tullamore), Niall Hand (Kilcormac/Killoughey), Oisin O'Neill (Birr).
Subs. Adrian Cahill (Birr) for Hogan. Peadar Bergin (Kinnitty), Eunan Martin (Sarsfields, Cork), Shane Buggy (Ballinamere-Durrow), Raymond Dooley (Coolderry), Mark Moloney (Coolderry), Johnny Carroll (Birr), Liam Clear (Shinrone), Brian Gath (Drumcullen), Adrian Cahill (Birr). Kevin Martin (Tullamore) was injured.

1992
LEINSTER FINAL: *Offaly 1-15, Kilkenny 2-10*
MUNSTER FINAL: *Waterford 0-17, Clare 1-12*
ULSTER FINAL: *Antrim 3-11, Down 3-4*
ALL IRELAND SEMI FINALS: *Offaly 3-17, Galway 1-5; Waterford 4-17, Antrim 2-8.*

1993 Final
Amazing Kilkenny rally secures draw.
12/9/1993 at O'Connor Park, Tullamore.
Galway 2-14. Kilkenny 3-11.

This final before an official attendance of 13,000 was a thrilling affair with an amazing climax. Galway had the wind in the first half. After an early exchange of points, the Tribesmen took the lead with a lovely point from Peter Kelly in the 4th minute. After 20 minutes Galway led by 0-6 to 0-3. Kilkenny conceded a goal just a minute from the interval. Liam Burke danced between three defenders before shooting high into the net, leaving Galway ahead at the break by 1-8 to 0-5. Galway drove 8 wides to Kilkenny's 5 in the first half.

Four minutes after the restart, Damien Coleman following a glorious run, pointed to put Galway seven points ahead. Then Kilkenny bagged five successive points in six minutes to reduce the deficit to two points. However, three lovely points by Francis Forde and a goal by Maurice Headd, followed by points from McGrath and Kirwan, left the Tribesmen ahead by 2-14 to 0-10, with 13 minutes left. Midfielder Canice Brennan initiated the Kilkenny recovery with a 49th minute point. Four minutes later, substitute Michael Owens goaled. With seven minutes left, Brennan blasted the ball to the roof of the Galway net from 35 metres. Time was almost up when Dermot Lawlor's blistering low shot earned Kilkenny a draw.

Galway, who had a Maurice Headd goal disallowed in the second half, had great performances from Morgan Darcy, Ronan Walsh, Michael Donoghue, William Burke, Francis Forde, Liam Burke and Maurice Headd.

Were it not for midfielders Canice Brennan and Patrick Farrell, who between them scored 1-6, Kilkenny would have lost. In their backline Dan O'Neill and David Beirne were superb, as was goalkeeper Joe Dermody. Of the starting Kilkenny forwards, only Dermot Lawlor scored.

The referee was Johnny McDonnell of Tipperary.

Galway scorers; Maurice Headd 1-3 (0-3fs), Francis Forde 0-4 (1lb), Liam Burke 1-1 (0-1f), Joe McGrath 0-2, Damien Coleman 0-2, Tony Kirwan 0-1, Peter Kelly 0-1.

Kilkenny scorers; Dermot Lawlor 1-5 (0-4fs), Canice Brennan 1-3, Paddy Farrell 0-3, Michael Owens 1-0,

Galway team. Morgan Darcy (Moycullen), Tony Headd (St. Thomas), William Burke (Oranmore-Maree), David Canning (Portumna), Ronan Walsh (Carnmore), Nigel Shaughnessy (Loughrea), Michael Donoghue (Clarinbridge), Liam Burke (Kilconieran), Capt., Michael Kilkelly (Kinvara), Francis Forde (Turloughmore), Joe McGrath (Sarsfields), Tony Kirwan (Fohenagh), Peter Kelly (Sarsfields), Damien Coleman (Portumna), Maurice Headd (St. Thomas).

Galway – All Ireland U21 Champions 1993
Back: William Burke, David Canning, Tony Headd, Joe McGrath, Damien Coleman, Morgan Darcy, Michael Kilkenny, Ronan Walsh.
Front Tony Kirwin, Michael Donoghue, Maurice Headd, Liam Burke (capt.), Nigel Shaughnessy, Francis Forde, Peter Kelly.
(Mascot: Thomas Durnin).

Subs. Colm O'Doherty (Ardrahan) for Shaughnessy. Pat Coyne (Castlegar) for Kelly. Damien Hawe (Meelick/Eyrecourt), Pat Diviney (Beagh), Michael Kearns (Loughrea), Brian Duffy (Castlegar), Michael Spellman (Clarinbridge), Martin Kenny (Meelick/Eyrecourt), Peter Mulrooney (Liam Mellows).

Kilkenny team. Joe Dermody (St. Lachtain's), David Beirne (Dicksboro), Capt., Michael Holohan (O'Loughlin's), James Carroll (Fenians), Dan O'Neill (Dicksboro), Eamon Kennedy (Dunamaggin), Philly Larkin (James Stephens), Canice Brennan (Conahy), Paddy Farrell (Carrickshock), Andy Comerford (O'Loughlin's), John Shefflin (Ballyhale), PJ Delaney (Fenians), Dermot Maher (Barrow Rangers), Sean Ryan (Dunamaggin), Dermot Lawlor (St. Martin's).

Subs. James McDermott (Young Irelands) for Shefflin. Michael Owens (Erin's Own) for Ryan. Mark Dowling (Dicksboro) for Maher. Martin Carey (Young Irelands), Sean Meally (Cloneen), Paul Long (Piltown), Peter Hennessy (Threecastles), Padraig Farrell (Ballyhale), Barry Power (O'Loughlin's).

1993 FINAL REPLAY
GALWAY DEFY CONDITIONS TO WIN REPLAY.
3/10/1993 AT O'CONNOR PARK, TULLAMORE.
Galway 2-9. Kilkenny 3-3.

Tough rain-soaked, the attendance of 10,000 enjoyed this absorbing replay. The slippery underfoot conditions and heavy rain took it's toll on the quality of hurling but the commitment and courage of both teams readily compensated. Given the defeats of their senior and minor teams in that year , the pressure was on Galway to deliver. They had the advantage of the elements in the first half but inaccuracy was undermining some excellent work further out. Early Galway points by Tony Kirwan and Francis Forde were cancelled out by two minors from Dermot Lawlor(1 free). In the 13th minute, Forde goaled for Galway. Seven minutes later, the same player sent over a great point from a lineball. Maurice Headd pointed two frees and Michael Kerins also pointed to leave the score at the break, Galway 1-6 Kilkenny 0-2. Galway shot ten wides in the first half.

Within two minutes of the restart, PJ Delaney goaled for Kilkenny. A minute later, Maurice Headd retaliated with a Galway goal. The same player pointed a free in the 46th minute to leave Galway ahead by 2-7 to 1-2. Canice Brennan pointed a lineball for Kilkenny and 11 minutes from the end, Dermot Lawlor goaled from close range. Forde responded with a great point from play. Kilkenny substitute Peter Hennessy fired home his side's third goal to leave two points between the sides. Forde provided the pass for Galway substitute Colm O'Doherty to point and seal Galway's win.

Morgan Darcy, Nigel Shaughnessy, Francis Forde, Liam Burke, Ronan Walsh and Michael Donoghue were outstanding for Galway. William Burke was a commanding figure at full back. Maurice Headd was Galway's second best forward after Forde.

Kilkenny lacked punch in the central attacking positions. That they lost was no fault of goalkeeper

Kilkenny – All Ireland U21 Finalists 1993
Back: Philip Larkin, John Shefflin, Andy Comerford, Michael Holohan, Canice Brennan, Sean Ryan, James Carroll, Dan O'Neill.
Front: Patrick Farrell, Eamon Kennedy, Joe Dermody, PJ Delaney, Dermot Lawlor, Dermot Maher, David Beirne (Captain).

Joe Dermody, defenders David Beirne, James Carroll and Dan O'Neill. Dermot Lawlor and PJ Delaney were best in attack for the Noresiders.

The referee was Johnny McDonnell of Tipperary.

Galway scorers; Francis Forde 1-3 (0-1lb), Maurice Headd 1-3 (0-2fs), Michael Kerins 0-1, Tony Kirwan 0-1, Colm O'Doherty 0-1.

Kilkenny scorers; Dermot Lawlor 1-2 (0-1f), PJ Delaney 1-0, Peter Hennessy 1-0, Canice Brennan 0-1 (lb).

Galway team. Morgan Darcy (Moycullen), Tony Headd (St. Thomas), William Burke (Oranmore-Maree), David Canning (Portumna), Ronan Walsh (Carnmore), Nigel Shaughnessy (Loughrea), Michael Donoghue (Clarinbridge), Liam Burke (Kilconieran), Capt., Michael Kerins (Loughrea), Francis Forde (Turloughmore), Joe McGrath (Sarsfields), Tony Kirwan (Fohenagh), Peter Kelly (Sarsfields), Damien Coleman (Portumna), Maurice Headd (St. Thomas).
Subs. Conor O'Donovan (Liam Mellowes) for Coleman. Colm O'Doherty (Ardrahan) for Kirwan. Michael Kilkelly (Kinvara) for Kelly. Liam Donoghue (Clarinbridge), Pat Diviney (Beagh), Brian Duffy (Castlegar), Martin Kenny (Meelick/Eyrecourt), Pat Coyne (Castlegar), Peter Mulrooney (Liam Mellowes).

Kilkenny team. Joe Dermody (St. Lachtain's), David Beirne (Dicksboro), Capt., Michael Holohan (O'Loughlin's), James Carroll (Fenians), Dan O'Neill (Dicksboro), Eamon Kennedy (Dunamaggin), Philly Larkin (James Stephens), Andy Comerford (O'Loughlin's), Canice Brennan (Conahy), Paddy Farrell (Carrickshock), James McDermott (Young Irelands), Dermot Maher (Barrow Rangers), Dermot Lawlor (St. Martin's), Sean Ryan (Dunamaggin), PJ Delaney (Fenians).
Subs. Michael Owens (Erin's Own) for McDermott). Peter Hennessy (Threecastles) for Ryan. Martin Carey (Young Irelands), Sean Meally (Cloneen), Mark Dowling (Dicksboro), John Shefflin (Ballyhale), Paul Long (Kilmacow), Austin Cleere (Emeralds), Robert Shortall (Clara), Barry Power (O'Loughlin's), Padraig Farrell (Ballyhale).

1993
LEINSTER FINAL: *Kilkenny 4-13, Wexford 2-7*
MUNSTER FINAL: *Cork 1-18, Limerick 3-9*
ULSTER FINAL: *Derry 2-13, Antrim 1-8*
ALL IRELAND SEMI FINALS: *Galway 4-9, Cork 2-10; Kilkenny 3-22, Derry 2-10.*

♦ *Galway captain Liam Burke also won an u-21 All-Ireland medal in 1991.*
♦ *Maurice and Tony Headd were brothers.*
♦ *Galway's panel contained players from 17 clubs.*

1994 FINAL
KILKENNY GAIN REVENGE FOR PREVIOUS YEAR'S LOSS.
11/9/1994 AT O'CONNOR PARK, TULLAMORE.
Kilkenny 3-10. Galway 0-11.

This All-Ireland final before an attendance of 17,200 was not up to the standard of the previous year's drawn final and replay. As the parade of the teams finished, an altercation between rival captains William Burke and Philip Larkin occurred. There were more wides than scores in the opening half. Galway with the assistance of the wind jumped into an early three point lead. The only goal of the first half came when Kilkenny's Robert Shortall kicked to the net in the 19th minute. That score rattled Galway and while they retaliated with four points before the interval to lead by 0-8 to 1-4, their hurling lacked conviction.

The shortcomings of the Galway attack were exposed in the second half, three points including two Daragh Coen frees were all they could muster. A spark of individual brilliance from PJ Delaney in the 43rd minute ended with Kilkenny's second goal, as he sped past two defenders and planted the ball in the Galway net. In the 49th minute, Kilkenny corner forward Brendan Ryan blasted to the net from an acute angle. Kilkenny completed a sweet revenge win with late points from substitute Ollie O'Connor, the strong finishing Dermot Maher and Robert Shortall.

Kilkenny's heroes were man-of-the-match Eddie Dwyer, Barry Power, Adrian O'Sullivan, Dermot Maher, PJ Delaney, Robert Shortall and Brendan Ryan. Full forward Denis Byrne also impressed as did substitute Ollie O'Connor.

Pat Diviney, William Burke and Nigel Shaughnessy performed solidly in a Galway backline, which had to endure some severe pressure. Midfielders Colm O'Doherty and Conor O'Donovan tried hard. Francis Forde and Peter Kelly were their team's liveliest forwards.

The referee was Pat Horan of Offaly.

Kilkenny scorers; PJ Delaney 1-3 (0-3fs), Robert Shortall 1-1, Brendan Ryan 1-0, Dermot Maher 0-2, Brian McEvoy 0-1, Seamus Dollard 0-1, Denis Byrne 0-1, Ollie O'Connor 0-1.

Galway scorers; Daragh Coen 0-5 (0-4fs), Peter Kelly 0-2, Francis Forde 0-2 (0-1lb), Colm O'Doherty 0-1, Ollie Fahy 0-1.

Kilkenny team. Martin Carey (Young Irelands), Sean Meally (Cloneen), Ed Drea (Barrow Rangers), Barry Power (O'Loughlins), Adrian O'Sullivan (John Lockes), Eddie Dwyer (Graigue/Ballycallan), Philip Larkin (James Stephens), Capt., Brian McEvoy (James Stephens), Dermot Maher (Barrow Rangers), Seamus Dollard (Glenmore), Peter Barry (James Stephens), PJ Delaney (Fenians), Brendan Ryan (Fenians), Denis Byrne (Graigue/Ballycallan), Robert Shortall (Clara).
Subs. Ollie O'Connor (St. Lachtain's) for Barry. Dan O'Neill (Dicksboro) for McEvoy. Francis

Kilkenny – All Ireland U21 Champions 1994

Back: Philip Larkin (Capt), Brian McEvoy, Ned Drea, Seamus Dollard, Peter Barry, Dermot Maher, Sean Meally, Barry Power.
Front: Eddie Dwyer, Robert Shortall, Brendan Ryan, Martin Carey, Adrian O'Sullivan, PJ Delaney, Denis Byrne.
Photo Tom Brett

Cantwell (James Stephens), Tobias White (James Stephens), Tom Henderson (Dicksboro), Ger Walsh (Graiguenamanagh), Michael Owens (Erin's Own), Jim Hickey (Dunamaggin), Sam Morrissey (Dicksboro), Malcolm Murphy (James Stephens), Richie Kelly (Rower Inistioge), Jarlath Bolger (Graignamanagh).

Galway team. Liam Donoghue (Clarinbridge), David Canning (Portumna), William Burke (Oranmore-Maree), Capt., Michael Spellman (Clarinbridge), Pat Diviney (Beagh), Nigel Shaughnessy (Loughrea), Michael Donoghue (Clarinbridge), Colm O'Doherty (Ardrahan), Conor O'Donovan (Liam Mellowes), Francis Forde (Turloughmore), Joe McGrath (Sarsfields), Daragh Coen (Clarinbridge), Peter Kelly (Sarsfields), Ollie Fahy (Gort), Maurice Headd (St. Thomas).

Subs. Damien Coleman (Portumna) for Fahy. Cathal Moore (Turloughmore) for Headd. Kenneth Walsh (Carnmore), Michael Kenny (Meelick/Eyrecourt), Michael Kilkelly (Kinvara), John O'Brien (Liam Mellowes), Fergal Fahy (Ardrahan), Tom Kavanagh (Abbey/Duniry), John Murray (Kilconieran).

Kilkenny captain Philly larkin and his father Fan with the Trophy after the 1994 Final

Photo Tom Brett

1994
LEINSTER FINAL: *Kilkenny 1-14, Wexford 0-15*
MUNSTER FINAL: *Waterford 1-12, Clare 0-12*
ULSTER FINAL: *Antrim 1-20, Down 1-4*
ALL IRELAND SEMI FINALS: *Galway 1-18, Antrim 0-6; Kilkenny 2-21, Waterford 3-6.*

1995 Final
Tipperary regain title after a six year lapse.
10/9/1995 at Semple Stadium, Thurles.
Tipperary 1-14. Kilkenny 1-10.

On a showery day in Thurles, before an attendance of 24,234, both the hurling and football u-21 finals were played. In the hurling final, Tipperary were up against the defending champions, who retained eight of of the 1994 winning side. Though Tipp had the wind in the first half, Kilkenny goaled after just three minutes when Brendan Ryan deflected a long ball from Brian McEvoy to the net. By the end of the first quarter Ryan and freetaker Damien Cleere had pushed Kilkenny into a 1-6 to 0-3 lead. A brilliant tackle by Tom Hickey on Tommy Dunne stopped Tipperary from goaling, just before the interval. At half time Kilkenny led by 1-6 to 0-5. Tipperary drove 7 wides in the first half to Kilkenny's 5.

At the start of the second half, Tipperary made three positional switches, which had a big influence on the outcome of the game. Kevin Tucker was brought out to the half forward line, Tommy Dunne reverted to wing forward where he had started and Liam McGrath went to midfield. The Munster champions also introduced teenager Philip O'Dwyer for his first outing in this grade, in place of Eddie Enright at half time. These changes made a profound difference. Terry Dunne ran through the Kilkenny defence for a point. His brother Tommy followed with three points, including a free and a 65. After seven minutes Tipp had reduced the deficit to two points. Then came the decisive score. Tucker soloed through the Kilkenny defence, laid the ball off to O'Dwyer and the youngster crashed it to the net. Kilkenny took the lead again with 2 great points from Cleere. With eleven minutes left, Tommy Dunne equalised with a huge pointed free from halfway. In the final ten minutes, O'Dwyer's speed led to Tipp's full forward line scoring a point each. O'Dwyer was fouled for the final free, which Tommy Dunne converted to ensure Tipperary's victory.

Key performers for Tipperary were Brendan Cummins, who made an outstanding save from Ryan in the 33rd minute, Liam Barron, Liam McGrath, Aidan Butler, Tommy Dunne, Kevin Tucker and Philip O'Dwyer.

Best for Kilkenny were goalkeeper, Martin Carey, Eddie Dwyer, John Costelloe, Damien Cleere and Brendan Ryan.

Each side had ten wides.

The referee was Terence Murray of Limerick.

Tipperary scorers; Tommy Dunne 0-7 (4fs &a 65), Philip O'Dwyer 1-0, Kevin Tucker 0-2, Aidan Butler 0-1, Terry Dunne 0-1, Liam McGrath 0-1, Darren O'Connor 0-1, David Bourke 0-1.

Kilkenny scorers; Damien Cleere 0-7 (4fs), Brendan Ryan 1-2, Liam Smith 0-1.

Tipperary – All Ireland U21 Champions 1995
Back:Tefry Dunne, Liam Barron, Tommy Dunne, Darren O'Connor,Brendan Cummins, Declan O'Meara, Aidan Butler, Brian Horgan, Liam McGrath.
Front: David Bourke, Eddie Enright, Philip Shanahan, Kevin Tucker,Paul Shelly, Brian Flannery, Noel Morris.
Photo: John Quirke

Kilkenny – All Ireland U21 Finalists 1995

Back Vincent O'Brien, Denis Byrne, Brian Lonergan, John Costello, Dermot Maher, Eddie O'Dwyer, Peter Barry, Ed Drea.
Front: Damien Cleere, Brian McEvoy, David Buggy, Martin Carey, Liam Smith, Tom Hickey, Brendan Ryan.
Photo: Tom Brett

Tipperary team. Brendan Cummins (Ballybacon/Grange), Liam Barron (Cashel), Paul Shelly (Killenaule), Philip Shanahan (Toomevara), Brian Horgan (Knockavilla) Capt., Keith Slevin (Borrisokane), Brian Flannery (Mount Sion), Aidan Butler (Clonoulty-Rossmore), Terry Dunne (Toomevara), Tommy Dunne (Toomevara), Liam McGrath (Burgess), Eddie Enright (Thurles Sarsfields), Kevin Tucker (Eire Og Nenagh), Darren O'Connor (Cahir), David Bourke (Holycross/Ballycahill).
Subs. Philip O'Dwyer (Boherlahan-Dualla) for Enright. Kevin O'Sullivan (Cashel), Sean Maher (Ballybacon/Grange), Pat Coman (Moycarkey-Borris), Aidan Flanagan (Boherlahan-Dualla), Noel Morris (Loughmore-Castleiney), Ger Flanagan (Boherlahan-Dualla), Pat Croke (Mullinahone), Robbie Tomlinson (Eire Og Nenagh).

Kilkenny team. Martin Carey (Young Irelands), Brian Lonergan (Galmoy), Ed Drea (Barrow Rangers), Tom Hickey (Dunamaggin), Vinny O'Brien (James Stephens), John Costelloe (St. Lachtains), Eddie Dwyer (Graig/Ballycallan), Dermot Maher (Barrow Rangers), Peter Barry (James Stephens), Capt., Damien Cleere (Graig/Ballycallan), Liam Smith (James Stephens), Brian McEvoy (James Stephens), Brendan Ryan (Fenians), Denis Byrne (Graig/Ballycallan), David Buggy (Erin's Own).
Subs. Michael Owens (Erin's Own) for Buggy. Ollie O'Connor (St. Lachtain's) for Smith. Francis Cantwell (James Stephens), Ciaran Connery (Conahy Shamrocks), Joe Philpott (Dicksboro), Trevor Dunphy (Mooncoin), Ger Walsh (Graiguenamanagh), Vincent Norton (Tullaroan), Niall Moloney (St.Martin's).

1995
LEINSTER FINAL: *Kilkenny 2-11, Wexford 1-12*
MUNSTER FINAL: *Tipperary 1-17, Clare 0-14*
ULSTER FINAL: *Antrim 2-18, Derry 1-7*
ALL IRELAND SEMI FINALS: *Kilkenny 3-7, Galway 1-13, Kilkenny 1-15, Galway 1-14 (Replay);*
Tipperary 4-12, Antrim 1-8.,

1996 FINAL
GALWAY WIN SEVENTH U-21 HURLING TITLE.
8/9/1996 AT SEMPLE STADIUM, THURLES.
Galway 1-14. Wexford 0-7.

Both u-21 finals, hurling and football, were played at Semple Stadium on a glorious day, before an attendance of 35,315. In the hurling final, Wexford were quickest off the mark racing into a three point lead after six minutes. Galway soon hauled them back to parity, as Alan Kerins contributed three opportunist points in the first twelve minutes. Cathal Moore pointed a mammoth

Galway – All Ireland U21 Champions 1996
Back: Gregory Kennedy; Fergal Healy, Eugene Cloonan, Alan Kerins, Vinny Maher, Peter Huban, Cathal Moore, Gordon Glynn, Liam Hodgins.
Front: Donal Moran, Ollie Canning, Michael Healy, Brian Higgins, Kevin Broderick, Daragh Coen.
Pic clare Express

Wexford – All Ireland U21 Finalists 1996
Back: Eddie Doyle, Martin Byrne, Tommy Radford, James Purcell, Michael O'Leary, Edward Cullen, Seanie Colfer.
Front: Jason Lawlor, Michael Jordan, Paul Codd, M. J. Cooper, P.J. Carley, Declan O'Connor, Conor Power, John Hegarty.
Photo: Sportsfile

90 yard free for Galway. Wexford edged in front again with points from Paul Codd (2) and Garry Laffan. A Kevin Broderick point and one from Donal Moran levelled for Galway, leaving the sides equal at the interval, 0-6 each. Wexford had scored only one point from play in the opening half.

The second half was all about Galway as Wexford could manage only one score, a pointed '65 from Paul Codd. Despite their growing dominance, Galway shot five wides in succession. They only led by 0-10 to 0-7 with ten minutes remaining. Eight minutes from time, Broderick's lightning pace left the Wxford defence for dead, before he planted the sliotar in Cooper's net. Further points from Kerins, Moran, Darragh Coen and Broderick gave Galway a wider winning margin.

Outstanding for Galway were Broderick, Kerins, Gordon Glynn, Ollie Fahy, Cathal Moore, Peter Huban and "man-of-the-match" Gregory Kennedy, who held Wexford's All-Ireland senior star Garry Laffan scoreless from play.

Great credit for achieving half time parity must go to Wexford goalkeeper, MJ Cooper. He made an outstanding triple save in the 22nd minute from Vinnie Maher, Kerins and Kerins again. He had to make another brilliant save from Coen at the end of the third quarter. Wexford's half backs especially Michael O'Leary, midfielder Martin Byrne and wing forward Eddie Cullen had marvellous first halves. The Slaneysiders were fortunate that Paul Codd was in such good freetaking form.

The referee was Pat O'Connor of Limerick.

Galway scorers; Kevin Broderick 1-2, Alan Kerins 0-4, Darragh Coen 0-4 (3fs & 65), Donal Moran 0-2, Fergal Healy 0-1, Cathal Moore 0-1 (f).

Wexford scorers; Paul Codd 0-5 (2fs & 2 65s), Garry Laffan 0-2 (fs).

Galway team. Eugene Cloonan (Athenry), Gregory Kennedy (Loughrea), Peter Huban (Kinvara), Capt., Liam Hodgins (Abbey-Duniry), Brian Higgins (Athenry), Cathal Moore (Turloughmore), Michael Healy (Castlegar), Gordon Glynn (Kiltormer), Ollie Fahy (Gort), Donal Moran (Athenry), Vinnie Maher (Loughrea), Fergal Healy (Craughwell), Alan Kerins (Clarinbridge), Darragh Coen (Clarinbridge), Kevin Broderick (Abbey-Duniry).
Subs. Martin Cullinane (Castlegar) for Higgins. Declan Walsh (Carnmore) for Fergal Healy. Nigel Murray (Loughrea), John Feeney (Athenry), Niall Linnane (Gort), Kieran Flaherty (Abbeyknockmoy), Brian Carr (Clarinbridge), Eddie Brady (Athenry), Finnbar Gantley (Beagh).

Wexford team. MJ Cooper (Adamstown), John Hegarty (Ballyfad), Eddie Doyle (Rathnure), Tommy Radford (St. Martin's), Declan Ruth (Shamrocks), James Purcell (Shanballymore), Michael O'Leary (Rathnure), Rory McCarthy (St. Martin's), Martin Byrne (Rathnure), Jason Lawlor (Adamstown), Seanie Colfer (Fethard), Eddie Cullen (Ferns St. Aidan's), Paul Codd (Rathnure), Capt., Garry Laffan (Glynn-Barntown), Michael Jordan (Jordanstown).
Subs. Denis Kent (Rathgarogue-Cushinstown) for Jordan. Declan O'Connor (Oulart-the Ballagh) for Laffan. PJ Carley (Glynn-Barntown) for Colfer. Cathal Donovan (Geraldine O'Hanrahan's), Simon McGrath (Rathnure), Conor Power (St. Martin's), Niall Shiel (Faythe Harriers), Barry Doyle (Buffer's Alley).

1996
LEINSTER FINAL: *Wexford 1-9, Offaly 0-12*
Wexford 2-16, Offaly 2-5
MUNSTER FINAL: *Cork 3-16, Clare 2-7*
ULSTER FINAL: *Antrim 1-13, Down 1-12*
ALL IRELAND SEMI FINALS: *Galway 1-13, Cork 1-9; Wexford 3-14, Antrim 1-6.*

♦ *Gregory Kennedy captained Galway to All-Ireland minor success in 1994.*

1997 FINAL
A MEEK PERFORMANCE FROM DEFENDING CHAMPIONS, AS CORK WIN FIRST U-21 TITLE SINCE 1988. 21/9/1997 AT SEMPLE STADIUM, THURLES.
Cork 3-11. Galway 0-13.

Galway with 12 of the team, who played in the All-Ireland u-21 victory in 1996, had first advantage of the strong breeze. Before a disappointing attendance of 10,378, they built up a lead of 0-3 to 0-1 in the first ten minutes. Cork got a crucial score when Joe Deane showed the requisite sharpness to blast the sliotar home for a 13th minute goal. The Leesiders scored three points without reply between the 17th and 20th minutes. Cork then goaled again through Darren Ronan following a fluid passing movement initiated by Sean Og O hAilpin. In response to Cork's goals, Galway were dependent on points from frees and 65s by Eugene Cloonan. Cork led by 2-6 to 0-7 at half time.

Galway's confidence was not helped when Kevin Broderick, a star of their 1996 win, had to retire at the interval with a recurrence of a hamstring injury. Cork began the second half with points from Michael O'Connell(free) and Ronan. In the eighth minute Cork goaled again. Sean O'Farrell, a Cork substitute, planed the ball in the top corner of the net from a very tight angle. There were now three clear goals between the sides. Galway responded with points from Martin Cullinane and Rory Gantley. Both sides exchanged further points as Cork wrapped up their first All-Ireland win in this grade since 1988.

Cork's half back line of sticky wing back, Derek Barrett, captain Dan Murphy and the outstanding Sean Og O hAilpin was the launch pad for their victory. John Browne, Diarmuid O'Sullivan and Wayne Sherlock were equally unyielding in front of an assured Donal Og Cusack. Pat Ryan scaled the heights at midfield, especially during the second half. Best of their attack were Darren Ronan, Joe Deane and highly effective substitute Sean O'Farrell.

For Galway, only Hodgins, Kennedy, Glynn Cullinane and Cloonan could garner any satisfaction from their individual performances. Far too many of their players had an off day, with the forward

Cork – All Ireland U21 Champions 1997

Back: Diarmuid O'Sullivan, Brian O'Driscoll, John Browne, Dan Murphy, Derek Barrett, Donal Og Cusack, Wayne Sherlock, Sean Óg Ó hAilpín.
Front Austin Walsh, Pat Ryan, Jimmy McCarthy, Michael O'Connell, Joe Deane, John O'Flynn, Sean O'Farrell.

sector especially disappointing. Before the final, Galway had faced Derry in their only competitive game.

The referee was Pat Horan of Offaly.

Cork scorers; Michael O'Connell 0-5 (4fs), Sean O'Farrell 1-1, Darren Ronan 1-1, Joe Deane 1-0, Pat Ryan 0-2, Brian O'Driscoll 0-1, John O'Flynn 0-1.

Galway scorers; Eugene Cloonan 0-7 (3fs & 2 65s), Rory Gantley 0-2, Martin Cullinane 0-2, Gordon Glynn 0-1, Fergal Healy 0-1.

Cork team. Donal Og Cusack (Cloyne), John Browne (Blackrock), Diarmuid O'Sullivan (Cloyne), Wayne Sherlock (Blackrock), Derek Barrett (Cobh), Dan Murphy (Ballincollig), Capt., Sean Og O hAilpin (Na Piarsaigh), Pat Ryan (Sarsfields), Austin Walsh (Kildorrery), Brian O'Driscoll (Kilavullen), Timmy McCarthy (Castlelyons), Michael O'Connell (Midleton), John O'Flynn (Blackrock), Darren Ronan (Ballyhea), Joe Deane (Killeagh).
Subs. Sean O'Farrell (Carrigtwohill) for O'Flynn. Brendan Coleman (Youghal) for McCarthy. Brian Hurley (St. Finbarr's), Donal Murphy (Na Piarsaigh), Tadhg Murphy (Glen Rovers), Colm Buckley (Banteer), Noel Sheehan (Ballymartle), John Anderson (Glen Rovers), Brian O'Keeffe (Blackrock), Barry Hennebry (Blackrock), Kieran O'Callaghan (Glen Rovers).

Galway team. Nigel Murray (Loughrea), Gregory Kennedy (Loughrea), Peter Huban (Kinvara), Finbarr Gantley (Beagh), Vinnie Maher (Loughrea), Michael Healy (Castlegar), Liam Hodgins (Abbey-Duniry), Capt., Rory Gantley (Beagh), Gordon Glynn (Kiltormer), Fergal Healy (Craughwell), Martin Cullinane (Castlegar), Kevin Broderick Abbey-Duniry), Alan Kerins (Clarinbridge), Eugene Cloonan (Athenry), Ollie Canning (Portumna).
Subs. Darren Shaughnessy (Turloughmore) for Broderick. Brian Higgins (Athenry) for Huban. Mark Kerins (Clarinbridge) for Canning. Peter Commins (Gort), Kieran Flaherty (Abbeyknockmoy), Brian Carr (Clarinbridge), Geoffrey Lynskey (Liam Mellowes), Keith Carr (Ballindereen).

1997
LEINSTER FINAL: *Wexford 2-13, Offaly 0-15*
MUNSTER FINAL: *Cork 1-11, Tipperary 0-13*
ULSTER FINAL: *Derry 2-11, Antrim 0-17*
Derry 0-22, Antrim 1-16 (Ex. time)
ALL IRELAND SEMI FINALS: *Cork 2-12, Wexford 1-6; Galway 8-26 Derry 0-7.*

1998 FINAL
LATE GALWAY GOALS FAIL TO DENT CORK'S SUPERIORITY.
20/9/1998 AT SEMPLE STADIUM, THURLES.
Cork 2-15. Galway 2-10.

Fielding eleven of the players who were involved in the previous year's All-Ireland final, the champions Cork again faced Galway in sweltering heat, before an attendance of 10,394. Galway, who had nine survivors from the previous year, took the game to Cork during the opening quarter. Cork goalkeeper Donal Og Cusack made a good save from Kevin Broderick in the 10th minute. At the time, the teams were tied at 0-2 each. Then the Galway defence began to needlessly concede frees which allowed Joe Deane and Micky O'Connell to share four points. Cork were ahead by a point in the 19th minute. Then Brian O'Keeffe intervened and scored a superb individual goal for them. Galway reduced the gap to two points by the 22nd minute. Cork's Micky O'Connell then thundered into the game. He picked off three fine points from play which left Cork leading at the interval by 1-7 to 0-6.

On the resumption , the Leesiders switched O'Connell to midfield and he scored two more excellent points from play during the third quarter. Cork had a penalty opportunity in the 42nd minute but Diarmuid O'Sullivan's well struck effort was brilliantly saved by Galway goalkeeper Terence Grogan. That encouraged the Tribesmen and they were still in with a chance when they trailed by 1-13 to 0-10 with nine minutes remaining. Their fate was effectively sealed when Brian O'Keeffe pounced for his second goal in the 54th minute. During the last five minutes, Galway scored two consolation goals from Eugene Cloonan(a free) and Mark Kerins.

Cork had many stars, the most outstanding of whom were Wayne Sherlock, O'Connell, O'Keeffe, Derek Barrett, Sean Og O hAilpin and goalkeeper Cusack. They were far and away the better team and the final score did not reflect their superiority.

For Galway, only Mark Kerins, Eugene Cloonan, the fleet-footed Fergal Healy, John Feeney and Terence Grogan played to their potential. Padraic Walsh and Alan Kerins, who shaded the midfield battle in the first half, struggled during the second period.

The referee was Dickie Murphy of Wexford.

Cork scorers; Michael O'Connell 0-7 (1f & 1 65), Joe Deane 0-7 (5fs), Brian O'Keeffe 2-0, John Anderson 0-1.

Galway scorers; Eugene Cloonan 1-5 (1-3fs), Mark Kerins 1-3, Alan Kerins 0-1, Padraic Walsh 0-1 (65).

Cork team. Donal Og Cusack (Cloyne), Mark Prendergast (Na Piarsaigh), Diarmuid O'Sullivan (Cloyne), Wayne Sherlock (Blackrock), Derek Barrett (Cobh), Dan Murphy (Ballincollig), Capt., Sean Og O hAilpin (Na Piarsaigh), Austin Walsh (Kildorrery), Luke Mannix (Fermoy), Neil

Cork – All Ireland U21 Champions 1998

Back: Diarmuid O'Sullivan, Donal Murphy (captain), Sean Farrell, Donal Óg Cusack, Derek Barrett, Wayne Sherlock, Sean Óg Ó hAilpín, John Anderson.
Front: Brian O'Keeffe, Austin Walsh, Michael O'Connell, Joe Deane, Thomas Fitzgibbon, Mark Prendergast, Timmy McCarthy.

Galway – All Ireland U21 Finalists 1998

Back: Colm Connaughton, Martin Cullinane, Padraic Walsh, Michael Healy, Darren O'Shaughnessy, Eugene Cloonan, Mark Kerins.
Front: Alan Kerins, John Feeney, Geoffrey Lynskey, Nigel Murray, Vennie Maher, Fergal Healy, Liam Madden, Kevin Broderick.

Ronan (Ballyhea), Timmy McCarthy (Castlelyons), Michael O'Connell (Midleton), Brian O'Keeffe (Blackrock), Sean O'Farrell (Carrigtwohill), Joe Deane (Killeagh).*Subs. John Anderson (Glen Rovers) for Mannix. Ben O'Connor (Newtownshandrum) for O'Farrell. Bernard Rochford (Killeagh), Will Twomey (Kilworth), John O'Dwyer (Ballincollig), John Murphy (Sarsfields), Pat Sexton (Kilbritain), Thomas Fitzgibbon (Rathluirc), Adrian Coughlan (Blackrock).*

Galway team. Terence Grogan (Castlegar), Vinny Maher (Loughrea), Capt., John Feeney (Athenry), Liam Madden (Clarinbridge), Fergal Healy (Craughwell), Michael Healy (Castlegar), Geoffrey Lynskey (Liam Mellowes), Padraic Walsh (Turloughmore), Alan Kerins (Clarinbridge), Rory Gantley (Beagh), Colm Connaughton (Kilconieran), Martin Cullinane (Castlegar), Kevin Broderick (Abbey-Duniry), Mark Kerins (Clarinbridge), Eugene Cloonan (Athenry).
Subs. Darren Shaughnessy (Turloughmore) for Connaughton. Ronan Cullinane (Castlegar) for Gantley. Nigel Murray (Loughrea), Eoin McDonagh (Ballindereen), Eamon Donoghue (Mullagh), David Tierney (Kilnadeema-Leitrim), Cathal Murray (Sarsfields), Colin Coen (Ballindereen), Justin Donnelly (Kiltormer).

1998
LEINSTER FINAL: Kilkenny 2-10, Dublin 0-12
MUNSTER FINAL: Cork 3-18, Tipperary 1-10
ULSTER FINAL: Antrim 3-20, Down 4-8
ALL IRELAND SEMI FINALS: Cork 3-15 Antrim 0-11; Galway 4-18 Kilkenny 3-7.

1999 FINAL
GALWAY LOSE THIRD SUCCESSIVE U-21 FINAL.
19/9/1999 AT O'CONNOR PARK, TULLAMORE.
Kilkenny 1-13. Galway 0-14.

With the dark and wet conditions not helping the standard of hurling, this final was always going to be a dour struggle. The early signs before an attendance of 8,000 had been encouraging for Galway, who had lost the previous two finals. They led by 0-5 to 0-1 after ten minutes. Galway spurned an obvious point scoring opportunity in the 25th minute , when Eugene Cloonan went for a goal from a free. His drive was parried to safety by Kilkenny goalkeeper Jamie Power. That miss served to lift Kilkenny's spirits and three minutes later Eddie Brennan goaled following a penetrating run by John O'Neill. Kevin Power added a point from a free for Kilkenny. Enda Linnane equalised for Galway before Eamon Donoghue gave them a single point advantage at the interval, 0-9 to 1-5.

Cloonan pointed a free shortly after the resumption. Kilkenny now hit form and points from

Kilkenny – All Ireland U21 Champions 1999
Back: Sean Dowling, John O'Neill, Henry Shefflin, John Paul Corcoran, Aidan Cummins, Jimmy Coogan, Kevin Power, Richie Mullally.
Front: Jamie Power, Michael Gordon, Alan Geoghegan, Michael Kavanagh, Noel Hickey (Capt), Eddie Brennan, Adrian Walpole.
Photo Tom O'Neill

Galway – All Ireland U21 Finalists 1999
Back: Eugene Cloonan, Steven Morgan, David Loughrey, Aidan Poinard, Mark Kerins, Darren
O'Shaughnessy, Enda Tannian, Nigel Murray.
Front: Eamon Donoghue, David Tierney, David Donoghue, Rory Gantley, Enda Linnane, Diarmuid
Cloonan, Shane McClearn, Michael Healy.

Michael Gordon, John O'Neill and three Henry Shefflin frees had the Leinster champions ahead by 1-10 to 0-11 after 40 minutes. Galway retaliated with points from Enda Tannion, Darren O'Shaughnessy(free) and a lovely effort from play by Eugene Cloonan, as they regained a narrow lead. Kilkenny drew level with Gordon's second point and took the lead with a pointed free from Shefflin. Kilkenny midfielder JP Corcoran settled the issue with a magnificent sideline cut from 35 yards in the 59th minute. Over the course of the game, Galway drove ten wides to Kilkenny's five.

Best for Kilkenny were goalkeeper Jamie Power, Noel Hickey, Michael Kavanagh, John O'Neill, JP Corcoran, Michael Gordon, Eddie Brennan, until his injury, and Henry Shefflin for his freetaking.

Enda Linnane was arguably Galway's most prominent player. Goalkeeper Nigel Murray was faultless between the posts. Enda Tannion tried his heart out at midfield. Up front was a struggle for Galway. Eugene Cloonan was their best forward , although restricted by a hand injury incurred early in the second half. The injury meant that he had to be withdrawn from freetaking duties.

The referee was Ger Harrington of Cork.

Kilkenny scorers; Henry Shefflin 0-8 (fs), Eddie Brennan 1-0, Michael Gordon 0-2, John O'Neill 0-1,

Noel Hickey – Kilkenny Captain 1999
Sportsfile

JP Corcoran 0-1 (lb), Kevin Power 0-1 (f).

Galway scorers; Eugene Cloonan 0-8 (7fs), Enda Linnane 0-1, Enda Tannion 0-1, Eamon Donoghue 0-1, Mark Kerins 0-1, David Donoghue 0-1, Darren O'Shaughnessy 0-1 (f).

Kilkenny team. Jamie Power (Carrickshock), Adrian Walpole (Bennettsbridge), Noel Hickey (Dunamaggin), Capt., Michael Kavanagh (St. Lachtain's), Aidan Cummins (Ballyhale), Sean Dowling (O'Loughlins), Richie Mullally (Glenmore), John O'Neill (John Lockes), JP Corcoran (John Lockes), Michael Gordon (Piltown), Jimmy Coogan (Tullaroan), Kevin Power (Fenians), Alan Geoghegan (O'Loughlins), Henry Shefflin (Ballyhale), Eddie Brennan (Graigue Ballycallan).
Subs. Podge Delaney (Fenians) for Geoghegan. John Barron (Tullogher/Rosbercon) for Brennan. Niall McCormack (Dunamaggin), Derek Lyng (Emeralds), Pat Tennyson (Carrickshock), Paul Buggy (Conahy), Dick Carroll (Young Irelands), Tom Drennan (Young Irelands), Martin Comerford (O'Loughlins).

Galway team. Nigel Murray (Loughrea), Eoin McDonagh (Ballindereen), Diarmuid Cloonan (Athenry), Shane McClean (Killimor), Enda Linnane (Gort), Rory Gantley (Beagh), Capt., Darren O'Shaughnessy (Turloughmore), Enda Tannion (St. Thomas), Eamon Donoghue (Mullagh), David Tierney (Kilnadeema-Leitrim), Mark Kerins (Clarinbridge), David Loughrey (Gort), Aidan Poinard (Athenry), Eugene Cloonan (Athenry), David Donoghue (Athenry).
Subs. Shane Lawless (Killimor) for Poinard. Ronan Cullinane (Castlegar) for Loughrey, John Culkin (Abbeyknockmoy) for E. Donoghue. Terence Grogan (Castlegar), Shane Donoghue (Athenry), Justin Cummins (Oranmore-Maree), Damien Huban (Kinvara), Cathal O'Reilly (Loughrea), David Huban (Kinvara).

1999
LEINSTER FINAL: *Kilkenny 1-17, Offaly 1-6*
MUNSTER FINAL: *Tipperary 1-18, Clare 1-15*
ULSTER FINAL: *Antrim 2-14, Derry 0-12*
ALL IRELAND SEMI FINALS: *Galway 3-12 Tipperary 1-16; Kilkenny 6-27, Antrim 0-10.*

♦ *This was a third successive defeat for Galway.*
♦ *They were to lose three more finals before their next win in 2005*

CHAPTER 5
ALL IRELAND U21
HURLING FINALS
2000-2009

Limerick – All Ireland U21 Champions 2000

Back : Mark Keane, Paul O'Grady, Paul O'Reilly, Brian Begley, Eugene Mulcahy, John Meskell, Sean O'Connor, Stephen Lucey.
Front: Willie Walsh, Damien Reale, Paudie Reale, Donnacha Sheehan, Timmie Houlihan, Dave Stapleton, Brian Geary.

2000 FINAL
LIMERICK WIN FIRST U-21 TITLE SINCE 1987 IN DOUR GAME.
17/9/2000 AT SEMPLE STADIUM, THURLES.
Limerick 1-13. Galway 0-13.

This final, before an attendance of 18,500, was punctuated by several stoppages as the heavy surface took it's toll on the quality of action. David Donoghue sent over two early points from frees for Galway. Limerick got a penalty in the 5th minute but Mark Keane's shot was superbly stopped on the line by Eoin McDonagh. Stephen Lucey pointed after ten minutes to open Limerick's account. The Treatysiders with the advantage of the wind, then had a string of points from Keane(free), Paul O'Grady, Sean O'Connor and David Stapleton. David Huban had Galway's only score from play in the first half, when he pointed in the 20th minute. David Donoghue's accuracy from frees kept Galway in touch before half-time. When Huban had his goal shot blocked in the 28th minute, it was a let-off for Limerick. At the interval, the Shannonsiders led by 0-8 to 0-6.

On the restart, Derek Hardiman scored a long range point for Galway after ninety seconds. In this crucial period of the match, points for Limerick by Donnacha Sheehan and Keane preceded the only goal of the game. In the 39th minute, Keane's ground stroke from 10 yards rifled past Ciaran Callanan in the Galway goal. Keane pointed a free shortly afterwards to extend Limerick's advantage to six. Points from the Donoghue brothers kept Galway in touch. Galway substitute Michael Greaney got the final point of the game.

Nobody typified Limerick's determination more than left corner back Paudie Reale, who was outstanding. His full back colleagues Eugene Mulcahy and Paudie's cousin Damien Reale also shone. Half backs Paul O'Reilly, Brian Geary and Willie Walsh excelled. Forwards Mark Keane, Donnacha Sheehan and Paul O'Grady were the pick of their attacking sextet.

Galway's cause was greatly hampered by the leg injury which prevented David Tierney from starting. The dual star came on as a sub in the 40th minute, but his movement was clearly restricted. Diarmuid Cloonan was Galway's most consistent player. Eoin McDonagh, Jamie Cannon and Conor Dervan were best in defence. Only David Donoghue and David Forde troubled the Limerick rearguard.

The referee was Pat Horan of Offaly.

Mark Keane scored 3-33 in the 2000 u-21 championship season.

Donncha Sheehan, Limerick Captain 2000
Sportsfile

Limerick scorers; Mark Keane 1-8 (0-7fs), Stephen Lucey 0-1, Paul O'Grady 0-1, Sean O'Connor 0-1, David Stapleton 0-1, Donnacha Sheehan 0-1.

Galway scorers; David Donoghue 0-6 (5fs), Eamon Donoghue 0-2, Derek Hardiman 0-1, Shane Donoghue 0-1, David Huban 0-1, Michael Greaney 0-1, Stephen Morgan 0-1 (f).

Limerick team. Timmy Houlihan (Adare), Damien Reale (Hospital/Herbertstown), Eugene Mulcahy (Knockainey), Paudie Reale (Hospital/Herbertstown), Paul O'Reilly (Patrickswell), Brian Geary (Monaleen), Willie Walsh (Murroe/Boher), John Meskell (Ahane), Stephen Lucey (Croom), Paul O'Grady (Patrickswell), Sean O'Connor (Ahane), David Stapleton (Doon), Donnacha Sheehan (Adare), Capt., Brian Begley (Mungret), Mark Keane (South Liberties).
Subs. Kevin Tobin (Murroe/Boher) for O'Connor. Dave Bulfin (Mungret), Mark O'Riordan (Croom), Conor FitzGerald (Adare), Shane Mullane (Monaleen), Kevin Holmes (Claughaun), Cathal O'Reilly (Ahane), Colm Hickey (Garryspillane), Colm Moriarty (Mungret).

Galway team. Ciaran Callanan (Ardrahan), Eoin McDonagh (Ballindereen), Diarmuid Cloonan (Athenry), Jamie Cannon (Clarinbridge), Derek Hardiman (Mullagh), Conor Dervan (Mullagh), Stephen Morgan (Loughrea), Capt., John Culkin (Abbeyknockmoy), Shane Donoghue (Athenry), David Forde (Clarinbridge), Eamon Hyland (Kilnadeema-Leitrim), Eamon Donoghue (Mullagh), Damien Joyce (Cappataggle), David Huban (Kinvara), David Donoghue (Athenry).
Subs. David Tierney (Kilnadeema-Leitrim) for Joyce. Brian Cunningham (Tynagh) for Hyland. Michael Greaney (Kiltormer) for Huban. Gavin Keary (Loughrea) for E. Donoghue. Johnny O'Loughlin (Loughrea), Michael Coughlan (Craughwell), Mark Ryan (Meelick/Eyrecourt), Joe Hession (Turloughmore), Ian Daniels (Craughwell).

2000
LEINSTER FINAL: *Offaly 3-14, Kilkenny 2-14*
MUNSTER FINAL: *Limerick 1-13, Cork 1-13*
Limerick 4-18, Cork 1-6
ULSTER FINAL: *Antrim 2-14, Derry 0-3*
ALL IRELAND SEMI FINALS: *Galway 4-13, Offaly1-10; Limerick 1-21, Antrim 1-9.*

2001 FINAL

LIMERICK WIN TWO IN A ROW AND GAIN REVENGE FOR SENIOR DEFEAT.
16/9/2001 AT SEMPLE STADIUM, THURLES.
Limerick 0-17. Wexford 2-10.

On a lovely September day before an attendance of 31,413, Limerick were attempting to defend their title. This final was of a very high standard featuring skilful hurling from both teams. Limerick lead by four points, 0-5 to 0-1, after 14 minutes. A goal from Michael Jacob for Wexford, followed by a point from his brother Rory had the sides on level terms. Limerick again assumed control and led by 0-11 to 1-3 at the interval.

The Shannonsiders fired three wides in four minutes on the resumption. They soon found the target again and fired over the points to lead by 0-16 to 1-5 at the end of the third quarter. The Model county men now shook off their inertia and scored 1-4 in the following six minutes. Substitute Paul Carley, who was introduced in the 48th minute, scored 1-2. Points from Michael Jacob and Barry Lambert reduced the deficit to one. Mark Keane with a pointed free in the 54th minute settled Limerick nerves. This was their only score of the last quarter. Ger Coleman again reduced the margin to the minimum, when he pointed in the 58th minute. Wexford's last minute chance to draw level evaporated, when Barry Lambert's 75 yard free was narrowly wide.

Star of the Limerick team was 17 year old left half back Maurice O'Brien, who gave an outstanding display. Not far behind him in the honours list were Damien Reale, Brian Geary, Peter Lawlor, Stephen Lucey, Eoin Foley, Kevin Tobin, Conor FitzGerald, Niall Moran and Mark Keane.

Paul Carley, Nicky Lambert, Michael and Rory Jacob and Ger Coleman were key players in Wexford's resurgence. Darren Stamp, David O'Connor and Rory Mallon also impressed.

The referee was Aodhan MacSuibhne of Dublin.

Limerick scorers; Mark Keane 0-7 (5fs & 1 65), Conor FitzGerald 0-3, Eoin Foley 0-2, Kevin Tobin 0-2, Niall Moran 0-2, Stephen Lucey 0-1.

Wexford scorers; Paul Carley 1-2 (0-1f), Michael Jacob 1-1, Rory Jacob 0-3 (2fs), Ger Coleman 0-2, Barry Lambert 0-2 (fs).

Limerick team. Timmy Houlihan (Adare), Capt., Damien Reale (Hospital/Herbertstown), Brian Carroll (Kilmallock), Eugene Mulcahy (Knockainy), Mark O'Riordan (Croom), Brian Geary (Monaleen), Maurice O'Brien (Garryspillane), Peter Lawlor (Croom), Stephen Lucey (Croom), Eoin Foley (Patrickswell), Kevin Tobin (Murroe/Boher), Pat Tobin (Murroe/Boher), Conor FitzGerald (Adare), Niall Moran (Ahane), Mark Keane (South Liberties).
Subs. Andrew O'Shaughnessy (Kilmallock) for P.Tobin. David Bulfin (Mungret), Kieran Bermingham (Na Piarsaigh), Michael Clifford (Adare), Niall Mullane (Claughaun), Donal O'Grady (Granagh/Ballingarry), Michael Clancy (Granagh/Ballingarry), Peter O'Reilly

Limerick – All Ireland U21 Champions 2001
Back : Mark Keane, Kevin Tobin, Brian Carroll, Stephen Lucey, Brian Geary, Eugene Mulcahy;
Front : Pat Tobin, Peter Lawlor, Mark O'Riordan, Eoin Foley, Timmie Houlihan, Damian Reale, Maurice O'Brien,
Conor Fitzgerald, Niall Moran.

Wexford – All Ireland U21 Finalists 2001
Back ; Robbie Kirwan, Redmond Barry, Barry McGee, David O'Connor, Nicky Lambert (captain), Diarmuid Lyng, Trevor Kelly, Michael Jacob.
Front: Niali Maguire, Barry Lambert, Matty White, Darren Stamp, Rory Mallon, Ger Coleman, Rory Jacob.

The Limerick team observe a minute's silence for the 9/11 victims before the 2001 All Ireland Final

Connor (St.Annes, Rathangan), Robbie Kirwan (Oulart-the- Ballagh), Rory Mallon (Faythe Harriers), Barry McGee (Shamrocks), Trevor Kelly (Monageer/Boolavogue), Nicky Lambert (Faythe Harriers), Capt., Darren Stamp (Oulart- the-Ballagh), Redmond Barry (St.Annes,Rathangan), Ger Coleman (Duffry Rovers), Rory Jacob (Oulart- the-Ballagh), Barry Lambert (St. Martins), Michael Jacob (Oulart-the-Ballagh), Diarmuid Lyng (St.Martins).

Subs. Pierce Donoghue (Glynn-Barntown) for Kirwan. Paul Carley (Glynn-Barntown) for N.Lambert. N.Lambert for Barry. Stephen Murphy (Monageer/Boolavogue), Des Mythen (Oulart-the-Ballagh), Joe Kavanagh (HWH-Bunclody), MJ Furlong (Cloughbawn), John O'Connor (Rathnure), Shane Fenlon (Monageer/Boolavogue), Tomas Mahon (Rapparees).

2001
LEINSTER FINAL: *Wexford 0-10, Kilkenny 1-5*
MUNSTER FINAL: *Limerick 3-14, Tipperary 2-16*
ULSTER FINAL: *Antrim 2-18, Derry 1-16*
ALL IRELAND SEMI FINALS: *Limerick 1-13, Galway 2-6; Wexford 2-17, Antrim 1-5.*

♦ *Limerick were without their senior star Sean O'Connor, who was suspended.*
♦ *Limerick were defeated by Wexford in the All-Ireland senior quarter final by 4-10 to 2-15, also a one point margin.*

2002 FINAL
U-21'S ARE THE FIRST TEAM FROM LIMERICK TO WIN 3 IN A ROW IN ANY GRADE.
15/9/2002 AT SEMPLE STADIUM, THURLES.
Limerick 3-17. Galway 0-8.

On a beautiful day in Thurles before an official attendance of 24,106, the gulf between the champions Limerick and the challengers Galway, was staggering. The final was as good as decided after twenty minutes, when Limerick had stormed into a convincing lead of 2-7 to 0-3. Limerick's physical power had Galway on the back foot from the throw-in. The pressure on the Galway backs was unrelenting and it was no surprise that their defence was breached so often. With the score at 0-3 to 0-2 in favour of Limerick in the eleventh minute, their 17 year old forward Andrew O'Shaughnessy scored a cracking individual goal. Further disaster ensued for Galway in the 20th minute, when Mark Keane's ground pull found the net. Limerick led by 2-10 to 0-4 at the interval.

Limerick – All Ireland U21 Champions 2002
Back: Mark Keane, Kevin Tobin, Eugene Mulcahy, Eoin Foley, Brian Carroll, Maurice O'Brien, Paudie O'Dwyer.
Front: James O'Brien, Michael Cahill, Patrick Kirby, Andrew O'Shaughnessy, Damien Reale, Timmie Houlihan, Conor Fitzgerald, Niall Moran.

Galway – All Ireland U21 Finalists 2002

Back: David Greene, Shane Kavanagh, Aidan Diviney, Conor Dervan, Michael Coughlan, Fergal Moore, Richie Murray.
Front Brian Mahony, David Forde, Michael John Quinn, Kevin Brady, Damien Hayes, Adrian Diviney, Adrian Cullinane, Ger Farragher.

Galway reshuffled their team on the resumption but there were too many gaps to fill. They required an early goal to spark a resurgence but instead Andrew O'Shaughnessy again goaled after only three minutes of the second period. The rest of the action was academic. Galway were demoralised and unable to stage a fightback. To compound their misery, substitute JP O'Connell was sent off in the 42nd minute. It was a surprisingly heavy defeat for a team who had won the minor All-Ireland three years previously.

Man of the match Eugene Mulcahy was magnificent at full back for Limerick. He presided over a very tight defensive unit. Captain Peter Lawlor and Niall Moran dominated at midfield. Andrew O'Shaughnessy was their leading light in attack. Mark Keane, Patrick Kirby and the strong-running James O'Brien made life very difficult for the Galway defence.

Of Galway's starting forward sextet, only Richie Murray scored. The rest of the Galway attack had a day to forget. Of Galway's backs only Shane Kavanagh and David Forde rose to the challenge.

The referee was Dickie Murphy of Wexford.

Mark Keane was the U-21 championship top scorer for 2002 with a total of 3-37.

Limerick scorers; Mark Keane 1-6 (0-5fs), Andrew O'Shaughnessy 2-2, Patrick Kirby 0-3 (2fs), James O'Brien 0-2, Peter Lawlor 0-2 (1f), Damien Reale 0-1, Conor FitzGerald 0-1.

Galway scorers; Ger Farragher 0-5 (4fs), Richie Murray 0-2, JP O'Connell 0-1.

Limerick team. Timmy Houlihan (Adare), Damien Reale (Hospital/Herbertstown), Eugene Mulcahy (Knockainey), Michael Cahill (Croom), Eoin Foley (Patrickswell), Paudie O'Dwyer (Kilmallock), Maurice O'Brien (Garryspillane), Peter Lawlor (Croom), Capt., Niall Moran (Ahane), Conor FitzGerald (Adare), James O'Brien (Bruree), Kevin Tobin (Murroe/Boher), Andrew O'Shaughnessy (Kilmallock), Patrick Kirby (Knockainey), Mark Keane (South Liberties).
Subs. Pat Tobin (Murroe/Boher) for FitzGerald. Brian Carroll (Kilmallock) for O'Dwyer. Raymond Hayes (Desmonds) for M. O'Brien. Eoghan Murphy (Patrickswell), John O'Connor (Murroe/Boher), Michael Clifford (Adare), Thomas Carmody (Croom), John Paul Healy (Adare).

Galway team. Aidan Diviney (Oranmore-Maree), Brian Mahony (Loughrea), Shane Kavanagh (Kinvara), John Culkin (Abbeyknockmoy), Fergal Moore (Turloughmore), Conor Dervan (Mullagh),

Peter Lawlor, Limerick Captain 2002
Sportsfile

David Forde (Clarinbridge), Tony Og Regan (Rahoon/Newcastle), Ger Farragher (Castlegar), Richie Murray (St. Thomas), Michael Coughlan (Craughwell), Kevin Brady (Castlegar), Damien Hayes (Portumna), Capt., Adrian Cullinane (Craughwell), David Green (Ardrahan).
Subs. JP O'Connell (Carnmore) for Regan. Michael J Quinn (Athenry) for Coughlan. Kenneth Burke (St. Thomas) for Green. Colm Callanan (Kinvara), Adrian Diviney (Beagh), John Conroy (St. Thomas), Hugh Whoriskey (Craughwell), Cathal Coen (Clarinbridge), Cathal Dervan (Mullagh).

2002
LEINSTER FINAL: *Wexford 1-15, Dublin 0-15*
MUNSTER FINAL: *Limerick 3-9, Tipperary 2-12*
Limerick 1-20, Tipperary 2-14
ULSTER FINAL: *Antrim 2-23, Down 0-6*
ALL IRELAND SEMI FINALS: *Galway 1-20, Wexford 1-10; Limerick 2-20, Antrim 2-6.*

2003 FINAL
KILKENNY CLINCH TREBLE OF SENIOR, MINOR AND U-21 TITLES.
21/9/2003 AT SEMPLE STADIUM, THURLES.
Kilkenny 2-13. Galway 0-12.

Before an attendance of 15,135, Galway started brightly with midfielder Kevin Brady firing over an inspirational long range point in the first minute. Shane Hennessy for Kilkenny and Ger Farragher for Galway exchanged points from frees, before Conor Phelan gave Kilkenny the lead in the fifth minute. Galway managed to stay in touch for most of the first half through Farragher's frees. Kilkenny punished them five minutes before the interval, when Aidan Fogarty unleashed an unstoppable shot to the Galway net. Kilkenny led by 1-7 to 0-7 at half time.

The decisive score of the final came just 50 seconds into the second half. A Galway defender was in possession, when he stumbled and fumbled the ball just yards from the goal. Kilkenny's Peter Cleere pounced on the loose ball and passed to Conor Phelan, who blasted to the net from close range. Hennessy added a forty yards free to put the Leinster champions seven points ahead with 25 minutes to go. Points from impressive substitutes Niall Healy and John Paul O'Connell gave Galway some hope. However, Kilkenny were too strong all over the park and were able to tag on a score or two, whenever Galway looked like threatening their lead. Kilkenny regained their seven point advantage by the final whistle.

Kilkenny – All Ireland U21 Champions 2003
Back : Shane Hennessy, Ken Coogan, Tommy Walsh, John Phelan, Jackie Tyrrell (capt.), Canice Hickey, Peter Cleere, Conor Phelan,
Colin Dunne, Sean O'Neill.
Middle: Ger Joyce, Aidan Fogarty, Michael Rice, Richie O'Neill, David Herrity, Mark Phelan, J.J. Delaney, Brian Dowling, Willie Dwyer
Chris O'Neill, Eoin McCormack, Michael Grace, Conor O'Loughlin, Niall Moran, Niall Doherty, Martin Phelan, Ned Sweeney.

Conor Phelan was man of the match. Aidan Fogarty, Peter Cleere and Michael Rice gave most support to the outstanding Phelan in the winners' attack. The Kilkenny half back line of Ken Coogan, Jackie Tyrrell and JJ Delaney formed a solid wall, which Galway could not breach. Tommy Walsh and Shane Hennessy held sway over midfield.

None of Galway's six starting forwards scored from play. Brave midfielder Kevin Brady tried his hardest to encourage his colleagues. Galway substitutes Healy and O'Connell improved their attack. Minor star Healy showed a willingness to engage the Kilkenny defence with direct running. David Collins and Fergal Moore were best of a besieged Galway defence.

The referee was Michael Wadding of Waterford.

Kilkenny scorers; Conor Phelan 1-4, Aidan Fogarty 1-1, Shane Hennessy 0-4 (4fs), Tommy Walsh 0-2, Peter Cleere 0-1, Brian Dowling 0-1.

Galway scorers; Ger Farragher 0-7 (7fs), Kevin Brady 0-2, Niall Healy 0-2, John Paul O'Connell 0-1.

Kilkenny team. David Herity (Dunamaggin), Mark Phelan (Glenmore), Canice Hickey (Dunamaggin), Ger Joyce (Emeralds), Ken Coogan (Tullaroan), Jackie Tyrrell (James Stephens),

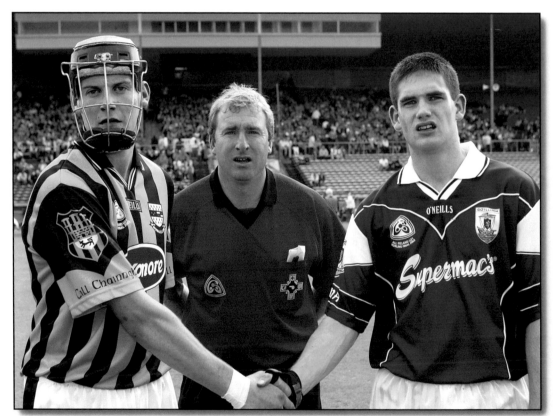

Captains Jackie Tyrrell (Kilkenny) and Fergal Moore (Galway) with Referee Michael Wadding before the 2003 Final

Capt., JJ Delaney (Fenians), Shane Hennessy (Tullaroan), Tommy Walsh (Tullaroan), Conor Phelan (Clara), Peter Cleere (Blacks & Whites), Willie O'Dwyer (Mullinavat), Aidan Fogarty (Emeralds), Michael Rice (Carrickshock), Brian Dowling (O'Loughlins).
Subs. Sean O'Neill (Dunamaggin) for Dowling. Eoin McCormack (James Stephens) for Cleere. Richie O'Neill (Kilmacow), Chris O'Neill (Graiguenamanagh), Colin Dunne (Erin's Own), Niall Doherty (Galmoy), Conor O'Loughlin (Dicksboro), Niall Moran (St. Martin's).

Galway team. Aidan Diviney (Oranmore-Maree), David Collins (Liam Mellowes), Tony Óg Regan (Rahoon/Newcastle), Fergal Moore (Turloughmore), Capt., Shane Kavanagh (Kinvara), Eoin Lynch (Portumna), Adrian Cullinane (Craughwell), Kevin Brady (Castlegar), Brian Mahony (Loughrea), Richie Murray (St. Thomas), Tom Tierney (Kilnadeema-Leitrim), Damien Hayes (Portumna), Kenneth Burke (St.Thomas), Ger Farragher (Castlegar), David Greene (Ardrahan).
Subs. Niall Healy (Craughwell) for Burke. John Paul O'Connell (Carnmore) for Greene. William Donnellan (Craughwell) for Tierney. Colm Callanan (Kinvara), David Hayes (Kiltormer), Peter Garvey (Sarsfields), Cathal Dervan (Mullagh), Adrian Diviney (Beagh), Kevin Briscoe (Mullagh).

2003
LEINSTER FINAL: *Kilkenny 0-12, Dublin 1-4*
MUNSTER FINAL: *Tipperary 1-18, Cork 3-12*
Tipperary 2-14, Cork 0-17 (after e.t.)
ULSTER FINAL: *Down 3-12, Derry 1-12*
ALL IRELAND SEMI FINALS: *Galway 2-20, Tipperary 2-16 (aet); Kilkenny 4-19, Down 1 -7.*

◆ *The result meant that Galway had lost six All-Ireland U-21 finals in seven years.*

2004 FINAL
RAMPANT KILKENNY HAVE RUNAWAY WIN BEFORE HOME SUPPORT.
18/9/2004 AT NOWLAN PARK, KILKENNY.
Kilkenny 3-21. Tipperary 1-6.

Tipperary, although winning the toss, opted to play against the stiff breeze before an attendance of 11,000. Kilkenny swept into the attack from the off and were on top in virtually every sector. Tipp scored their first point after 12 minutes. Kilkenny had 1-5 on the board at that stage. The lead had increased to 13 points before Michael Farrell had a superbly taken goal for the Munster champions. It was only a temporary respite as the Leinster champions finished off the
half with unanswered points to lead 2-12 to 1-1 at the interval. Kilkenny lost their captain "Cha" Fitzpatrick with a collarbone injury just before half time.

Kilkenny – All Ireland U21 Champions 2004

Back: Padraig Holden, Mark Heffernar,John Tennyson, Seaghan O,Äô Neill, P.J. Delaney, Eddie Campion, Stephen Maher, Willie O,Äô Dwyer.

3rd Row: Ned Quinn (Co. Board Chairman) Michael Dempsey (Trainer) Anthony Owens, John Murphy, JohnPhelan, Pat Robinson, Peter Cleere, Colin Dunne, Ciar√¨n Hoyne, Tom Doheny (Selector)

2nd Row: Martin Fogarty (Manager) Brian Dowling, Eoin Larkin, Richie Power, David Herrity, James Fitzpatrick (Capt.) Conor Phelan, Keith Nolan, Michael Fennelly, Martin Phelan, Richard Mulrooney (Selector)

Front: Niall Moran, Tom√¨s Frisbey, James Maher, Tommy Walsh, Eoin Reid, Michael Rice, Niall Doherty. (Absent Robbie Dowling.)

tPhoto Eoin Hennessy

On the resumption, Willie O'Dwyer increased Kilkenny's lead with a point. Two points from Joe Caesar and one from Tony Scroope were all that the Munster champions could muster in reply. They were still 13 points down at the three -quarter stage. Kilkenny scored the next four points. Tony Scroope pointed a free in reply. Kilkenny were to score a further 1-3 to a solitary Tipp point before the final whistle. Tipperary's woes were further compounded in the closing stages as Scroope was sent off, on receipt of a second yellow card. They were down to 13 men at the end, as the injured Darragh Walton could not be replaced----5 substitutes having already been introduced.

Kilkenny's Willie O'Dwyer was named as man of the match. All of the Kilkenny team could have been candidates for the award. From goalkeeper David Herity to corner forward Richie Power, there was menace and method in their play. They could afford to lose their captain at half time and yet win comfortably.

With the exception of their midfielder Joe Caesar, Tipperary were beaten in every position on the field. Their starting sextet of forwards could only manage 1-0 from play. Their scoring problems were underlined by the fact that Tony Scroope who had hit 5-18 in the run to the final, did not score until the 39th minute. Tipperary recorded their second lowest score in 14 appearances in the U-21 decider.

The referee was Barry Kelly of Westmeath.

Kilkenny scorers; Richie Power 0-7 (4fs,1 65), Willie O'Dwyer 1-3, Conor Phelan 1-1, James "Cha" Fitzpatrick 1-1 (0-1f), Sean O'Neill 0-3, Brian Dowling 0-2, Ciaran Hoyne 0-1, Shane Hennessy 0-1, Eoin Reid 0-1, Michael Rice 0-1.

Tipperary scorers; Joe Caesar 0-3, Michael Farrell 1-0, Tony Scroope 0-2 (fs), Willie Ryan 0-1.

Kilkenny team. David Herity (Dunamaggin), Stephen Maher (Tullaroan), John Tennyson (Carrickshock), Michael Fennelly (Ballyhale), Tommy Walsh (Tullaroan), PJ Delaney (Fenians), Ciaran Hoyne (Graigue/Ballycallan), Shane Hennessy (Tullaroan), Peter Cleere (Blacks & Whites), Sean O'Neill (Dunamaggin), Willie O'Dwyer (Mullinavat), Eoin Reid (Ballyhale), James Fitzpatrick (Ballyhale), Capt., Conor Phelan (Clara), Richie Power (Carrickshock).
Subs. Michael Rice (Carrickshock) for Fitzpatrick. Brian Dowling (O'Loughlins) for Cleere. Eoin Larkin (James Stephens) for Reid. John Phelan (Clara) for O'Neill. Niall Doherty (Galmoy) for Delaney. Padraig Holden (Ballyhale), Niall Moran (St. Martins), Eddie Campion (Tullaroan), John Murphy (Carrickshock).

James "Cha Fitzpatrick
Kilkenny Captain 2004

Tipperary – All Ireland U21 Finalists 2004
Back: Shane McGrath, Damian O'Brien, Joe Caesar, Francis Devanney, Tommy Fitzgerald, Tony Scroope, Evan Hanley, Pat Buckley,
Willie Ryan, Wayne Culley, Conor O'Mahony, Ger Griffin, David Morrissey, David Kennedy,
Front: David Sheppard, Evan Sweeney, Hugh Moloney, Michael Farrell, Patrick McCormack, Andrew Morrissey, Diarmuid Fitzgerald (capt.),
Shane Sweeney, Conor O'Brien, Richie Ruth, Gerry Kennedy.

Tipperary team. Patrick McCormack (Thurles Sarsfields), Andrew Morrissey (Galtee Rovers), Conor O'Mahoney (Newport), Darragh Walton (Ballingarry), Evan Hanley (Lattin/Cullen), Diarmuid Fitzgerald (Roscrea), Capt., Hugh Moloney (Nenagh), Joe Caesar (Killenaule), Wayne Cully (Thurles Sarsfields), Pat Buckley (Emly), Shane Sweeney (Ballybacon/Grange), Francis Devaney (Toomevara), Evan Sweeney (Loughmore), Tony Scroope (Burgess), Michael Farrell (Killenaule).

Subs. Willie Ryan (Toomevara) for Morrissey. David Sheppard (Moycarkey) for Buckley. David Morrissey (Galtee Rovers) for E.Sweeney. Tommy Fitzgerald (Roscrea) for S.Sweeney. Pat Shortt (Upperchurch) for Cully. Gerry Kennedy (Killenaule), Richie Ruth (Thurles Sarsfields), Shane McGrath (Ballinahinch), Damien O'Brien (Burgess).

2004
LEINSTER FINAL: *Kilkenny 1-16, Wexford 2-3*
MUNSTER FINAL: *Tipperary 1-16, Cork 1-13*
ULSTER FINAL: *Down 5-8, Derry 4-7*
ALL IRELAND SEMI FINALS: *Kilkenny 0-20, Galway 0-15; Tipperary 4-20, Down 0-5.*

2005 FINAL
GALWAY STRIKE LATE TO END POOR RUN IN U-21 FINALS.
18/9/2005 AT GAELIC GROUNDS, LIMERICK.
Galway 1-15. Kilkenny 1-14.

Kilkenny went in search of their first three in a row at U-21 level before 7,363 spectators at Limerick. They began well when "Cha" Fitzpatrick made a goal for Eoin Larkin after only two minutes. Galway responded with intensity and scored a fine goal through Aonghus Callanan in the 12th minute. Larkin was the main man for Kilkenny with successive points from frees. Galway captain Kenneth Burke contributed well in this half scoring two fine points and having another effort, which was clearly a point, signalled wide. Kilkenny missed a fine chance of a goal in the 15th minute, when two unmarked forwards couldn't find the target. Galway led by 1-7 to 1-5 at the break.

On the resumption, Galway managed just three points in the third quarter, whereas Kilkenny scored six. With Michael Rice very prominent at midfield for Kilkenny, Galway's attack found it very difficult to gain possession during that quarter. Kilkenny led by three points, 1-14 to 1-11, with fifty five minutes gone. It looked probable that Galway would suffer their seventh U-21 final defeat

Galway – All Ireland U21 Champions 2005

Back Mark Herlihy, Kerrill Wade, Cathal Dervan, Thomas Mannion, Martin Nestor, Mark Lane, Niall Earls, Paul Madden, Alan Garvey, Kevin Huban, Joe Gantley, David Collin, Ger Mahon, Aonghus Callanan, Brendan Lucas, Kevin Briscoe, Brian Costello.
Front: Aidan Ryan, Roderick White, Finian Coone, Damien Kelly, Paul Flynn, Barry Cullinane, Niall Healy, Alan Gaynor, Kenneth Burke (capt), Enna Ryan, Donal Reilly.

Kilkenny - All Ireland U21 Finalists 2005
Back: Pat Hartley, Alan Healy, Liam Tierney, Gavin Nolan, Eoin McGrath, Shane Cadogan, T.J. Reid, Padraig Holden.
Middle: Maurice Nolan, Eoin Guinan, David McCormack, P.J. Delaney, Donnacha Cody, Stephen Maher, Michael Fennelly,
Austin Murphy, Michael Rice, John Tennyson, Ciaran Hoyne, Tomás Frisby, Paul O'Flynn.
Front: Peter O'Donovan, Keith Nolan, John Dalton, Damien Fogarty, Eoin Reid, Eoin Larkin, Richie Power,
Willie O'Dwyer, Cha Fitzpatrick, Eamon O'Gorman, Andrew McCarthy, Sean Cummins.
Photo: Eoin Hennessy

in nine seasons. Kilkenny had scored 0-8 since half time to Galway's 0-4 and looked very comfortable when "Cha" Fitzpatrick scored their 14th point. However, they had seven wides in the second half to none from Galway. The Galway comeback was initiated by David Collins, who pointed a long-range free in the 56th minute. Substitute Cathal Dervan reduced the margin to one.

As the game moved into injury time Kerill Wade equalised from a free. In the 62nd minute, Niall Healy and Kenneth Burke combined to find Wade and he fired over the winning point. Kilkenny's wing-back John Dalton had a chance to level the match but missed the target.

For Galway, Alan Gaynor, Paul Flynn and Kevin Briscoe were a solid full back line in front of reliable goalkeeper, Aidan Ryan. Barry Cullinane and David Collins were prominent in the outer line of defence. In attack, top scorer Wade, Aonghus Callanan and Kenneth Burke contributed most.

Kilkenny's half back line of John Dalton, PJ Delaney and Ciaran Hoyne were impressive. Midfielders Michael Fennelly and Michael Rice had the better of their tussle with the Galway duo. Their attack was too dependent on the freetaking of Eoin Larkin. "Cha" Fitzpatrick was their most dangerous forward.

The referee was John Sexton of Limerick.

Kenneth Burke
Galway Captain 2005

Galway scorers; Kerill Wade 0-8 (5fs &1 65), Aonghus Callanan 1-1, Kenneth Burke 0-2, Niall Healy 0-1, Cathal Dervan 0-1, Brendan Lucas 0-1, David Collins 0-1 (f).

Kilkenny scorers; Eoin Larkin 1-9 (0-8fs), James "Cha" Fitzpatrick 0-2, Michael Fennelly 0-1, Willie O'Dwyer 0-1, Eoin Reid 0-1.

Galway team. Aidan Ryan (Craughwell), Paul Flynn (Tommie Larkins), Alan Gaynor (Mullagh), Kevin Briscoe (Mullagh), Ger Mahon (Kinvara), Barry Cullinane (Turloughmore), David Collins (Liam Mellowes), Brendan Lucas (Meelick-Eyrecourt), Alan Garvey (Tommie Larkins), Joe Gantley (Beagh), Aonghus Callanan (Liam Mellowes), Eanna Ryan (Killimordaly), Kenneth Burke (St. Thomas), Capt., Niall Healy (Craughwell), Kerill Wade (Sarsfields).
Subs. Finian Coone (Mullagh) for Ryan. Cathal Dervan (Mullagh) for Gantley. Damien Kelly (Tommie Larkins) for Cullinane. Mark Herlihy (Kilnadeema-Leitrim). Brian Costelloe (Abbeyknockmoy), Roderick White (Tommie Larkins), Kevin Huban (Tommie Larkins), Donal Reilly (Mullagh), Niall Earls (Killimordaly).

Kilkenny team. Damien Fogarty (Erin's Own), Stephen Maher (Tullaroan), John Tennyson (Carrickshock), Donncha Cody (James Stephens), John Dalton (Carrickshock), PJ Delaney (Fenians), Ciaran Hoyne (Graigue/Ballycallan), Michael Fennelly (Ballyhale), Michael Rice (Carrickshock), James Fitzpatrick (Ballyhale), Austim Murphy (Clara), Willie O'Dwyer (Mullinavat), Eoin Reid (Ballyhale), Capt., Richie Power (Carrickshock), Eoin Larkin (James Stephens).
Subs. David mcCormack (James Stephens) for Murphy. Liam Tierney (Rower/Inistioge), Padraic Holden (Ballyhale), TJ Reid (Ballyhale), Eamon O'Gorman (Emeralds), Andrew McCarthy (Piltown), Alan Healy (Conahy), Tomas Frisby (Mullinavat), Paul O'Flynn (Dicksboro).

2005
LEINSTER FINAL: Kilkenny 0-17, Dublin 1-10
MUNSTER FINAL: Cork 4-8, Tipperary 0-13
ULSTER FINAL: Antrim 3-12, Down 0-16
ALL IRELAND SEMI FINALS: Galway 1-19, Cork 1-13; Kilkenny 6-33, Antrim 1-8.

♦ *Barry Cullinane completed the U-21 double as he had won the football All-Ireland at the grade in May.*

2006 Final
Supersub Richie Hogan snatches a draw at the death.
10/9/2006 at Croke Park.
Kilkenny 2-14. Tipperary 2-14.

Both sides played some great hurling before an attendance of 20,685. In a nervy opening quarter, Tipperary conceded some soft frees which "Cha" Fitzpatrick converted. Seven minutes had elapsed before Tipperary opened their account with a point from a long-range Stephen Lillis free. Kilkenny led by three points by the fourteenth minute. Further points by Lillis and Darragh Egan(2) had the sides level by the 19th minute. Three points each were then exchanged, before a "Cha" Fitzpatrick point from a free ensured that Kilkenny led by 0-9 to 0-8 at the break.

In the 36th minute, Darragh Egan blasted a 21 yard free to the Kilkenny net, to give Tipperary a two point lead. They had extended their lead to three at the end of the third quarter. Kilkenny retaliated with a goal from Richie Power in the 48th minute, following a pass from David McCormack. Substitute Richie Hogan gave Kilkenny the lead with a point in the 52nd minute but Tipp drew level a minute later. A 53rd minute goal from Niall Teehan seemed to have the Munster champions in the driving seat but Kilkenny levelled with a goal from Richie Hogan at the end of the third minute of injury time. Kilkenny finished with 14 players, having substitute Maurice Nolan sent off in the 58th minute, two minutes after coming on.

Best for Kilkenny were John Dalton, "Cha" Fitzpatrick, Richie Power and supersub Richie Hogan. For Tipperary, goalkeeper Gerry Kennedy made some outstanding saves. Paddy Stapleton, David Young, James Woodlock, Stephen Lillis, Niall Teehan and Darragh Egan also starred in a wonderful game.

The referee was Michael Haverty of Galway.

Kilkenny scorers; James "Cha" Fitzpatrick 0-6 (fs), Richie Hogan 1-1, Richie Power 1-1, Austin Murphy 0-3, TJ Reid 0-2, Paddy Hogan 0-1.

Tipperary scorers; Darragh Egan 1-5 (1-3fs), Niall Teehan 1-1, Stephen Lillis 0-3 (2fs), James Woodlock 0-2, David Young 0-1, Ryan O'Dwyer 0-1, David Sheppard 0-1.

Kilkenny team. Liam Tierney (Rower/Inistioge), Kieran Joyce (Rower/Inistioge), John Tennyson (Carrickshock), Sean Cummins (Rower/Inistioge), Pat Hartley (Tullogher Rosbercon), John Dalton (Carrickshock), Damien Fogarty (Erin's Own), James Fitzpatrick (Ballyhale), Michael Fennelly (Ballyhale), Capt., TJ Reid (Ballyhale), Austin Murphy (Clara), Paddy Hogan (Danesfort), Alan Healy (Conahy), Richie Power (Carrickshock), David McCormack (James Stephens).
Subs. Richie Hogan (Danesfort) for Healy. Maurice Nolan (O'Loughlins) for P. Hogan. Bill Beckett (St. Lachtain's) for Murphy. Danny Loughnane (O'Loughlins). Eamon Walsh (Ballyhale), Eddie

Kilkenny – All Ireland U21 Champions 2006

Back: Darren O'Neill, Neal Prendergast, Richie Power, Niall Kennedy, Richie Dollard, John Tennyson, Sean Cummins, Sean Mahony, John Dalton, David Prendergast, Shane Prendergast, Kieran Joyce.

Third Row: Adrian Finan (Manager) James Maher, David McCormack, T.J. Reid, Mark Aylward, Pat Hartley, Eamon Walsh, Donnacha Coady, Bill Beckett, Paddy Hogan, Austin Murphy, Matthew Ruth, Tom Doheny, Tom Hogan, Ger Fennelly.

Second Row: Colin Grant, Damien Fogarty, Shane Cadogen, Liam Tierney, Michael Fennelly, Danny Loughnane, Peter Donovan, James ,"Cha" Fitzpatrick, Richie Hogan.

Front: Chris O'Neill, Eoin McCormack, Michael Grace, Conor O'Loughlin, Niall Moran, Niall Doherty, Martin Phelan, Ned Sweeney.

Photo Eoin Hennessy

Drawn Final 2006

Captains Michael Fennelly (Kilkenny) and David Young (Tipperary) with referee Michael Haverty (Galway) before the drawn Final 2006. (Eoin Hennessy)

O'Donoghue (Dicksboro), Shane Cadogan (St. Martin's), Gavin Nolan (Conahy), Peter O'Donovan (Erin's Own), Neal Prendergast (Clara).

Tipperary team. Gerry Kennedy (Killenaule), Paddy Stapleton (Borris Ileigh), Alan Byrne (Shannon Rovers), Conor O'Brien (Annacarty), David Young (Toomevara), Capt., Jim Bob McCarthy (Golden/Kilfeacle), Sean Horan (St. Patrick's), James Woodlock (Drom &Inch), Stephen Lillis (Thurles Sars), Ryan O'Dwyer (Cashel), Niall Teehan (Gortnahoe/Glengoole), David Sheppard (Moycarkey), Richie Ruth (Thurles Sars), Darragh Egan (Kildangan), Ray McLoughney (Kilruane).

Subs. Danny O'Hanlon (Carrick Swans) for McLoughney. Darragh Hickey (Boherlahan) for Ruth. Kevin Quinlan (Kilruane) for McCarthy). Matthew Ryan (Templederry), Kevin Lanigan (Carrick Swans), Philip Austin (Borrisokane), Stephen Murphy (Kilruane), Joe Dixon (Moycarkey), Ian Murphy (Killenaule).

2006 FINAL REPLAY
KILKENNY WIN THIRD U-21 TITLE IN FOUR YEARS.
16/9/2006 AT SEMPLE STADIUM, THURLES.
Kilkenny 1-11. Tipperary 0-11.

The large attendance of 18,578 resulted in a ten minute delay before throw in. From the start, Kilkenny looked better prepared than for the drawn game. The pace of the game was electric and there was no holding back from either side. Six minutes had elapsed before the first score, which fell to Richie Ruth of Tipperary. Austin Murphy soon equalised for Kilkenny. The Leinster champions led by two points at the end of the first quarter. Tipperary soon equalised through a Darragh Egan free and a Danny O'Hanlon point from play. In the 23rd minute Austin Murphy set up Paddy Hogan for the only goal of the final. Kilkenny led at the interval by 1-6 to 0-7.

Tipperary introduced Philip Austin for the second half. He made an immediate impact by scoring a point. Kilkenny led by three points at the end of the third quarter. Richie Power increased their lead to four, when he converted a free from the sideline. James Woodlock narrowed the gap with a point and a Darragh Egan free with ninety seconds remaining reduced the margin to two. Richie Hogan pointed for Kilkenny seconds into injury time. With time almost up, Woodlock was pulled to the ground. Darragh Egan shot for the equalising goal from the free but there were too many bodies in the way. The referee immediately blew for full time.

Quality hurling was evident all through. Kilkenny were slightly the better side. Austin Murphy, Richie Power and Paddy Hogan were very dangerous forwards. In defence, John Dalton was outstanding and was the recipient of the man of the match award. "Cha" Fitzpatrick and Michael Fennelly won the midfield duel.

Tipperary did not play as well as in the drawn game but Gerry Kennedy, Paddy Stapleton, Conor O'Brien, Danny O'Hanlon, James Woodlock and pacy substitute Philip Austin put in huge efforts.

The referee was Brian Gavin of Offaly.

Kilkenny scorers; Richie Power 0-6(5fs), Austin Murphy 0-3, Paddy Hogan 1-0, James "Cha" Fitzpatrick 0-1, Richie Hogan 0-1.

Tipperary scorers; Darragh Egan 0-5 (4fs), Philip Austin 0-2, Danny O'Hanlon 0-2, James Woodlock 0-1, Richie Ruth 0-1.

Kilkenny team. Liam Tierney (Rower/Inistioge), Kieran Joyce (Rower/Inistioge), John Tennyson (Carrickshock), Sean Cummins (Rower/Inistioge), Pat Hartley (Tullogher/Rosbercon), John Dalton (Carrickshock), Damien Fogarty (Erin's Own), James "Cha" Fitzpatrick (Ballyhale), Michael Fennelly (Ballyhale), Capt., TJ Reid (Ballyhale), Austin Murphy (Clara), Paddy Hogan (Danesfort), Richie Hogan (Danesfort), Richie Power

Tipperary – All Ireland U21 Finalists 2006

Back: Ian Murphy (Killenaule), Kevin Lanigan (Carrick Swan), Richie McGrath (Carrick Davins), Darragh Egan (Kildangan), Joe Dixon (Moycarkey -Borris), David Sheppard (Moycarkey-Borris), Ray McLoughney (Kilruane MacDonaghs), Ryan O'Dwyer (Cashel King Cormacs), Sean Horan (St. Patricks), Niall Teehan (Gortnahoe-Glengoole), Alan Byrne (Shannon Rovers), Danny O'Hanlon (Carrick Swan), Philip Austin (Borrisokane), Stephen Murphy (Kilruane MacDonaghs)

Front: Matthew Ryan (Templederry), Kevin Quintan (Kilruane MacDonaghs), Darragh Hickey (Boherlahan-Dualla), Jim Bob McCarthy (Golden-Kilfeacle), Paddy Stapleton (Borris-Ileigh), James Woodlock (Drom & Inch), Gerry Kennedy (Killenaule), Richie Ruth (Thurles Sarsfields), Stephen Lillis (Thurles Sarsfields), David Young (Toomevara - Captain), Conor O'Brien (Éire Óg Annacarty), Michael Coleman (Cashel King Cormacs), Shane Scully (JK Brackens), Ian Delaney (JK Brackens)

(Carrickshock), David McCormack (James Stephens).

Subs. Alan Healy (Conahy) for McCormack. Danny Loughnane (O'Loughlins), Eamon Walsh (Ballyhale), Eddie O'Donoghue (Dicksboro), Bill Beckett (St. Lachtains), Shane Cadogan (St. Martins), Gavin Nolan (Conahy), Peter O'Donovan (Erin's Own), Neal Prendergast (Clara).

Tipperary team. Gerry Kennedy (Killenaule), Paddy Stapleton (Borris-Ileigh), Alan Byrne (Shannon Rovers), Conor O'Brien (Annacarty), David Young (Toomevara), Capt., Jim Bob McCarthy (Golden/Kilfeacle), Sean Horan (St.Patricks), James Woodlock (Drom&Inch), Stephen Lillis (Thurles Sars), Ryan O'Dwyer (Cashel), Niall Teehan (Gortnahoe/Glengoole), David Sheppard (Moycarkey/Borris), Richie Ruth (Thurles Sars), Danny O'Hanlon (Carrick Swans), Darragh Egan (Kildangan).

Subs. Philip Austin (Borrisokane) for Sheppard. Kevin Lanigan (Carrick Swans) for Horan. Darragh Hickey (Boherlahan) for Teehan. Kevin Quinlan (Kilruane) for Lillis. Matthew Ryan (Templederry), Stephen Murphy (Kilruane), Joe Dixon (Moycarkey/Borris), Ian Murphy (Killenaule), Ray McLoughney (Kilruane).

2006
LEINSTER FINAL: Kilkenny 2-18, Dublin 2-10
MUNSTER FINAL: Tipperary 3-11, Cork 0-13
ULSTER FINAL: Antrim 2-15, Down 2-11
ALL IRELAND SEMI FINALS: Kilkenny 1 -24, Galway 2-12; Tipperary 5-19, Antrim 0-7.

2007 FINAL
GALWAY'S SECOND U-21 TITLE IN THREE YEARS.
9/9/2007 AT CROKE PARK.
Galway. 5-11. Dublin 0-12.

An official attendance of 33,154 watched this final. Another 1,000 spectators got free admission as there was a glitch in the ticketing arrangements. A Kerill Wade point for Galway opened the scoring after only 20 seconds. Alan McCrabbe quickly replied for Dublin. Conor Kavanagh goaled for Galway in the 8th minute. Another Galway goal followed in the 10th minute through Sean Glynn. This was quickly followed by another goal from Kavanagh. As a result, Galway led by 3-4 to 0-1 at the end of the first quarter. The Dublin defence now tightened up and McCrabbe was unerring in his free-taking as they reduced the deficit to more manageable proportions. Then further disaster struck for Dublin, when Glynn placed Wade for a Galway goal, leaving the interval score at 4-6 to 0-8.

Galway – All Ireland U21 Champions 2007

Back: Paul Loughnane, Paul Callanan, Enda Collins, John Lee, Sean Glynn, James Skehill, Martin Ryan, Ciaran O'Donovan, Joe Canning, Ger Mahon,
Andrew Keary, Kevin Keane, Paddy Cormican, John Greene, Enda Concannon.
Front: Niall Forde, Paul Madden, Aidan Harte, David Kennedy, Keith Kilkenny, Kerril Wade, Kevin Hayes, Conor Kavanagh, Finnian Cooney, Alan Leech,
Barry Hanley, Noel Kelly, Danny White, Benny Kenny, Mark Herlihy, Vinny Faherty.

Photo SPORTSFILE

Dublin – All Ireland U21 Finalists 2007

Back: Ross O'Connell, Richie Walker, Joey Boland, Kevin O'Reilly, Peter O'Callaghan, Eoin Moran, Danny Webster, Diarmuid Connolly, Keith Dunne, Ronan Drumgoole, Sam Lehane, Keith Nolan, Ian Fleming, Eugene Farrell, Stephen Ennis, Ciaran Lane, Eoin Ryan, Declan O'Dwyer, Alan McCrabbe.

Front: Stephen Bennett, Peadar Carton, Shane Durkin, Johnny McCaffrey (Capt) Stephen Loughlin, Michael McGarry, Gary Kelly, Barry Aird, Joey Maher, Paddy Curtin, Jack Gilligan, Tomas brady, Kevin Davis.

n the first five minutes of the second half, McCrabbe scored two points from frees for the Leinster champions. Dublin had now stepped up the pressure considerably. However, Galway held their composure and after a scuffle which led to three players being yellow-carded, they picked off a few points to copper fasten their dominance. The best of their second half scores was a point, which teenager Joe Canning scored from a sideline cut over 60 yards out. Galway's fire-power was in contrast to Dublin's lack of scoring power. Dublin's four points in the second half all came from frees. Galway substitute Noel Kelly added a goal and a point in the last few minutes.

Galway goalkeeper James Skehill was inspirational under the high ball. Senior players Ger Mahon and John Lee showed great leadership in the centre of their defence. Kerill Wade and Conor Kavanagh shone in attack.

Dublin relied heavily on the free-taking of Alan McCrabbe for scores. Midfield was the one area where Dublin shared possession through McCrabbe and Johnny McCaffrey. Full back Peter O'Callaghan was best in their defence. The fact that their attacking sextet only managed 0-2 showed that Dublin had big problems in scoring.

The referee was Johnny Ryan of Tipperary.

Galway scorers; Kerill Wade 1-4 (0-2fs), Conor Kavanagh 2-0, Noel Kelly 1-1, Sean Glynn 1-0, Joe Canning 0-3 (1 lb), Finian Cooney 0-2, Keith Kilkenny 0-1.

Dublin scorers; Alan McCrabbe 0-9 (7fs), Johnny McCaffrey 0-1, Diarmuid Connolly 0-1, Peadar Carton 0-1.

Galway team. **James Skehill (Cappataggle), Alan Leech (Kinvara), Gerard Mahon (Kinvara), Ciaran O'Donovan (Athenry), Martin Ryan (Kilconieron), John Lee (Liam Mellowes), Andrew Keary (Killimor), David Kennedy (Ardrahan), Keith Kilkenny (Kiltormer), Sean Glynn (Athenry), Kevin Hynes (Sarsfields), Capt., Finian Cooney (Mullagh), Conor Kavanagh (Kinvara), Joe Canning (Portumna), Kerril Wade (Sarsfields).**
Subs. Barry Hanley (Carnmore) for Glynn. Aidan Harte (Gort) for Kennedy. John Greene (Ardrahan) for Cooney. Noel Kelly (Sarsfields) for Kavanagh. Paul Loughnane (Cappataggle) for Leech. Mark Herlihy (Kilnadeema-Leitrim), Niall Forde (Gort), Paul Callanan (Clarinbridge), Enda Collins (Clarinbridge).
Dublin team. **Paddy Curtin (St. Oliver Plunketts Eoghan Ruadh), Ronan Drumgoole (St. Vincents), Peter O'Callaghan (Lucan Sarsfields), Danny**

Kevin Hynes
Galway Captain 2007

Webster (O'Toole's), Keith Dunne (Erin's Isle), Tomas Brady (Na Fianna), Joseph Boland (Na Fianna), Johnny McCaffrey (Lucan Sarsfields), Capt., Alan McCrabbe (Craobh Chiarain), Eoin Moran (Round Towers, Clondalkin), Diarmuid Connolly (St. Vincents), Shane Durkin (Ballyboden St. Endas), Peadar Carton (O'Toole's), Declan O'Dwyer (St. Olafs), Ross O'Carroll (Kilmacud Crokes).

Subs. Michael McGarry (Ballyboden St.Endas) for Webster. Ian Fleming (St. Vincents) for O'Carroll. Sam Lehane (St. Judes) for Connolly. Joey Maher (Ballinteer St. Johns), Gary Kelly (Craobh Chiarain), Conor Connolly (Liffey Gaels), Ciaran Lane (Ballinteer St.Johns), Stephen Ennis (Craobh Chiarain), Stephen Loughlin (St.Vincents).

2007
LEINSTER FINAL: *Dublin 2-18, Offaly 3-9*
MUNSTER FINAL: *Cork 1-20, Waterford 0-10*
ULSTER FINAL: *Derry 2-16, Antrim 1-18*
ALL IRELAND SEMI FINALS: *Dublin 3-18, Derry 2-11; Galway 4-21, Cork 2-18 (aet).*

2008 FINAL
KILKENNY WIN THEIR FIRST EVER HURLING CHAMPIONSHIP GRAND SLAM.
14/9/2008 AT CROKE PARK.
Kilkenny 2-13. Tipperary 0-15.

Before an attendance of 18,727, Kilkenny went in search of a clean sweep of hurling titles, having already won senior, minor and intermediate. Both sides started tentatively. Tipperary led by 0-3 to 0-1 after six minutes and the sides were level at 0-4 each at the end of the first quarter. Kilkenny pulled away with goals from Matthew Ruth in the 15th and 30th minutes. The creators of the goals, TJ Reid and Richie Hogan, were unchallenged before giving passes to Ruth. Tipperary's poor second quarter, which they lost by 2-3 to 0-3, was to cost them dearly. Kilkenny led at the interval by 2-7 to 0-7.

Tipperary scored five points without reply on either side of half-time. By the three-quarter mark, they had reduced the deficit to two points with Pa Bourke pointing two frees for fouls on Seamus Callanan to Kilkenny's one point from a Richie Hogan free. Despite points from Richie Hogan and John Mulhall, Tipp reduced the margin again to two points, following scores from Bourke and Gearoid Ryan, with ten minutes to go. In the 59th minute and with Kilkenny still leading by two points, Tipperary's Patrick Maher was rugby tackled to the ground. Despite appeals for a penalty, referee James Owens gave a free out for overcarrying. Two points in injury time from TJ Reid and Richie Hogan sealed Kilkenny's victory.

Kilkenny – All Ireland U21 Champions 2008

Back: Kieran Mooney, Joe Maher, Niall Walsh, Eoin Cody, Richie Dollard, Kevin Reid, TJ Reid, John Joe Farrell, Martin Walsh, David Lyng.

Third Row: Robbie Walsh, Brian Healy, Michael Grace, David Langton, PJ Rowe, Paul Murphy, Michael Murphy, Lester Ryan,
Kieran Grehan, Eoin O'Shea.

Second Row: James Nolan, Paddy Nolan, Keith Hogan, Colin McGrath, Neil Pendergast, James Norris, Kieran Joyce, Paddy Hogan, Mark Kelly,

Front: Mark Bergin, John Mulhall, Colin Fennelly, Matthew Ruth, James Dowling (Capt), Nicky Cleere, Richie Hogan, Liam Ryan, Niall Tennyson.

(Photo Eoin Hennessy)

Tipperary – All Ireland U21 Finalists 2008

Back: *Pa Bourke, Sliane Bourke, Seamus Callinan, Gearoid Ryan, Matthew Ryan, Pádraig Maker, Mark O'Meara, Seanius Hennessy (captain), Thomas McGrah.*

Front: *Brendan Maker, Patrick Maker, Mickael Cahill, Kevin Maher, Tiiomas Stapleton, Kevin Lanigan.*

In a superb Kilkenny defence, goalkeeper Colin McGrath made some vital saves. Kieran Joyce and Paddy Hogan held the centre of the defence in a vice-like grip. Niall Walsh hurled well at midfield. Matthew Ruth and TJ Reid were their most productive forwards.

Tipperary's downfall can be attributed to the fact that their forward division only scored two points from play. Patrick "Bonnar" Maher was best of their attack, while Pa Bourke was unerring from frees. The Tipperary full back line of Michael Cahill, Padraic Maher and Kevin Maher all gave fine displays. In the half back line, Thomas Stapleton and Brendan Maher played very well. Gearoid Ryan was outstanding at midfield and contributed three points from play.

The referee was James Owens of Wexford.

Kilkenny scorers; Matthew Ruth 2-2, Richie Hogan 0-6 (fs), TJ Reid 0-2, John Mulhall 0-2, Niall Walsh 0-1.

Tipperary scorers; Pa Bourke 0-8 (fs), Gearoid Ryan 0-3, Kevin Lanigan 0-1, Brendan Maher 0-1, Seamus Callanan 0-1, Shane Bourke 0-1.

Kilkenny team. Colin McGrath (St. Martin's), Paul Murphy (Danesfort), Kieran Joyce (Rower/Inistioge), Eoin O'Shea (Clara), Lester Ryan (Clara), Paddy Hogan (Danesfort), Neal Prendergast (Clara), James Dowling (St. Martin's), Capt., Niall Walsh (Slieverue), Colin Fennelly (Ballyhale), Nicky Cleere (Bennettsbridge), TJ Reid (Ballyhale), Matthew Ruth (James Stephens), John Mulhall (St. Martin's), Richie Hogan (Danesfort).
Subs. JJ Farrell (Thomastown) for Cleere. Joe Maher (St. Martin's) for Dowling. Mark Bergin (O Loughlins) for Farrell. James Norris (Piltown), Kieran Mooney (Conahy), David Langton (Clara), Richie Dollard (Tullogher/Rosbercon), Martin Walsh (Tullaroan), PJ Rowe (Mooncoin).

Tipperary team. Matthew Ryan (Templederry), Michael Cahill (Thurles Sarsfields), Padraic Maher (Thurles Sarsfields), Kevin Maher(Lorrha), Kevin Lanigan (Carrick Swans), Thomas Stapleton (Templederry), Brendan Maher (Borris-Ileigh), Gearoid Ryan (Templederry), Seamus Hennessy (Kilruane), Capt., Patrick Maher(Lorrha), Seamus Callanan (Drom&Inch), Thomas McGrath (Ballingarry), Pa Bourke (Thurles Sarsfields), Mark O'Meara (Knockshegowna), Shane Bourke (JK Brackens).
Subs. John O'Keefe (Clonoulty) for Lanigan. Danny O'Hanlon(Carrick Swans) for O'Meara. Philip Ivors (Ballingarry) for Shane Bourke. Johnny Ryan

James Dowling, Kilkenny Captain 2008

(Drom&Inch) for McGrath. Toss Lowry (Holycross), George Hannigan (Shannon Rovers), Ronan Sherlock (Silvermines), Ray McLoughney(Kilruane), Timmy Hammersley(Clonoulty).

2008
LEINSTER FINAL: *Kilkenny 2-21, Offaly 2-9*
MUNSTER FINAL: *Tipperary 1-16, Clare 2-12*
ULSTER FINAL: *Derry won round robin c'ship.*
ALL IRELAND SEMI FINALS: *Kilkenny 2-14, Galway 1-13; Tipperary 1-20, Derry 0-10.*

2009 FINAL
CLARE WIN THEIR FIRST U-21 HURLING FINAL.
13/9/2009 AT CROKE PARK.
Clare 0-15. Kilkenny 0-14.

The attendance of 25,924 observed a tightly contested low scoring game that saw the sides level on eight occasions. During the first half it was point for point as both sides gave their all in the quest for the "Cross of Cashel" trophy. Two Kilkenny defenders shadowed Clare's Darach Honan, who though doubtful before the final, was seen as the Banner's dangerman. The final minutes of the first half saw three scores, as Colin Ryan converted two frees for Clare and Mark Kelly responded for Kilkenny. The Munster champions led by 0-8 to 0-6 at the interval.

On the restart, Richie Hogan pointed for the Leinster champions. James Nolan then equalised and Colin Fennelly put them a point ahead. John Conlon equalised for Clare. Nolan pointed again for Kilkenny and Richie Hogan increased their lead to two points. In the 43rd minute, Cormac O'Donovan pointed for Clare to leave them only one point behind. In the 49th minute, a crucial save by Clare goalkeeper Donal Touhy deprived Richie Hogan of a goal. Conlon equalised in the 51st minute. Mark Kelly, with his third point from play, put the Noresiders ahead again. Colin Ryan equalised for the Banner with a point from a long-range free. To their supporters great delight, Cormac O'Donovan after a mazy run, pointed in the last minute and sealed Clare's first title at U-21 level. There were only seven frees in the second half, four to Kilkenny. Over the hour, Clare had only four wides to Kilkenny's twelve. At the final whistle, despite the best efforts of the stewards, the Clare supporters gathered in their thousands to celebrate on Croke Park.

Clare goalkeeper Donal Touhy made vital saves during the game. Their full back line of Glynn, Dillon and Doherty were superb. Nicky O'Connell was a colossus at centre back. Midfielder Cormac O'Donovan ranged upfield to score two long-range points, including the winner. John Conlon de servedly won man-of-the-match for his performance at centre forward. Colin Ryan was unerring from placed balls.

Colin McGrath performed soundly in the Kilkenny goal. Paul Murphy and Lester Ryan were best in

Clare - All Ireland U21 Champions 2009

Back: Martin Tierney, Colm Quinn, Colm Maddan, Joe Meaney, Diarmuid Hehir, Cillian Duggan Joe O'Connor, Cian Dillion, Colin Ryan, Darach Honan ,Nicky O'Connell, John Conlon, Ciarán O'Doherty (capt.) Conor Tierney, Camin Morey, Eoin Hayes, Cathal Chaplin, Noel Casey,
Liam Markham, Jamie Roughan.
Front: Conor McGrath, Patrick O'Connor, Conor Neylon, George Waterstone, Patrick Kelly, Cormac O'Donovan, Eamon Glynn, James Gunning,
Domhall O'Donovan, Enda Barrett, Sean Collins, John Moloney, Blaine Earley, Niall Keane, Derek Fahy.

Kilkenny – All Ireland U21 Finalists 2009
Back: Shane Maher, Martin Phelan, Keith Hogan, David Lyng, Michael Walsh, Nicky Cleere, Colin McGrath, Martin Walsh, David Langton, John Joe Farrell, Paul Murphy, Mark Kelly, Colin Fennelly, Peter McCarthy.
Front: Richie Hogan, Thomas Breen, John Mulhall, Paddy Nolan, Eoin Murphy, James Nolan, Conor Fogarty, Lester Ryan, Mark Bergin, Liam Ryan.   *(Photo Eoin Hennessy)*

Clare Captain, Ciarán O'Doherty receives the trophy from Uachtarán CLG Criostóir Ó Cuanaigh.

their defence. Midfielder Mark Kelly was outstanding, scoring three points from play. In attack, Colin Fennelly's searching runs tested the Clare defence. Richie Hogan and John Mulhall also contributed strongly.

The referee was Cathal McAllister of Cork.

Clare scorers; Colin Ryan 0-9 (8fs, I 65), John Conlon 0-3, Cormac O'Donovan 0-2, Caimin Morey 0-1.

Kilkenny scorers; Richie Hogan 0-5 (1f), Mark Kelly 0-3, Colin Fennelly 0-2, John Mulhall 0-2, James Nolan 0-2.

Clare team. Donal Touhy (Crusheen), Eamon Glynn (Inagh/Kilnamona), Cian Dillon (Crusheen), Ciaran O'Doherty (Crusheen), Capt.,Domhall O'Donovan (Clonlara), Nicky O'Connell (Clonlara), James Gunning (Broadford), Enda Barrett (Newmarket), Cormac O'Donovan (Clonlara), Caimin Morey (Sixmilebridge), John Conlon (Clonlara), Sean Collins

(Cratloe), Conor Tierney (Inagh/Kilnamona), Darach Honan (Clonlara), Colin Ryan (Newmarket).

Subs. Conor McGrath (Cratloe) for Tierney. Patrick O'Connor (Tubber) for Morey. Eoin Hayes (Newmarket) for Gunning. Derek Fahy (Sixmilebridge), Cathal Chaplin (Broadford), Patrick Kelly (Clarecastle), Cillian Duggan (Clooney), Liam Markham (Cratloe), Joe O'Connor (Parteen).

Kilkenny team. Colin McGrath (St.Martin's), Paul Murphy (Danesfort), Paddy Nolan (St. Martin's), Conor Fogarty (Erin's Own), Lester Ryan (Clara), David Langton (Clara), Martin Walsh (Tullaroan), Mark Kelly (O'Loughlins), Liam Ryan (Clara), Colin Fennelly (Ballyhale), Mark Bergin (O'Loughlins), John Mulhall (St. Martin's), Richie Hogan (Danesfort), John Joe Farrell (Thomastown), James Nolan (Clara).

Subs. Nicky Cleere (Bennettsbridge) for Bergin. Eoin Murphy (Glenmore), Michael Walsh (Young Irelands), Kieran Mooney (Conahy), Andy Kearns (O'Loughlins), James Dowling (St. Martin's), Thomas Breen (St. Martin's), Shane Maher (Dicksboro), Capt., Peter McCarthy (Piltown).

2009

LEINSTER FINAL: *Kilkenny 2-20, Dublin 1-19*
MUNSTER FINAL: *Clare 2-17, Waterford 2-12*
ULSTER FINAL: *Antrim 1-18, Derry 0-9*
ALL IRELAND SEMI FINALS: *Kilkenny 2-22, Antrim 2-7; Clare 3-23, Galway 5-15 (aet).*

CHAPTER 6
ALL IRELAND U21
HURLING FINALS
2010-2014

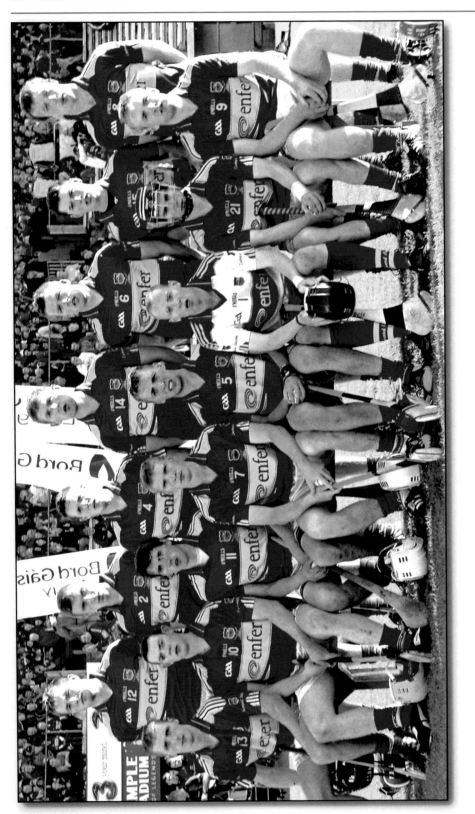

Tipperary - All Ireland U21 Champions 2010

Back: Brian O'Meara, Kevin O'Gorman, Michael Cahill, Paddy Murphy, Pádraig Maher (Capt), John O'Dwyer, Seamus Hennessy.
Front: Michael Heffernan, Sean Carey, Patrick Maher, Brendan Maher, James Barry, James Logue, Ciarán Hough, Noel McGrath.

2010 FINAL
TIPPERARY ACHIEVE SENIOR AND U-21 DOUBLE IN SIX DAYS.
11/9/2010 AT SEMPLE STADIUM, THURLES.
Tipperary 5-22. Galway 0-12.

Galway weren't happy about having to travel to Thurles for this final, which attracted an attendance of 21,110. Tipperary contained five starters from the senior team, who had deprived Kilkenny of 5-in-a-row. Goals in the first three minutes from Brian O'Meara and John O'Dwyer made Galway's difficult task almost impossible. In the 15th minute Patrick Maher galloped through the Galway defence and set up Sean Carey for another Tipperary goal. They led at that stage by 3-4 to 0-2. Galway had wind advantage in the first half and they scored four points without reply between the 16th and 23rd minutes. At the interval, the Munster champions led by 3-7 to 0-9. Galway had nine wides in that first half, but had outscored Tipperary by 0-7 to 0-2 in the second quarter.

With wind assistance in the second half, Tipp piled on the points. Patrick Maher cut through the Galway defence in the 41st minute for the Premier side's fourth goal. In the 47th minute, Noel McGrath's free from inside his own half went all the way to the Galway net. Tipperary now led by 5-13 to 0-10. There was no easing up as they scored nine of the last eleven points as the game petered out to a close. The Tribesmen's distress was added to when centre forward Niall Quinn was sent off in the 52nd minute. Tipperary had outscored Galway in the second half by 2-15 to 0-3. The 25 point gap at the final whistle was the biggest margin in a final in the 47 year history of the competition.

James Logue, Michael Cahill, Padraic Maher, Brendan Maher, Sean Carey, Seamus Hennessy, Noel McGrath, Patrick Maher, man-of-the-match Brian O'Meara, Paddy Murphy and John O'Dwyer were all outstanding for the winners.

Only David Burke, Johnnie Coen, Gerard O'Halloran, James Regan and Gerard Burke performed anywhere near the required standard for Galway, while subs Bernard Burke and Joseph Cooney made an impression when introduced.

The referee was James McGrath of Westmeath.

Tipperary scorers; Brian O'Meara 1-3, John O'Dwyer 1-3, Sean Carey 1-3, Noel McGrath 1-3 (1-0f), Patrick Maher 1-0, Seamus Hennessy 0-3 (1f & 1 65), Paddy Murphy 0-2, Michael Heffernan 0-2, Brendan Maher 0-1 (f), John O'Neill 0-1, Kieran Morris 0-1 (f).

Pádraig Maher, Tipperary Captain 2010

Galway - All Ireland U21 Finalists 2010

Back: Eoin Forde, James Regan, Niall Quinn, Niall Donoghue, Paul Gordan, Ger O'Halloran,
Front: Richie Cummins, Barry Daly, Johnny Coen, Kris Finnegan, Sylvie Og Linnane, David Burke, Gary Burke, Declan Connolly, Gerard Kelly.

Photo: SPORTSFILE

Galway scorers; David Burke 0-2 (1f), Johnnie Coen 0-2, Barry Daly 0-1, James Regan 0-1, Niall Quinn 0-1, Gerard Burke 0-1, Gerard Kelly 0-1, Joseph Cooney 0-1, Bernard Burke 0-1, Jason Grealish 0-1.

Tipperary team. James Logue (Ballingarry), Kevin O'Gorman (Thurles Sarsfields), Padraic Maher (Thurles Sars), Capt. Michael Cahill (Thurles Sars), James Barry (Upperchurch/Drombane), Brendan Maher (Borris-Ileigh), Ciaran Hough (Lorrha), Seamus Hennessy (Kilruane), Noel McGrath (Loughmore/Castleiney), Sean Carey (Moyle Rovers), Paddy Murphy (Nenagh), Patrick Maher (Lorrha), Michael Heffernan (Nenagh), Brian O'Meara (Kilruane). John O'Dwyer (Killenaule).
Subs. Christy Coughlan (Templederry) for O'Gorman. John O'Neill (Clonoulty) for O'Dwyer. Adrian Ryan (Templederry) for Murphy. Joe Gallagher (Kildangan) for McGrath. Kieran Morris (Moycarkey/Borris) for Heffernan. Bill McCormack (Thurles Sars), Thomas Butler (Clonoulty), Sean Curran (Mullinahone), John Coughlan (Moyne/Templetouhy).

Galway team. Kris Finnegan (Gort), Declan Connolly (Killimordaly), Paul Gordon (Tynagh-Abbey-Duniry), Gerard O'Halloran (Craughwell), Niall Donoghue (Kilbeacanty), David Burke (St.Thomas), Capt., Sylvie Og Linnane (Gort), Johnnie Coen (Loughrea), Barry Daly (Clarinbridge), James Regan (St.Thomas), Niall Quinn (Sarsfields), Eoin Forde (Clarinbridge), Richie Cummins (Gort), Garry Burke (Turloughmore), Gerard Kelly (Tommy Larkins).
Subs. Joseph Cooney (Sarsfields) for Forde. Bernard Burke (St.Thomas) for G. Burke. Jason Grealish (Gort) for Linnane. Davy Glennon (Mullagh) for Cummins. Brian Flaherty (Abbeyknockmoy) for Gordon. Jamie Ryan (Craughwell), Mark McMahon (Gort), Ronan Burke (Turloughmore)., Niall Burke (Oranmore-Maree).

2010
LEINSTER FINAL: *Dublin 2-15, Wexford 0-15*
MUNSTER FINAL: *Tipperary 1-22, Clare 1-17*
ULSTER FINAL: *Antrim 0-21, Armagh 0-16*
ALL IRELAND SEMI FINALS: *Tipperary 2-32, Antrim 1-7; Galway 2-14, Dublin 1-10.*

♦ *Padraic Maher, Michael Cahill, Brendan Maher, Seamus Hennessy, Noel McGrath, Patrick Maher and Michael Heffernan all completed the full set of Minor, U-21 and Senior All Ireland medals.*

2011 Final
Galway complete under age double to match achievements of 1983 and 2005.
10/9/2011 at Semple Stadium, Thurles.
Galway 3-14. Dublin 1-10.

Eight of Galway's starting 15 returned to the scene of their hammering in the previous year's final. A very disappointing attendance of 5,352 saw Galway take an early lead with points by James Regan and Tadhg Haran. Dublin scored their only goal of the game in the 3rd minute, when Tomas Connolly netted. Galway's first goal came from a Haran penalty in the 9th minute. Declan Connolly and Niall Donoghue were rock solid in the Galway full back line, as Dublin found it difficult to get scoring opportunities. The Galway attack hadn't the same problem as James Regan set up Davy Glennon for their second goal after 27 minutes. Regan then quickly followed up with another goal featuring a great catch and a wonderful finish. Galway led by 3-6 to 1-4 at the interval.

Dublin made two changes at the break with Fionan Clabby and Sean McGrath replacing Mark Schutte and Darren Kelly. Glennon pointed for the first score of the second half. This left nine points between the sides. Dublin had to wait 17 minutes before another substitute Robert Mahon hit their first score from play in the second half. Try as they did, Dublin could not get back into the game. Galway were firmly on top. The Westerners closed out the game with two David Burke frees. Their victory was assured long before the referee blew the final whistle.

Davy Glennon just about deserved the man of the match award. There were also tremendous performances from Niall Donoghue, Ger O'Halloran, Jason Grealish, David and Niall Burke, Rory Foy, Johnnie Coen, Tadhg Haran, James Regan and team captain Barry Daly.

Senior regular Liam Rushe was Dublin's best player. The only others who performed to the required standard were Conor Gough, Tomas Connolly, Niall McMorrow and the very effective substitute Robert Mahon.

The referee was Tony Carroll of Offaly.

Galway scorers; Tadhg Haran 1-3 (1-0pen.), Davy Glennon 1-2, James Regan 1-2, David Burke 0-3 (2fs), Niall Burke 0-3 (2fs), Conor Cooney 0-1.

Dublin scorers; Tomas Connolly 1-2 (0-2fs), Kevin O'Loughlin 0-5 (fs), Robert Mahon 0-2, Niall McMorrow 0-1.

Galway team. Jamie Ryan (Craughwell), Declan Connolly (Killimordaly), Niall Donoghue (Kilbeacanty), Ger O'Halloran (Craughwell), Jason Grealish (Gort), Paul Gordon (Tynagh-Abbey-Duniry), Rory Foy (Ballinderreen), Johnny Coen (Loughrea), David Burke (St. Thomas), Barry Daly (Clarinbridge), Capt., Niall Burke (Oranmore-Maree), Tadhg Haran (Liam

Galway - All Ireland U21 Champions 2011
Back: Davy Glennon, Donal Cooney, James Regan, Rory Foy, Niall Donoghue, Niall Burke, Declan Connolly, Paul Gordan, Gerry O'Halloran, John Brehony, Ronan Burke
Front: Bernard Burke, Eoin Fahy, Tadhg Haran, Jason Grealish, Barry Daly (Capt.), Jamie Ryan, Conor Cooney, Davy Burke, Johnny Coen, Stephen Page.

Dublin - All Ireland U21 Finalists 2011

Back: Stephen O'Connor, Darren Kelly, Conor Murphy, Odhran Ó Maoileidigh, Martin Ouilty, Mark Schutte, Robbie Mahon, Dean Curran, Sean McGrath, Eamon Dillon, Daire Plunkett, Gerard McManus, Damian Gallagher.

Front: Kevin O'Loughlin, Jack Doughan, Tomas Connolly, Kevin Fitzgerald, Fionnan Clabby, Niall McMorrow, Bill O'Carroll, Danny Sutcliffe, Liam Rushe (Capt.), Conor Gough, Ben Quinn.

Mellowes), James Regan(St. Thomas), Conor Cooney (St. Thomas), Davy Glennon (Mullagh).

Subs. Ronan Burke (Turloughmore) for Gordon. Bernard Burke (St. Thomas) for Haran. Donal Fox (Carnmore) for Cooney. Niall Quinn (Sarsfields) for N.Burke. Donal Cooney (St. Thomas) for D.Burke. Fergal Flannery (Padraig Pearses), Eoin Fahy (Killimor), Colm Flynn (Tommie Larkins), John Brehony (Tynagh-Abbey-Duniry).

Dublin team. Ger McManus (St.Jude's), Bill O'Carroll (Kilmacud Crokes), Darren Kelly (Craobh Chiarain), Jack Doughan (Kilmacud Crokes), Dean Curran (Ballyboden St. Enda's), Liam Rushe (St.Patrick's, Palmerstown), Capt., Martin Quilty (Na Fianna), Conor Gough (Cuala), Danny Sutcliffe (St.Jude's), Daire Plunkett (St.Brigid's), Mark Schutte (Cuala), Tomas Connolly (St.Vincent's), Kevin O'Loughlin (Kilmacud Crokes), Niall McMorrow (Ballyboden St.Enda's), Eamon Dillon (Naomh Fionnbara).

Barry Daly, Galway Captain 2011

Subs. Fionnan Clabby (Ballinteer St. John's) for Kelly. Sean McGrath (Kilmacud Crokes) for Schutte. Robert Mahon (Craobh Chiarain) for O'Loughlin. Ben Quinn (Good Counsel) for Connolly.Damian Gallagher (St. Patrick's Palmerstown), Stephen O'Connor (Ballyboden St. Enda's), Conor Murphy (Crumlin), Odhran O Maoleidigh (Na Fianna), Ciaran Brennan (Faughs).

2011

LEINSTER FINAL: Dublin 1-18, Wexford 0-11
MUNSTER FINAL: Limerick 4-20, Cork 1-27 (after e.t.)
ULSTER FINAL: Antrim 0-15, Armagh 2-7
ALL IRELAND SEMI FINALS: Galway 0-22, Limerick 2-14; Dublin 3-23, Antrim 0-6.

2012 Final
Clare dominate after the interval to win their second U-21 title.
15/9/2012 at Semple Stadium, Thurles.
Clare 2-17. Kilkenny 2-11.

Although Kilkenny captain Kevin Kelly pointed from play after only 15 seconds, Clare retaliated in whirlwind fashion before an attendance of 9,250. The Banner's Cathal McInerney immediately equalised. After only 7 minutes, Clare led by 1-5 to 0-2. Cathal O'Connell scored their opening goal. In the last 20 minutes of the first half, Clare scored just a single point, though driving 10 wides. Kilkenny scored 2-3 in the same period. The two Kilkenny goals came from a John Power penalty and a ground stroke from Ger Aylward. Thus Kilkenny led by 2-7 to 1-7 at the interval.

Kilkenny had the wind in the second half but Clare upped their performance hugely. The Clare forwards began to take over and attacked Kilkenny straight down the middle with great success. Kilkenny were a physically bigger team but Clare had the more skilful and wristy hurlers. The Banner men had four early second half points to wipe out the Leinster champions half time lead. Then in the 44th minute came the game changer, as Clare captain Conor McGrath goaled. McGrath, Shane Golden and Cathal O'Connell all pointed between the 45th and 48th minutes with a single reply for Kilkenny from Kevin Kelly. The Noresiders scored just one point from play in the second half. Clare were dominant during the last quarter and O'Connell, McInerney and Tony Kelly all pointed before the final whistle.

All of the Clare team had their moments, but particularly outstanding were Paul Flanagan, David McInerney, Conor Ryan, Pat O'Connor, Seadna Morey with his amazing pace, and the full forward line of Cathal McInerney, Conor McGrath and Cathal O'Connell, who were responsible for 2-11. Best for Kilkenny were Luke Harney, Richie Doyle, Kevin Kelly, Walter Walsh, John Power and Ger Aylward.

The referee was Diarmuid Kirwan of Cork.

Clare scorers; Cathal O'Connell1-6 (0-4fs), Conor McGrath 1-1, Cathal McInerney 0-4, Seadna Morey 0-1, Pat O'Connor 0-1, Colm Galvin 0-1, Shane Golden 0-1, Aaron Cunningham 0-1, Tony Kelly 0-1 (f).

Kilkenny scorers; Kevin Kelly 0-6 (4fs), Ger Aylward 1-1, John Power 1-0 (pen), Walter Walsh 0-2, Geoff Brennan 0-1, Padraig Walsh 0-1.

Clare team. Ronan Taaffe (Tubber), Paul Flanagan (Ballyea), David McInerney (Tulla), Killian Ryan (Ruan), Seadna Morey (Sixmilebridge), Conor Ryan (Cratloe), Pat O'Connor (Tubber), Colm Galvin (Clonlara), Shane Golden (Sixmilebridge), Aaron Cunningham (Wolfe Tones), Padraic Collins (Cratloe), Tony Kelly (Ballyea), Cathal McInerney (Cratloe), Conor McGrath (Cratloe),Capt., Cathal O'Connell (Clonlara).
Subs. Peter Duggan (Clooney-Quin) for Cunningham. Niall Arthur (Inagh/Kilnamona) for

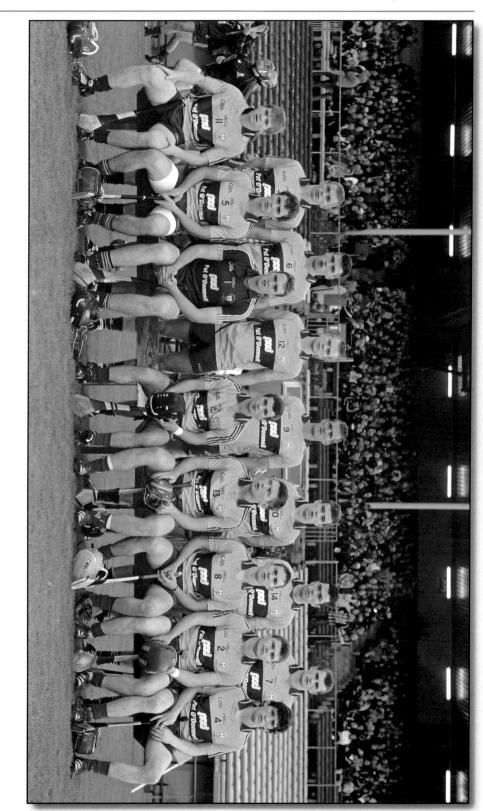

Clare - All Ireland U21 Champions 2012

Back :David McInerney, Conor Ryan, Tony Kelly, Shane Golden, Aaron Cunningham, Conor McGrath, Pat O'Connor.
Front: Padraic Collins, Seadna Morey, Ronan Taaffe, Cathal O'Connell, Cathal McInerney, Colm Galvin, Paul Flanagan, Killian Ryan.

Photo SPORTSFILE

Kilkenny - All Ireland U21 Finalists 2012

Back: James Cassin, Luke Harney, Richie Doyle, Cillian Buckley, Owen McGrath, Richie Reid, Ian Duggan, Cathal Kenny, Pat Carroll, Ger Aylward, Dylan Walsh, Willie Phelan, Martin Gaffney, Walter WalshFront: James Gannon, Michael Brennan, Padraig Walsh, John Power, Geoff Brennan, Kevin Kelly, Brian Kennedy, Jason Corcoran, Paul Buggy, Ollie Walsh, Joe Lyng. *Photo Eoin Hennessy*

Captains, Kevin Kelly (Kilkenny) and Conor McGrath (Clare), with referee Diarmuid Kirwan (Cork) before the 2012 Final. Photo SPORTSFILE

Collins. Niall Woods (Newmarket), David O'Halloran (Eire Og,Ennis), Stephen O'Halloran (Clarecastle), Cillian Fennessy (Clonlara), Jarlath Colleran (St. Joseph's, Doora-Barefield), Enda Boyce (Cratloe), Pa Sheehan (Sixmilebridge).

Kilkenny team. Dylan Walsh (Thomastown), Jason Corcoran (John Lockes), Willie Phelan (Dunamaggin), Brian Kennedy (St. Lachtain's), Joe Lyng (Rower/Inistioge), Richie Doyle (Barrow Rangers), Luke Harney (Kilmacow), Geoff Brennan (St. Patrick's), Cillian Buckley (Dicksboro), Ollie Walsh (Dicksboro), John Power (Carrickshock), Kevin Kelly (St.Patrick's), Capt., Walter Walsh (Tullogher-Rosbercon), Padraig Walsh (Tullaroan), Ger Aylward (Glenmore).
Subs. Martin Gaffney (Dicksboro) for O.Walsh. Cathal Kenny (Barrow Rangers) for P.Walsh. Richie Reid (Ballyhale), Owen McGrath (John Lockes), Ian Duggan (Mullinavat), Paul Buggy (Tullaroan), James Cassin (Rower/Inistioge), Michael Brennan (St. Patrick's), James Gannon (St Patrick's).

2012
LEINSTER FINAL: *Kilkenny 4-24, Laois 1-13*
MUNSTER FINAL: *Clare 1-16, Tipperary 1-14*
ULSTER FINAL: *Antrim 2-20, Derry 1-12*
ALL IRELAND SEMI FINALS: *Kilkenny 4-16, Galway 2-15; Clare 4-24, Antrim 0-8.*

◆ *Conor McGrath and Pat O'Connor were each collecting their second All-Ireland U-21 medal.*

2013 FINAL
CLARE EASILY WIN THIRD TITLE IN FIVE YEARS.
14/9/2013 AT SEMPLE STADIUM, THURLES.
Clare 2-28. Antrim 0-12.

Clare, who had retained the Munster title for the first time, met Antrim, who had previously lost 32 All-Ireland semi finals, in Semple Stadium, before an attendance of 11,148. It was the first appearance by an Ulster side in an All-Ireland U-21 hurling final. Clare had four of the starting side that had played in the previous Sunday's All-Ireland senior final.

Antrim used Eoghan Campbell as a sweeper but to no great effect. Cathal O'Connell pointed seven frees for Clare in the first half. Davy O'Halloran scored Clare's first goal after 23 minutes. Shane O'Donnell scored their second after 27 minutes. Antrim finished the first half with a lovely point from a sideline cut by Ciaran Clarke. Clare led by 2-16 to 0-4 at the interval.

Seven minutes after the resumption, Clare replaced all four of their senior players. They had then extended their lead by four points. In the remaining 23 minutes, both sides scored almost the same number of points, eight for Clare and seven for Antrim. The closest that Antrim came to scoring a goal was an effort from Clarke that was saved by Clare goalkeeper Ronan Taaffe.

Clare were the hottest of favourites before the final and easily justified that rating. There was never any prospect during the game of Antrim repeating their shock semi final heroics. Clare were never troubled and all players used contributed to their victory. Davy O'Halloran, who scored 1-4 from play, was selected as man-of-the-match. Their senior players, David McInerney, Tony Kelly, Colm Galvin and Podge Collins all contributed to their victory. Cathal "Tots" O'Connell was unerring from frees and play.

It was a great achievement on Antrim's part to reach the final. The occasion proved too much for them as they could not reproduce their performance against Wexford in the semi final. Their best players in the final were goalkeeper Ger Dixon, Paddy McNaughton, Chris McGuinness, Jackson McGreevy, Stephen McAfee and Ciaran Clarke.

Clare scorers; Cathal O'Connell 0-11 (9fs), Davy O'Halloran 1-4, Colm Galvin 0-3, Tony Kelly 0-3, Shane O'Donnell 1-0, Seadna Morey 0-2, Cathal Malone 0-2, Jarlath Colleran 0-1, Enda Boyce 0-1, Alan O'Neill 0-1.

Antrim scorers; Ciaran Clarke 0-7 (5fs &1lb), Chris McGuinness 0-1, Jackson McGreevy 0-1, Stephen McAfee 0-1, Conor McCann 0-1, Michael Bradley 0-1.

The referee was Colm Lyons of Cork.

Clare team. Ronan Taaffe (Tubber), Paul Flanagan (Ballyea), Capt., David McInerney (Tulla), Jack Browne (Ballyea), Seadna Morey (Sixmilebridge), Alan O'Neill (St.Joseph's,

Clare - All Ireland U21 Champions 2013

Back: Enda Boyce, Darragh Corry, Jarlath Colleran, Daire Keane, Stephen O'Halloran, Alan O'Neill, Cathal Malone, Peter Duggan, Shane O'Donnell,
Paul Flanagan, captain, Kevin Lynch, John Guilfoyle, Conor Cleary, Bobby Duggan, Keith Hogan, Noel Purcell, Paudge Collins.
Front: Pa Sheehan, Mikey O'Neill, Tony Kelly, Ronan Taaffe, Seadna Morey, David McInerney, Jack Browne, Colm Galvin, Davy O'Halloran,
Cathal O'Connell, Aaron Cunningham, Niall Arthur, Gearoid O'Connell, Eibhear Quilligan, Jamie Shanahan.

Antrim - All Ireland U21 Finalists 2013

Back: David Kearney, Paddy McNaughton, Ciarán Clarke, Stephen Beaty, Darragh McGuinness, Stephen McAfee, Conor McCann, Conal Morgan, Tomás O'Ciarán, Ciarán Johnston, Conor McAlister, Micheál Bradley.

Front: Micheál Dudley, Tiernan Coyle, Matthew Donnelly, Shane Dooey, Niall McKenna, Jackson McGreavey (capt), Ger Dixon, Daniel McKernan, Christoher McGuinness, Eoghan Campbell.   Photo/John McIlwaine

Doora-Barefield), Stephen O'Halloran (Clarecastle), Colm Galvin (Clonlara), Tony Kelly (Ballyea), Peter Duggan (Clooney Quin), Podge Collins (Cratloe), Cathal Malone (Ennistymon), Cathal O'Connell (Clonlara), Shane O'Donnell (Eire Og), Davy O'Halloran (Eire Og).
Subs. Jarlath Colleran (St.Joseph's, Doora-Barefield) for McInerney. Kevin Lynch (Sixmilebridge) for Kelly. Niall Arthur (Inagh/Kilnamona) for Collins. Enda Boyce (Cratloe) for Galvin. Aaron Cunningham (Wolfe Tones) for O'Donnell. Daire Keane (Kilmaley), Mikey O'Neill (Kilmaley), Bobby Duggan (Clarecastle), Gearoid Ryan (Clarecastle), Jamie Shanahan (Sixmilebridge), Pa Sheehan (Sixmilebridge), Noel Purcell (Sixmilebridge), Oisin Hickey (Meelick).

Liam O'Neill, Uachtarán CLG, presents the Cross of Cashel trophy to Clare Captain, Paul Flanagan. Photo John McIlwaine

Antrim team. Ger Dixon (Dunloy), Conal Morgan (St. John's), Matthew Donnelly (Ballycastle), Tiernan Coyle (Loughiel), Tomas O Ciarain (St.Gall's), Paddy McNaughton (Cushendall), Chris McGuinness (O'Donovan Rossa), Jackson McGreevy (St.John's), Capt.,Eoghan Campbell (Cushendall), Shane Dooey (Dunloy), Stephen McAfee (Ballycastle), Niall McKenna (Patrick Sarsfields), Daniel McKernan (Patrick Sarsfields), Conor McCann (Creggan Kickhams), Ciaran Clarke (Ballycastle).
Subs. David Kearney (Cushendall) for O Ciarain. Michael Bradley for Donnelly. Stephen Beattie for Dooey. M.Dudley for McKernan. D. McGuinness for McCann. Ciaran Johnson (St.John's), C. McAllister.

2013

LEINSTER FINAL: Wexford 1-21, Kilkenny 0-21 (a.e.t)
MUNSTER FINAL: Clare 1-17, Tipperary 2-10
ULSTER FINAL: Antrim 7-17, Down 1-5
ALL IRELAND SEMI FINALS: Clare 1-16, Galway 0-7; Antrim 2-15, Wexford 1-16.

2014 FINAL
CLARE WIN THIRD SUCCESSIVE TITLE.
13/9/2014 AT SEMPLE STADIUM, THURLES.
Clare 2-20. Wexford 3-11.

This U-21 final was yet another marvellous occasion for the attendance of 15,081 who enjoyed fantastic colour and atmosphere and a truly absorbing battle. The game ebbed and flowed. Wexford threw everything at the defending champions from the throw-in. Clare kept finding ways of counteracting their efforts.

Early points for Clare from Tony Kelly and Aaron Cunningham were answered by a brace of points from frees by Jack Guiney for Wexford. The first decisive turning point of the final arrived in the 13th minute. A goal-bound shot by Wexford's Kevin Foley hit the crossbar and rebounded back into play. From the resulting goalmouth scramble, Colm Galvin emerged with the ball, powered forward and passed to Shane O'Donnell, whose searing run ended with David Reidy flicking to the net. Tony Kelly then ruthlessly moved through the gears with four opportunist points. At the interval Clare had 1-8 on the board, all scored from play, with Kelly responsible for five of those points. Wexford were on 0-6, with four points from frees by Jack Guiney and two from play by Gary Moore.

Wexford made their intentions extremely clear at the start of the second half as Conor McDonald fielded and fired over a point. A minute later, a pointed free from Jack Guiney reduced the arrears to a goal as the large contingent of Wexford supporters made their presence felt. Bobby Duggan fed Galvin for a Clare point. Duggan followed up with a pointed free. Aaron Cunningham scored Clare's second goal in the 38th minute to leave the score at 2-11 to 0-9. Galvin followed with another point. In the 44th minute, Wexford substitute David Dunne broke through and goaled to add to a pointed free from Guiney. Clare then rattled off four unanswered points to move nine clear. Dunne and then McDonald got further goals for Wexford. The scoreboard now read: Clare 2-17 Wexford 3-11, following another Guiney free for the Model county. The exchanges were ferocious, the supporters were roaring their sides on and the decibels reached a crescendo.

During the anxious final few minutes, Wexford substitute Peter Sutton saw a goal effort whiz past the post and a McDonald effort was saved by the Clare goalkeeper. Clare were not to be denied. Their shining stars Tony Kelly and Colm Galvin registered the final three points of the final to seal victory for the Banner county..

Kelly with seven points and Galvin with four lit up Semple Stadium with the majesty of their displays. Beside Galvin at midfield, Eoin Enright covered every blade of grass in a tireless display. The youngest member of the Clare team Bobby Duggan did not let the pressure of a very intense second half affect him. Full-back Jack Browne kept Wexford's dangerman Conor McDonald largely in check , until McDonald moved further out the field. Gearoid O'Connell hurled brilliantly from wing back, less than a fortnight after his father lost his life in a tragic farm accident. Aaron Cunningham chipped in with his seventh goal of the campaign. Jamie Shanahan epitomised Clare's work ethic.

Wexford contributed hugely to an intense battle. Liam Ryan, Aidan Nolan, Gary Moore, Conor McDonald and substitute David Dunne were superb. They were unfortunate in that they came up against an outstanding team. Wexford did not let a nine point deficit as the final entered the last twenty minutes inhibit them and they battled to the end.

Clare - All Ireland U21 Champions 2014

Back: Shane Gleeson, Brian Carey, Micheal Ryan, Jamie Shanahan, Bobby Duggan, Conor Cleary, Keith Hogan, Peter Duggan , Alan O'Neill, Seadna Morey, Jack Browne, Niall Deasy, Shane McGrath.

Front: Shane O'Brien, Aidan McGuane, Gearoid O'Connell, Tony Kelly, Aaron Cunningham, Shane O'Donnell, David Reidy, Colm Galvin, Eoin Enright, Jarlath Colleran, Eibhear Quilligan, Cathal O'Connell, David Conroy.

Photo: SPORTSFILE

Wexford - All Ireland U21 Finalists 2014

Back: Garrett Foley, Rúairí Tubrid, Jim White, Pádraig Foley, Jack O'Connor, Conor McDonald, Tony French, Oliver O'Leary, Aidan Nolan, James Cash, David Dunne, Peter Sutton, Conor O'Leary, Andrew Kenny.

Front: Kevin Foley, Conor Devitt, Jack Guiney, Gary Moore, Shane O'Gorman (capt.), Eoin Conroy, Rhys Clarke, Luke White, Gavin Bailey, Liam Ryan.

Photo SPORTSFILE

The referee was Cathal McAllister of Cork.

Clare scorers; Tony Kelly 0-7, Aaron Cunningham 1-2, Colm Galvin 0-4, Bobby Duggan 0-4 (3fs), David Reidy 1-1, Gearoid O'Connell 0-1, Jamie Shanahan 0-1.

Wexford scorers; Jack Guiney 0-7 (6fs & 1 65), David Dunne 2-0, Conor McDonald 1-1, Gary Moore 0-2, Conor Devitt 0-1.

Clare team. Keith Hogan (Clooney-Quin), Jarlath Colleran (St. Joseph's Doora/Barefield), Jack Browne (Ballyea), Seadna Morey (Sixmilebridge), Gearoid O'Connell (Ballyea), Conor Cleary (Kilmaley), Jamie Shanahan (Sixmilebridge), Colm Galvin (Clonlara), Eoin Enright (Kilmaley), Peter Duggan (Clooney-Quin), Tony Kelly (Ballyea), Capt., Bobby Duggan (Clarecastle), Shane O'Donnell (Eire Og), Aaron Cunningham (Wolfe Tones), David Reidy (Eire Og).
Subs. Cathal O'Connell (Clonlara) for O'Connell. Alan O'Neill (St.Joseph's Doora/Barefield) for O'Donnell. Shane

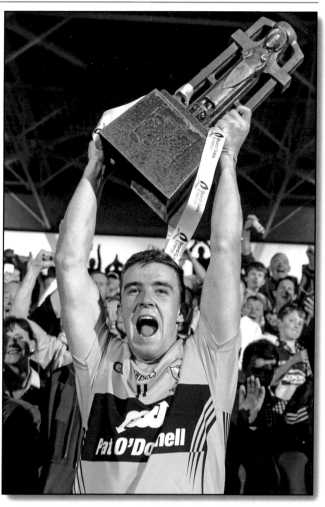

Tony Kelly, Clare Captain 2014
Photo SPORTSFILE

O'Brien (Clonlara) for Colleran. Eibhear Quilligan (Feakle), Shane Gleeson (Cratloe), Shane McGrath (Feakle), David Conroy (St. Joseph's Doora/Barefield), Niall Deasy (Ballyea), Aidan McGuane (Kilmaley), Brian Carey (Sixmilebridge).

Wexford team. Oliver O'Leary (Buffers Alley), Andrew Kenny (Buffers Alley), Liam Ryan (Rapparees), Jim White (Oylegate-Glenbrien), Shane O'Gorman (Adamstown), Capt., Eoin Conroy (Naomh Eoin), Jack O'Connor (St. Martin's), Aidan Nolan (Half Way House Bunclody), Conor Devitt (Ballyfad), Jack Guiney (Rathnure), Gary Moore (Glynn-Barntown), Padraig Foley (Crossabeg-Ballymurn), Kevin Foley (Rapparees), Conor McDonald (Naomh Eanna), Rhys Clarke (Faythe Harriers).
Subs. David Dunne (Davidstown-Courtnacuddy) for O'Connor. James Cash (Shelmaliers) for White. Conor O'Leary (Oulart-the-Ballagh) for Moore. Peter Sutton (Oulart-the-Ballagh) for Cash. Luke White (St. Martin's), Garrett Foley (Fethard), Ruairi Tubrid (Fethard), Gavin Bailey (Ferns St. Aidan's), Tony French (Adamstown).

Clare goalkeeper Keith Hogan and full back Jack Browne, defend a first half Wexford free.
Bord Gais Energy GAA Hurling Under 21 All-Ireland 'A' Championship Final 2014,
Clare v Wexford. Semple Stadium, Thurles, Co. Tipperary.
Photo Ray McManus SPORTSFILE

2014

LEINSTER FINAL: *Wexford 1-20, Dublin 0-18*
MUNSTER FINAL: *Clare 1-28, Cork 1-13*
ULSTER FINAL: *Antrim 7-17, Down 1-5*
ALL IRELAND SEMI FINALS: *Wexford 1-21, Galway 1-19;   Clare 4-28, Antrim 1-10.*

♦ *Seven of the Clare Panel won 3 All-Ireland U-21 medals in-a-row; Tony Kelly, Seadna Morey, Colm Galvin, Aaron Cunningham, Cathal O'Connell, Peter Duggan and Jarlath Colleran.*

CHAPTER 7
ALL IRELAND U21
HURLING FINAL
RECORDS ETC.

REFEREES OF ALL-IRELAND U-21 HURLING FINALS

1964 Aubrey Higgins (Galway)	1989 Paschal Long
1965 Jimmy Duggan (Galway)	1990 Pat Delaney (Laois)
1966 Donie Nealon (Tipperary)	1991 Terence Murray (Limerick)
1966 Gerry FitGerald (Limerick) Replay	1992 Willie Barrett (Tipperary)
1966 Gerry Fitzgerald 2nd Replay	1992 Willie Barrett Replay
1967 Aubrey Higgins	1993 Johnny McDonnell (Tipperary)
1968 Seamus Power (Waterford)	1993 Johnny McDonnell Replay
1969 Paddy Johnson (Kilkenny)	1994 Pat Horan (Offaly)
1970 Jim Dunphy (Waterford)	1995 Terence Murray
1970 Jim Dunphy Replay	1996 Pat O'Connor (Limerick)
1971 Paddy Buggy (Kilkenny)	1997 Pat Horan
1972 Sean O'Grady (Limerick)	1998 Dickie Murphy (Wexford)
1973 John Moloney (Tipperary)	1999 Ger Harrington (Cork)
1974 Sean O'Grady	2000 Pat Horan
1975 Sean O'Meara (Tipperary)	2001 Aodhan MacSuibhne (Dublin)
1976 Gerry Kirwan (Offaly)	2002 Dickie Murphy
1977 Jimmy Rankins (Laois)	2003 Michael Wadding (Waterford)
1978 Noel O'Donoghue (Dublin)	2004 Barry Kelly (Westmeath)
1978 Noel O'Donoghue Replay	2005 John Sexton (Limerick)
1979 Noel Dalton (Waterford)	2006 Michael Haverty (Galway)
1980 John Denton (Wexford)	2006 Brian Gavin (Offaly) Replay
1981 Neilly Duggan (Limerick)	2007 Johnny Ryan (Tipperary)
1982 Gerry Kirwan	2008 James Owens (Wexford)
1983 Michael Kelleher (Kildare)	2009 Cathal McAllister (Cork)
1984 Kevin Walsh (Limerick)	2010 James McGrath (Westmeath)
1985 John Denton	2011 Tony Carroll (Offaly)
1986 Gerry Long (Tipperary)	2012 Diarmuid Kirwan (Cork)
1987 Paschal Long (Kilkenny)	2013 Colm Lyons (Cork)
1988 John Moore (Waterford)	2014 Cathal McAllister (Cork)

VENUES FOR ALL-IRELAND U-21 HURLING FINALS

1964 Nowlan Park, Kilkenny		
1965 Nowlan Park		
1966 Nowlan Park		
1966 Gaelic Grounds, Limerick	Replay	
1966 Croke Park, Dublin	2nd Replay	
1967 Croke Park		
1968 Walsh Park, Waterford		
1969 Walsh Park		
1970 Croke Park		
1970 Croke Park	Replay	
1971 Croke Park		
1972 Gaelic Grounds		
1973 Davin Park, Carrick-on-Suir		
1974 Semple Stadium, Thurles		
1975 Fraher Park, Dungarvan		
1976 Walsh Park		
1977 Semple Stadium		
1978 Gaelic Grounds		
1978 Gaelic Grounds	Replay	
1979 O'Moore Park, Portlaoise		
1980 Walsh Park		
1981 Walsh Park		
1982 St Brendan's Park, Birr		
1983 O'Connor Park, Tullamore		
1984 Walsh Park		
1985 Walsh Park		
1986 Semple Stadium		
1987 Cusack Park, Ennis		
1988 St Brendan's Park		

1989 O'Moore Park	
1990 O'Moore Park	
1991 Gaelic Grounds	
1992 Nowlan Park	
1992 Nowlan Park	Replay
1993 O'Connor Park	
1993 O'Connor Park	Replay
1994 O'Connor Park	
1995 Semple Stadium	
1996 Semple Stadium	
1997 Semple Stadium	
1998 Semple Stadium	
1999 O'Connor Park	
2000 Semple Stadium	
2001 Semple Stadium	
2002 Semple Stadium	
2003 Semple Stadium	
2004 Nowlan Park	
2005 Gaelic Grounds	
2006 Croke Park	
2006 Semple Stadium	Replay
2007 Croke Park	
2008 Croke Park	
2009 Croke Park	
2010 Semple Stadium	
2011 Semple Stadium	
2012 Semple Stadium	
2013 Semple Stadium	
2014 Semple Stadium	

TOP SCORERS IN ALL-IRELAND

1964 Michael "Babs" Keating (Tipperary) 2-3 (0-1f)

1965 Tony Doran (Wexford) 1-2; Con Dowdall (Wexford) 1-2 (fs)

1966 (Draw) Seanie Barry (Cork) 2-8 (1-1fs)

1966 (1st Replay) Andrew Flynn (Cork) 3-0

1966 (2nd Replay) Seamus Barron (Wexford) 2-4 (1-4fs)

1967 Pat O'Connor (Tipperary) 1-3

1968 Bernard Meade (Cork) 1-12 (0-9fs)

1969 Ray Cummins (Cork) 2-4

1970 (Draw) Mick Butler (Wexford) 1-10 (0-9fs)

1970 (Replay) Connie Kelly (Cork) 2-7 (1-2fs)

1971 John Rothwell (Cork) 4-0

1972 Gerry Holland (Galway) 1-4 (0-1f)

1973 John Allen (Wexford) 2-0

1974 Billy Fitzpatrick (Kilkenny) 1-2; Tom Casey (Waterford) 1-2 (0-1f)

1975 John Fenton (Cork) 0-9 (8fs)

1976 Pat Horgan (Cork) 1-5 (0-4fs)

1977 Brendan Fennelly (Kilkenny) 1-2; Brian Waldron (Kilkenny) 0-5 (fs)

1978 (Draw) Mattie Conneely (Galway) 2-2; Seamus Bourke (Tipperary) 2-2 (1-0f)

1978 (Replay) Gerry Kennedy (Galway) 0-8 (fs)

1979 Michael Doyle (Tipperary) 1-2; John Ryan (Galway) 1-2

1980 Michael Murphy (Tipperary) 1-1 (1-0f); Willie Purcell (Kilkenny); 0-4 Michael Nash (Kilkenny) 0-4 (1f)

1981 Billy Walton (Kilkenny) 1-7 (1-5fs)

1982 Michael Haverty (Galway) 0-5 (3fs)

1983 Arthur Browne (Tipperary) 1-1

1984 Ray Heffernan (Kilkenny) 1-4 (1-0pen, 0-3fs)

1985 Michael Scully (Tipperary) 0-5 (4fs)

1986 Joe Cooney (Galway) 0-4 (2fs); Paul Carton (Wexford) 1-1

1987 Leo O'Connor (Limerick) 2-5 (0-5fs)

1988 Dan O'Connell (Cork) 2-1

1989 Dan Quirke (Tipperary) 3-2

U-21 HURLING FINALS

1990 Liam Sheedy (Tipperary) 0-7 (5fs)

1991 Johnny Dooley (Offaly) 1-5 (1-0pen, 0-4fs)

1992 (Draw) Sean Daly (Waterford) 3-0

1992 (Replay) Paul Flynn (Waterford) 0-5

1993 (Draw) Dermot Lawlor (Kilkenny) 1-5 (0-4fs)

1993 (Replay) Francis Forde (Galway) 1-3 (0-1 lb); Maurice Headd (Galway) 1-3 (0-2fs)

1994 PJ Delaney (Kilkenny) 1-3 (0-3fs)

1995 Tommy Dunne (Tipperary) 0-7 (4fs, 1 65); Damien Cleere (Kilkenny) 0-7 (4fs)

1996 Kevin Broderick (Galway) 1-2 Paul Codd; (Wexford) 0-5 (2fs, 2 65s)

1997 Eugene Cloonan (Galway) 0-7 (3fs, 2 65s)

1998 Eugene Cloonan (Galway) 1-5 (1-3fs)

1999 Eugene Cloonan (Galway) 0-8 (7fs); Henry Shefflin (Kilkenny) 0-8 (fs)

2000 Mark Keane (Limerick) 1-8 (0-7fs)

2001 Mark Keane (Limerick) 0-7 (5fs, 1 65)

2002 Mark Keane (Limerick) 1-6 (0-5fs)

2003 Conor Phelan (Kilkenny) 1-4; Ger Farragher (Galway) 0-7 (fs)

2004 Richie Power (Kilkenny) 0-7 (4fs 1 65)

2005 Eoin Larkin (Kilkenny) 1-9 (0-8fs)

2006 (Draw) Darragh Egan (Tipperary) 1-5 (1-3fs)

2006 (Replay) Richie Power (Kilkenny) 0-6 (5fs)

2007 Alan McCrabbe (Dublin) 0-9 (7fs)

2008 Matthew Ruth (Kilkenny) 2-2; Pa Bourke (Tipperary) 0-8 (fs)

2009 Colin Ryan (Clare) 0-9 (8fs 1 '65)

2010 Sean Carey (Tipperary) 1-3; Brian O'Meara (Tipperary); 1-3 John O'Dwyer (Tipperary) 1-3; Noel McGrath (Tipperary) 1-3 (1-0f)

2011 Tadhg Haran (Galway) 1-3 (1-0 pen)

2012 Cathal O'Connell (Clare) 1-6 (0-4fs)

2013 Cathal O'Connell (Clare) 0-11 (9fs)

2014 Tony Kelly (Clare) 0-7; Jack Guiney (Wexford) 0-7 (6f, 1 '65)

WINNING CAPTAINS OF ALL-IRELAND U-21H TEAMS

1964 Francis Loughnane(Tipperary & Roscrea)

1965 Willie O'Neill (Wexford & Kilmore)

1966 Gerald McCarthy (Cork & St Finbarr's)

1967 PJ Ryan (Tipperary & Carrick Davins)

1968 Pat Hegarty (Cork & Youghal)

1969 Michael McCarthy (Cork & Na Piarsaigh)

1970 Teddy O'Brien (Cork & Glen Rovers)

1971 Pat McDonnell (Cork & UCC)

1972 Iggy Clarke (Galway & Mullagh)

1973 Martin O'Doherty (Cork & GlenRovers)

1974 Ger Fennelly (Kilkenny & Ballyhale Shamrocks)

1975 Kevin Fennelly (Kilkenny & Ballyhale Shamrocks)

1976 Tadhg Murphy (Cork & Sarsfields)

1977 Michael Lyng (Kilkenny & Rower/Inistioge)

1978 Bernie Forde (Galway & Ardrahan)

1979 Michael Doyle (Tipperary & Holycross/Ballycahill)

1980 Philip Kennedy (Tipperary & Nenagh Eire Og)

1981 Philip Kennedy (Tipperary & Nenagh Eire Og)

1982 Martin McCarthy (Cork & Na Piarsaigh)

1983 Peter Casserley (Galway & Beagh)

1984 Seamus Delahunty (Kilkenny & Mooncoin)

1985 Michael Scully (Tipperary & Roscrea)

1986 Anthony Cunningham (Galway & St Thomas)

1987 Gus Ryan (Limerick & Claughaun)

1988 Christy Connery (Cork & Na Piarsaigh)

1989 Declan Ryan (Tipperary & Clonoulty/Rossmore)

1990 Jamesie Brennan (Kilkenny & Erin's Own)

1991 Brian Feeney (Galway & Athenry)

1992 Tony Browne (Waterford & Mount Sion)

1993 Liam Burke (Galway & Kilconieran0

1994 Philly Larkin (Kilkenny & James Stephens)

1995 Brian Horgan (Tipperary & Knockavilla Kickhams)

1996 Peter Huban (Galway & Athenry)

1997 Dan Murphy (Cork & Ballincollig)

1998 Dan Murphy (Cork & Ballincollig)

1999 Noel Hickey (Kilkenny & Dunamaggin)

2000 Donnacha Sheehan (Limerick & Adare)

2001 Timmy Houlihan (Limerick & Adare)

2002 Peter Lawlor (Limerick & Croom)

2003 Jackie Tyrrell (Kilkenny & James Stephens)

2004 James Fitzpatrick (Kilkenny & Ballyhale Shamrocks)

2005 Kenneth Burke (Galway & St Thomas)

2006 Michael Fennelly (Kilkenny & Ballyhale Shamrocks)

2007 Kevin Hynes (Galway & Sarsfields)

2008 James Dowling (Kilkenny & St Martin's)

2009 Ciaran O'Doherty (Clare & Crusheen)

2010 Padraic Maher (Tipperary & Thurles Sarsfields)

2011 Barry Daly (Galway & Clarinbridge)

2012 Conor McGrath (Clare & Cratloe)

2013 Paul Flanagan (Clare & Ballyea)

2014 Tony Kelly (Clare & Ballyea)

ALL IRELAND U-21H ROLL OF HONOUR

Cork (11) - 1966, 1968, 1969, 1970, 1971, 1973, 1976, 1982, 1988, 1997, 1998.
Kilkenny (11) -1974, 1975, 1977, 1984, 1990,1994,1999,2003,2004,2006,2008.
Galway (10) - 1972, 1978,1983,1986, 1991, 1993, 1996,2005,2007,2011.
Tipperary (9) - 1964,1967,1979,1980,1981,1985,1989,1995,2010.
Limerick (4) - 1987, 2000., 2001, 2002.
Clare (4) - 2009, 2012, 2013, 2014.
Wexford (1) - 1965.
Waterford (1) - 1992.

ALL IRELAND U-21 FINALS RESULTS

1964 Tipperary 8-9, Wexford 3-1.	1989 Tipperary 4-10, Offaly 3-11
1965 Wexford 3-7, Tipperary 1-4.	1990 Kilkenny 2-11, Tipperary 1-11
1966 Cork 3-12, Wexford 5-6	1991 Galway 2-17, Offaly 1-9
Cork 4-9, Wexford 4-9	1992 Waterford 4-4, Offaly 0-16
Cork 9-9, Wexford 5-9	Waterford 0-12, Offaly 2-3
1967 Tipperary 1-8, Dublin 1-7.	1993 Galway 2-14, Kilkenny 3-11
1968 Cork 2-18, Kilkenny 3-9	Galway 2-9, Kilkenny 3-3
1969 Cork 5-13, Wexford 4-7.	1994 Kilkenny 3-10 Galway 0-11
1970 Cork 3-8, Wexford 2-11	1995 Tipperary 1-14, Kilkenny 1-10
Cork 5-17, Wexford 0-8	1996 Galway 1-14, Wexford 0-7
1971 Cork 7-8, Wexford 1-11.	1997 Cork 3-11, Galway 0-13
1972 Galway 2-9, Dublin 1-10.	1998 Cork 2-15, Galway 2-10
1973 Cork 2-10, Wexford 4-2.	1999 Kilkenny 1-13, Galway 0-14
1974 Kilkenny 3-8, Waterford 3-7.	2000 Limerick 1-13, Galway 0-13
1975 Kilkenny 5-13, Cork 2-19.	2001 Limerick 0-17, Wexford 2-10
1976 Cork 2-17, Kilkenny 1-8.	2002 Limerick 3-17, Galway 0-8
1977 Kilkenny 2-9, Cork 1-9.	2003 Kilkenny 2-13 Galway 0-12
1978 Galway 3-5, Tipperary 2-8	2004 Kilkenny 3-21, Tipperary 1-6
Galway 3-15, Tipperary 2-8	2005 Galway 1-15, Kilkenny 1-14
1979 Tipperary 2-12, Galway 1-9.	2006 Kilkenny 2-14, Tipperary 2-14
1980 Tipperary 2-9, Kilkenny 0-14.	Kilkenny 1-11, Tipperary 0-11
1981 Tipperary 2-16, Kilkenny 1-10.	2007 Galway 5-11, Dublin 0-12
1982 Cork 0-12, Galway 0-11	2008 Kilkenny 2-13, Tipperary 0-15
1983 Galway 0-12, Tipperary 1-6	2009 Clare 0-15, Kilkenny 0-14
1984 Kilkenny 1-12, Tipperary 0-11	2010 Tipperary 5-22, Galway 0-12
1985 Tipperary 1-10, Kilkenny 2-6	2011 Galway 3-14, Dublin 1-10
1986 Galway 0-14, Wexford 2-5	2012 Clare 2-17, Kilkenny 2-11
1987 Limerick 2-15, Galway 3-6	2013 Galway 2-28, Antrim 0-12
1988 Cork 4-11, Kiikenny 1-5.	2014 Clare 2-20, Wexford 3-11

PROVINCIAL U21H FINALS RESULTS

LEINSTER U21 HURLING FINALS

1964 Wexford 4-7, Laois 2-2
1965 Wexford 7-9, Dublin 1-5
1966 Wexford 7-10, Laois 2-8
1967 Dublin 2-10, Offaly 2-9
1968 Kilkenny 4-10, Dublin 5-4
1969 Wexford 3-16, Kilkenny 4-3
1970 Wexford 2-15, Kilkenny 5-4
1971 Wexford 2-16, Kilkenny 2-9
1972 Dublin 2-11, Offaly 0-15
1973 Wexford 2-13, Offaly 2-10
1974 Kilkenny 3-8, Wexford 1-5
1975 Kilkenny 3-14, Wexford 0-8
1976 Kilkenny 3-21, Wexford 0-5
1977 Kilkenny 3-11, Wexford 1-10
1978 Offaly 2-14, Laois 2-7
1979 Wexford 0-14, Kilkenny 2-8
       Wexford 1-8, Kilkenny 0-10
1980 Kilkenny 2-14, Wexford 2-9
1981 Kilkenny 6-11, Wexford 2-10
1982 Kilkenny 5-20, Offaly 2-6
1983 Laois 3-13, Wexford 4-8
1984 Kilkenny 0-18, Wexford 1-10
1985 Kilkenny 4-18, Wexford 1-4
1986 Wexford 2-9, Offaly 2-9
       Wexford 1-16, Offaly 0-10
1987 Wexford 4-11, Offaly 0-5
1988 Kilkenny 3-13, Offaly 2-5
1989 Offaly 3-16, Kilkenny 3-9
1990 Kilkenny 2-9, Laois 1-10
1991 Offaly 2-10, Kilkenny 0-12
1992 Offaly 1-15, Kilkenny 2-10
1993 Kilkenny 4-13, Wexford 2-7
1994 Kilkenny 1-14, Wexford 0-15
1995 Kilkenny 2-11, Wexford 1-12
1996 Wexford 1-9, Offaly 0-12
       Wexford 2-16, Offaly 2-5
1997 Wexford 2-13, Offaly 0-15
1998 Kilkenny 2-10, Dublin 0-12
1999 Kilkenny 1-17, Offaly 1-6
2000 Offaly 3-14, Kilkenny 2-14
2001 Wexford 0-10, Kilkenny 1-5
2002 Wexford 1-15, Dublin 0-15
2003 Kilkenny 0-12, Dublin 1-4
2004 Kilkenny 1-16, Wexford 2-3
2005 Kilkenny 0-17, Dublin 1-10
2006 Kilkenny 2-18, Dublin 2-10
2007 Dublin 2-18, Offaly 3-9
2008 Kilkenny 2-21, Offaly 2-9
2009 Kilkenny 2-20, Dublin 1-19
2010 Dublin 2-15, Wexford 0-15
2011 Dublin 1-18, Wexford 0-11
2012 Kilkenny 4-24, Laois 1-13
2013 Wexford 1-21, Kilkenny 0-21 (a.e.t)
2014 Wexford 1-20, Dublin 0-18

MUNSTER U21 HURLING FINALS

1964 Tipperary 8-9, Waterford 3-1
1965 Tipperary 4-9, Galway 3-3
1966 Cork 5-12, Limerick 2-6
1967 Tipperary 3-9, Galway 3-5
1968 Cork 4-10, Tipperary 1-13
1969 Cork 3-11, Tipperary 1-5
1970 Cork 3-11, Tipperary 2-7
1971 Cork 5-11, Tipperary 4-9
1972 Tipperary 4-10, Clare 3-10
1973 Cork 4-11, Limerick 2-7
1974 Waterford 2-5, Clare 1-3
1975 Cork 3-12, Limerick 2-6
1976 Cork 2-11, Clare 3-6
1977 Cork 5-9, Limerick 1-8
1978 Tipperary 3-13, Cork 4-10
       Tipperary 3-8, Cork 2-9
1979 Tipperary 1-13, Cork 2-7
1980 Tipperary 4-11, Cork 2-9
1981 Tipperary 1-15, Cork 0-10
1982 Cork 1-14, Limerick 1-4
1983 Tipperary 2-17, Clare 3-8
1984 Tipperary 0-12, Limerick 1-8
1985 Tipperary 1-16, Clare 4-5
1986 Limerick 3-9, Clare 3-9
       Limerick 2-10, Clare 0-3
1987 Limerick 3-14, Cork 2-9
1988 Cork 4-12, Limerick 1-7
1989 Tipperary 5-16, Limerick 1-6
1990 Tipperary 2-21, Limerick 1-11
1991 Cork 0-17, Limerick 1-7
1992 Waterford 0-17, Clare 1-12
1993 Cork 1-18, Limerick 3-9
1994 Waterford 1-12, Clare 0-12
1995 Tipperary 1-17, Clare 0-14
1996 Cork 3-16, Clare 2-7
1997 Cork 1-11, Tipperary 0-13
1998 Cork 3-18, Tipperary 1-10
1999 Tipperary 1-18, Clare 1-15
2000 Limerick 1-13, Cork 1-13
       Limerick 4-18, Cork 1-6
2001 Limerick 3-14, Tipperary 2-16
2002 Limerick 3-9, Tipperary 2-12
       Limerick 1-20, Tipperary 2-14
2003 Tipperary 1-18, Cork 3-12
       Tipperary 2-14, Cork 0-17 (a.e.t)
2004 Tipperary 1-16, Cork 1-13
2005 Cork 4-8, Tipperary 0-13
2006 Tipperary 3-11, Cork 0-13
2007 Cork 1-20, Waterford 0-10
2008 Tipperary 1-16, Clare 2-12
2009 Clare 2-17, Waterford 2-12
2010 Tipperary 1-22, Clare 1-17
2011 Limerick 4-20, Cork 1-27 (a.e.t)
2012 Clare 1-16, Tipperary 1-14
2013 Clare 1-17, Tipperary 2-10
2014 Clare 1-28, Cork 1-13

ULSTER U21 HURLING FINALS

1964 Antrim only team entered
1965 Antrim 5-8, Down 4-7
1966 Antrim 4-5, Down 0-8
1967 Antrim 3-8, Down 2-7
1968 Down 7-6, Armagh 2-9 (Roinn 'B' final)
       (Antrim represented province in All-Ireland series.)
1969 Down 5-17, Antrim 2-11
1970 Antrim 6-12, Down 2-10
1971 Down 5-11, Antrim 2-9
1972 Antrim 4-9, Down 1-11
1973 Antrim 1-6, Down 1-6
       Antrim 3-19, Down 3-3
1974 Antrim 3-8, Down 0-3
1975 Down 3-10, Antrim 1-3
1976 Antrim 1-9, Down 0-4
1977 Down 3-7, Antrim 0-9
1978 Antrim 5-18, Down 3-9
1979 Antrim 9-13, Armagh 2-2
1980 Antrim 4-16, Down 0-9
1981 Antrim 2-9, Down 1-5
1982 Antrim 9-14, Down 4-5
1983 Down 2-7, Antrim 0-7
1984 Down 1-14, Antrim 0-15
1985 Down 1-12, Antrim 1-10
1986 Derry 2-9, Down 2-9
       Derry 3-9, Down 1-2
1987 Down 3-12 Derry 2-9
1988 Antrim 6-11, Down 1-4
1989 Antrim 4-18, Derry 0-4
1990 Down 2-9, Antrim 2-6
1991 Antrim 2-19, Down 2-6
1992 Antrim 3-11, Down 3-4
1993 Derry 2-13, Antrim 1-8
1994 Antrim 1-20, Down 1-4
1995 Antrim 2-18, Derry 1-7
1996 Antrim 1-13, Down 1-12
1997 Derry 2-11, Antrim 0-17
       Derry 0-22, Antrim 1-16 (a.e.t)
       Normal time:- Derry 0-15, Antrim 1-12.)
1998 Antrim 3-20, Down 4-8
1999 Antrim 2-14, Derry 0-12
2000 Antrim 2-14, Derry 0-3
2001 Antrim 2-18, Derry 1-16
2002 Antrim 2-23, Down 0-6
2003 Down 3-12, Derry 1-12
2004 Down 5-8, Derry 4-7
2005 Antrim 3-12, Down 0-16
2006 Antrim 2-15, Down 2-11
2007 Derry 2-16, Antrim 1-18
2008 Derry won round robin c'ship.
2009 Antrim 1-18, Derry 0-9
2010 Antrim 0-21, Armagh 0-16
2011 Antrim 0-15, Armagh 2-7
2012 Antrim 2-20, Derry 1-12
2013 Antrim 6-22, Derry 0-6
2014 Antrim 7-17, Down 1-5

Galway are the only team to win the Connacht championship and it has only been played on 8 occasions due to a lack of a competitive side to compete with in Connacht. Otherwise, Galway have been nominated to represent the province. `From 1959 to 1969 Galway played in Munster.

ALL IRELAND U21H SEMI-FINALS RESULTS

1964	Tipperary 11-6, Roscommon 2-6; Wexford 5-8, Antrim 2-3.
1965	Tipperary 8-16, Roscommon 0-4; Wexford 8-13, Antrim 0-4.
1966	Cork 11-18, Roscommon 5-1; Wexford 4-13, Antrim 1-5.
1967	Dublin 3-13, Antrim 0-7.
1968	Cork 4-17, Antrim 2-4.
1969	Wexford 12-10, Down 2-1.
1970	Cork 3-10, Antrim 1-4; Wexford 8-22, Galway 2-9.
1971	Cork 11-10, Down 2-11; Wexford 4-8, Galway 0-9.
1972	Dublin 4-12, Antrim 2-8; Galway 2-11, Tipperary 1-11.
1973	Cork 2-16, Galway 1 -8; Wexford 2-9, Antrim 0-7. *(Abandoned after 50 minutes. Wexford awarded match.)*
1974	Kilkenny 4-12, Galway 3-6; Waterford 3-18, Antrim 1-2.
1975	Cork 4-14, Down 1-4; Kilkenny 3-13, Galway 2-9.
1976	Cork 1-16, Galway 2-6; Kilkenny 4-15, Antrim 1-8.
1977	Cork 1-8, Galway 0-5; Kilkenny 4-19, Down 1-2.
1978	Galway 2-13, Offaly2-9; Tipperary 3-9, Antrim 1-8.
1979	Galway 1 -12, Wexford 2-8; Tipperary 7-13, Antrim 4-6.
1980	Kilkenny 2-13, Antrim 1-11; Tipperary 3-11, Galway 2-12.
1981	Kilkenny 3-23, Antrim 0-3; Tipperary 3-17, Galway 0-7.
1982	Cork 4-21, Antrim 1-10; Galway 1-13, Kilkenny 1-10.
1983	Galway 2-10, Laois 1-7; Tipperary 1-16, Down 3-7.
1984	Kilkenny 5-16, Down 1-9; Tipperary 3-10, Galway 2-8.
1985	Kilkenny 2-12, Down 0-4; Tipperary 1-15, Galway 2-7.
1986	Galway 2-10, Limerick 2-6; Wexford 5-16, Derry 2-3.
1987	Galway 0-11, Wexford1 -7; Limerick 2-14, Down 1 -6.
1988	Cork 4-21, Antrim 1-3; Kilkenny 0-19, Galway 2-9.
1989	Offaly 5-18, Antrim 0-9; Tipperary 1-14, Galway 1 -7.
1990	Kilkenny 2-16, Galway 1-13; Tipperary 6-13, Down 0-8.
1991	Galway 2-19, Cork 4-10; Offaly 2-19, Antrim 1-8.
1992	Offaly 3-17, Galway 1-5; Waterford 4-17, Antrim 2-8.
1993	Galway 4-9, Cork 2-10; Kilkenny 3-22, Derry 2-10.
1994	Galway 1-18, Antrim 0-6; Kilkenny 2-21, Waterford 3-6.
1995	Kilkenny 3-7, Galway 1-13, Kilkenny 1-15, Galway 1-14 *(Replay)*; Tipperary 4-12, Antrim 1-8.,
1996	Galway 1-13, Cork 1-9; Wexford 3-14, Antrim 1-6.
1997	Cork 2-12, Wexford 1-6; Galway 8-26 Derry 0-7.
1998	Cork 3-15 Antrim 0-11; Galway 4-18 Kilkenny 3-7.
1999	Galway 3-12 Tipperary 1-16; Kilkenny 6-27, Antrim 0-10.
2000	Galway 4-13, Offaly1-10; Limerick 1-21, Antrim 1-9.
2001	Limerick 1-13, Galway 2-6; Wexford 2-17, Antrim 1-5.
2002	Galway 1-20, Wexford 1-10; Limerick 2-20, Antrim 2-6.
2003	Galway 2-20, Tipperary 2-16 *(aet)*; Kilkenny 4-19, Down 1 -7.
2004	Kilkenny 0-20, Galway 0-15; Tipperary 4-20, Down 0-5.
2005	Galway 1-19, Cork 1-13; Kilkenny 6-33, Antrim 1-8.
2006	Kilkenny 1 -24, Galway 2-12; Tipperary 5-19, Antrim 0-7.
2007	Dublin 3-18, Derry 2-11; Galway 4-21, Cork 2-18 *(aet)*.
2008	Kilkenny 2-14, Galway 1-13; Tipperary 1-20, Derry 0-10.
2009	Kilkenny 2-22, Antrim 2-7; Clare 3-23, Galway 5-15 *(aet)*.
2010	Tipperary 2-32, Antrim 1-7; Galway 2-14, Dublin 1-10.
2011	Galway 0-22, Limerick 2-14; Dublin 3-23, Antrim 0-6.
2012	Kilkenny 4-16, Galway 2-15; Clare 4-24, Antrim 0-8.
2013	Clare 1-16, Galway 0-7; Antrim 2-15, Wexford 1-16.
2014	Wexford 1-21, Galway 1-19; Clare 4-28, Antrim 1-10.

Mick Malone

Ger Fennelly

UNDER 21H FINAL FACTS

Michael Doyle

Kevin Fennelly

⋆ Mick Malone of Cork is the only hurler to have won 4 U-21 All-Ireland medals.

⋆ Michael Doyle of Tipperary captained his county to an All-Ireland U-21 title in 1979 and managed Tipp to the same title in 1995.

⋆ The Fennelly brothers, Ger and Kevin captained Kilkenny to successive All-Ireland U-21 titles in 1974 and 1975.

⋆ Philip Kennedy of Tipperary captained his county to successive U-21 All-Ireland titles in 1980 and 1981.

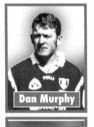
Dan Murphy

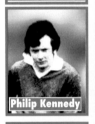
Philip Kennedy

⋆ Dan Murphy of Cork also captained his county to successive U-21 All-Ireland titles in 1997 and 1998.

⋆ Clare played and lost in 12 Munster U-21 finals, before winning the Munster and All-Ireland finals of 2009. They went on to win the Munster and All-Ireland titles in 2012, 2013 and 2014.

⋆ U-21 finalists who later became priests include Seanie Barry (Cork 1966), Martin Casey (Wexford 1969, 1970 & 1971), Iggy Clarke (Galway 1972), Fergus Farrell (Kilkenny 1968), Peter Brennan (Tipperary 1981).

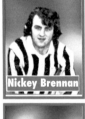
Nickey Brennan

Joe McDonagh

⋆ The U-21 Hurling Trophy is a replica of an old Celtic Cross of the 10th century from the Rock of Cashel and was first presented in 1967 by Most Rev. Dr. Morris, then Archbishop of Cashel and Emly.

Seanie Barry

Iggy Clarke

⋆ Clare's winning margin over Antrim in 2013 was 22 points (2-28 to 0-12). However, in 2010 Tipperary had 25 points in hand when defeating Galway by 5-22 to 0-12.

⋆ Only two GAA Presidents have won All-Ireland U-21 Hurling medals. Galway's Joe McDonagh was a member of their 1972 winning panel while Nickey Brennan played for Kilkenny in their 1974 triumph.

Martin Casey

John Rothwell

⋆ When Wexford took their lone title in 1965, ten of the starting fifteen from the previous year's heavy loss were back on duty.

⋆ The record number of goals in a final is the 14 recorded in the 2nd replay of the 1966 final with Cork beating Wexford by 9-9 to 5-9.

⋆ John Rothwell of Cork raised four green flags against Wexford in 1971.

Fergus Farrell

Peter Brennan

BORD GAIS AND THE U-21 HURLING CHAMPIONSHIP

**Bord Gais have sponsored the U-21 hurling championship since 2008.
They introduced U-21 Hurler of the Year Awards in 2009
and All Star Teams in 2013.**

U21 HURLER OF THE YEAR WINNERS FROM 2009 TO 2014

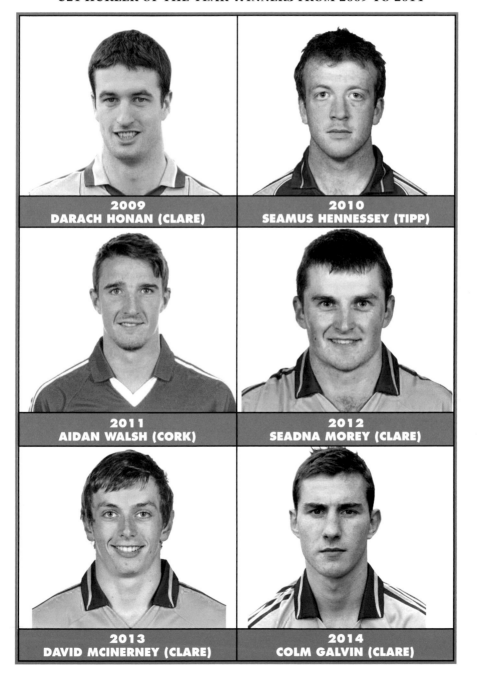

2009 DARACH HONAN (CLARE)	2010 SEAMUS HENNESSEY (TIPP)
2011 AIDAN WALSH (CORK)	2012 SEADNA MOREY (CLARE)
2013 DAVID MCINERNEY (CLARE)	2014 COLM GALVIN (CLARE)

BORD GAIS 2013 U21 HURLING TEAM OF THE YEAR

(1)

Ronan Taaffe *(Clare)*

(2)

Paul Flanagan *(Clare)*

(3)

David McInerney *(Clare)*

(4)

Brian Kennedy *(Kilkenny)*

(5)

Séadna Morey *(Clare)*

(6)

Alan O'Neill *(Clare)*

(7)

Ray Barry *(Waterford)*

(8)

Colm Galvin *(Clare)*

(9)

Lee Chin *(Wexford)*

(10)

Tony Kelly *(Clare)*

(11)

Padraic Collins *(Clare)*

(12)

Stephen McAfee *(Antrim)*

(13)

Stephen Quirke *(Offaly)*

(14)

Jason Forde *(Tipperary)*

(15)

Ciaran Clarke *(Antrim)*

BORD GAIS 2014 U21 HURLING TEAM OF THE YEAR

(1)

Oliver O'Leary *(Wexford)*

(2)   **(3)**   **(4)**

Cathal Barrett *((Tipperary)*   **Liam Ryan** *(Wexford)*   **Séadna Morey** *(Clare)*

(5)   **(6)**   **(7)**

Andrew Kenny *(Wexford)*   **Conor Cleary** *(Clare)*   **Jamie Shanahan** *(Clare)*

(8)   **(9)**

Colm Galvin *(Clare)*   **Eoin Enright** *(Clare)*

(10)   **(11)**   **(12)**

Jack Guiney *(Wexford)*   **Tony Kelly** *(Clare)*   **Padraig Brehony** *(Galway)*

(13)   **(14)**   **(15)**

Jason Forde *(Tipperary)*   **Conor McDonald** *(Wexford)*   **Aaron Cunningham** *(Clare)*